To Nancy

the story of
an upland community

All good wishes –

Katharine,

September 16th. 2000

Gaelic

It lies in pockets in the hills,
A wink of gold that has not been panned
From the older veins and worn faces,

And sometimes on a dark river of night,
Imagine it returning from the seas of its struggle
Like salmon to the birthright of the spring.

written in Abriachan by Ken Steven

ABRIACHAN

the story of
an upland community

Katharine Stewart.

abriachan forest trust

2000

This book has been supported by the Heritage Lottery Fund under the Awards for All programme.

Abriachan Forest Trust also gratefully acknowledges the support given by the Post Office, the Inverness Gaelic Society, the Inverness Field Club and Scottish Natural Heritage.

THE POST OFFICE

SCOTTISH
NATURAL
HERITAGE

A catalogue record
for this book is
available from the British Library

ISBN 09538715-0-9

published by the Abriachan Forest Trust
Abriachan
Inverness
2000

CONTENTS

THE HISTORY OF ABRIACHAN

ABRIACHAN TODAY

ACKNOWLEDGEMENTS

In writing this book, we have received help from many people. Our grateful thanks go to them all, in particular: the staff at the National Archives of Scotland; staff at the Inverness Library, the Highland Council genealogist, Alistair Macleod, and his assistant, Anne Wood; the Highland Archivist, Robert Steward and his staff; staff at the Museum in Inverness, especially Catherine Niven, Jane Petrie and Patricia Weekes; also staff at the Post Office Archives, Mount Pleasant, London; members of the Inverness Gaelic Society and the Inverness Field Club. We particularly acknowledge the skills of Norman MacMillan and Fred Macaulay of the Gaelic Society in translating some of the Gaelic poetry, and Hugh Barron for giving us so much of his time and allowing us to tap into his enormous fund of local knowledge. We are grateful also to Duncan Macdonald, Drumnadrochit.

Our inspiration has always come from Abriachan itself, and we would like to pay tribute here to the help given by some of the older residents, past and present. Hugh Macdonald, Balchraggan, has dug deep into a long lifetime of memories to help at every stage. Donald Fraser, Lower Milton, Drumnadrochit kindly allowed us to use the beautiful photograph of himself and his family for our cover. Dr Ian Macdonald, son of James Macdonald, Achbuie, gave us permission to use his father's account of life in Abriachan in a different age. Many people, some of them friends and neighbours now for half a century, others their descendants, have also contributed; we thank in particular Elizabeth Brownell, Peter Fraser Grant, and Miss Nan Macdonald, all with Abriachan antecedents, for much valued information and photographs.

For permission to quote from their writing, we would thank Eona MacNicol, Mollie Hunter and Ken Steven; for help with providing photographs and other illustrations we thank Eileen Pizzey, Michael Rother, Steve Austin, Suzann Barr, Christine Matheson, Jack Hesling, Mark Foster, John Macdonald, Mary Hesling and also Graham Hanks and Rita Farragher for their technical expertise. We are grateful to the Directors of the Abriachan Trust for placing their confidence in this project and particularly Suzann Barr for her support at all stages. We thank all those who wrote pieces for inclusion. We are grateful for the kind words of Dr James Hunter in his introduction and those of John Ward in his preface.

Abriachan Forest Trust wishes to thank Hilda Hesling and Christine Matheson for their work in preparing the text for publication.

The illustration on page 18 is by kind permission of Arthur Ackermann and Peter Johnson Ltd. and Sothebys. Quotations from the Seafield papers and the reproduction of the painting on page 53 are by permission of Lord Seafield. For permission to quote from Jessie Kesson's short story 'The Road of No Return' from the collection entitled 'Where the Apple Ripens' (1984) we thank the Hogarth Press; for permission to reproduce the map on pages 42-43 and the photographs on page 89 and page 158 we thank Inverness Museum and Art Gallery; for permission to reproduce the maps on pages 10-11 and 12-13 we thank the Ordnance Survey and the trustees of the National Library of Scotland; for permission to reproduce the photograph on page 143 we thank the editor of the Inverness Courier.

We have referred to the following texts on many occasions and recommend them to anyone wishing to embark on further study:

William Mackay: 'Urquhart and Glenmoriston,' 1893
Reports of the Royal Commissioners of 1884 and 1892
Stuart Piggott: 'Scotland before History'
Statistical Account of Scotland 1791-1799
Proceedings of the Society of Antiquaries
Reports on the Annexed Estates 1755-1769, Scottish Record Office, 1973
William Fraser: 'The Chiefs of Grant,' 1883
Alexander Mackenzie: 'History of the Frasers of Lovat,' Inverness, 1896
Transactions of the Gaelic Society of Inverness
Transactions of the Inverness Field Club
Alexander Macdonald: 'Song and Story from Loch Ness-side,' Inverness, 1914
Charles Fraser-Mackintosh: 'Antiquarian Notes,' Inverness, 1897
James Barron: 'The Northern Highlands in the Nineteenth Century,' 3 vols, 1903-14
'The Wardlaw Manuscript'- Chronicles of the Frasers, Scottish History Society, 1905

the illustration on the front cover, haymaking in Abriachan, c1920
by kind permission of Mr Donald Fraser, Lower Milton, Drumnadrochit

PREFACE

In a post-modernist age, when relativity, subjectivity and the Internet have conspired to challenge so many traditional ways of thinking and of doing things, Katharine Stewart's story of Abriachan is like a bracing breath of clean Highland air.

Rural communities such as are found all over Scotland, and for many of which Abriachan stands as symbol, have always been a mixture of economic fragility and great personal strength. The fact that so many communities survive - flourish, often - is a huge tribute to the spirit and adaptability of the people who choose to make the Highlands and other remoter parts their home.

Apart from the fact that Katharine was a distinguished postmistress of Abriachan (her daughter has continued the tradition), the role of the Post Office in rural communities has always been significant. The postie and Postmaster or Postmistress have brought the outside world to the community; and helped to take a little of home to those who have moved away. They have also provided a social service over and above their official duties. The reward for this is that they are possibly unique in the respect and affection they command throughout Scotland.

As Katharine says in her authoritative chapter on the Post, social changes are afoot which bring new communication opportunities for the people of Abriachan and other rural areas. The task will be to embrace them while retaining the friendly whistle of the postie and smile of the Postmistress. As with all things, the rural post office and the post must be used and will go into decline if not.

It but remains for me to congratulate Katharine on her scholarship, elegant prose and energy. Her readers are in for a treat.

John Ward, CBE
Chairman, Scottish Post Office Board
April, 2000

iii

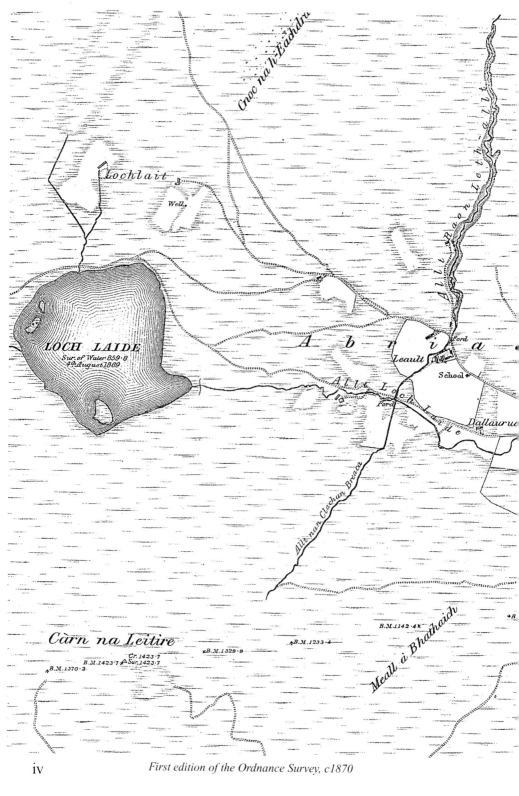

First edition of the Ordnance Survey, c1870

iv

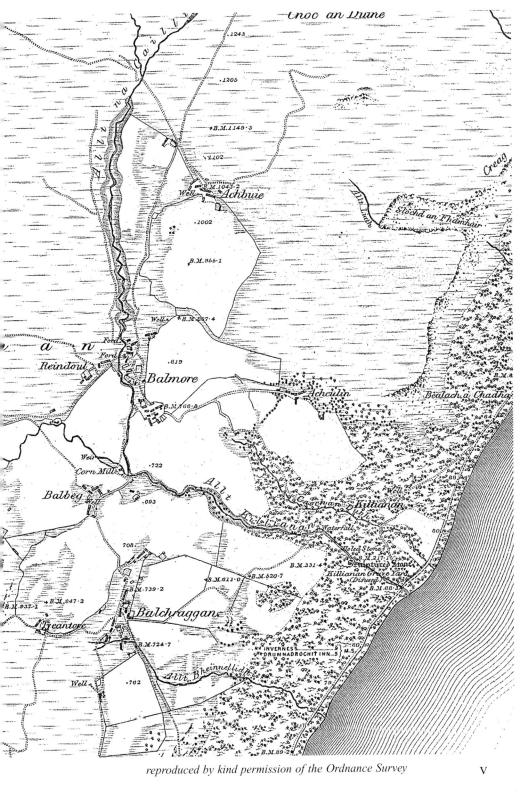

Cnoc an Duane

.1243

.1205

·B.M.1149·3

.1102

B.M.1045·2
Well   Achbuie

.1002

B.M.965·1

Well· ·B.M.867·4

Creag

Allt Coiltie

Slochd an Thamhar

a   n
Ford
Ford

Reindoul

.819

Balmore

B.M.768·8

Acheilin

Bealach a Chadha

B.M.8

84

Weir
Corn Mill

.722

Balbeg   .693
Well

Allt Killianan

Well

88

Creaman Killianan

Waterfall

Holed Stone

80

.708

B.M.331·4

B.M.217

.60

B.M.611·0 B.M.620·7

Sculptured Stone
Killianan Grave Yard
(Disused)
B.M.68·3

B.M.937·1 ·B.M.847·2

B.M.739·2

Treantore

Balchraggan

B.M.724·7

INVERNESS
DRUMNADROCHIT INN 5

80

78

Well   .762

Allt Bheinneltidh

79

B.M.89·2

reproduced by kind permission of the Ordnance Survey   V

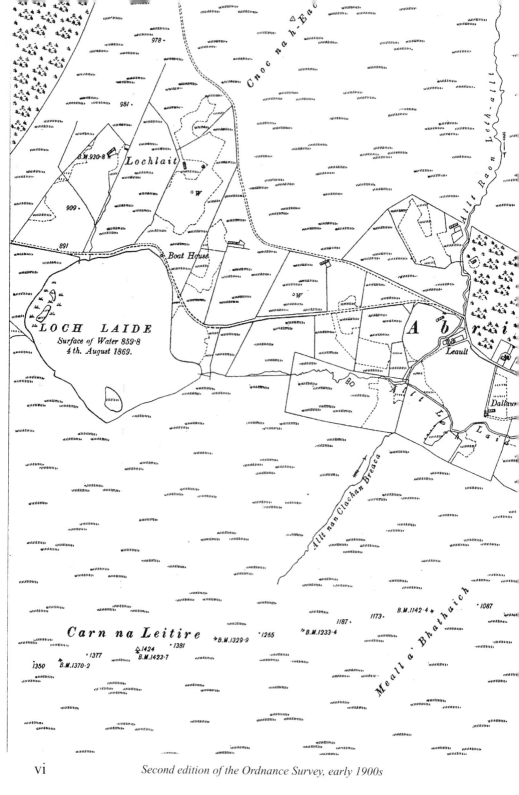

Second edition of the Ordnance Survey, early 1900s

reproduced by kind permission of the Ordnance Survey

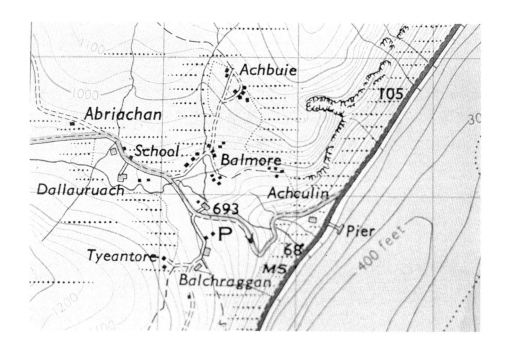

Introduction

On a warm summer's afternoon in 1999, I was one of a whole host of people who, in the company of a couple of government ministers, took a stroll through Abriachan. We were there because the Scottish Executive - the Edinburgh-based administration which, following devolution, had been established some weeks earlier - chose to launch in Abriachan its proposals for land reform. At the heart of those proposals was, and is, the notion that rural communities should be given greater opportunities to shape their own future by acquiring the ownership of the natural assets on their doorsteps. Abriachan residents have shown something of a lead in this regard - by taking over the management of an extensive tract of woodland. Hence the Scottish Executive's decision to stage a land reform press conference in Abriachan's village hall rather than in one of the Edinburgh venues usually selected on such occasions.

People do not assume responsibilities of the sort which have been assumed in Abriachan unless the community to which they belong is one that's confident in its own abilities. And there was plenty such confidence on display that summer's day in 1999. But something else was evident on the part of the Abriachan folk I then met and talked with: a very real sense of pride in, and attachment to, this little piece of territory on the shores of Loch Ness.

Those same emotions are to be detected in this book which is an altogether outstanding example of how to research, compile and write the history of a Highland locality. Like most other such localities, Abriachan is changing. For reasons explored in those pages, lots of families left the place in the course of the last two centuries. But other people are making their homes in Abriachan today. And as has been shown by the success of the Abriachan Forest Trust, formed in January 1997 with a view to purchasing 1,336 acres of land which had previously belonged to the Forestry Commission, Abriachan people - irrespective of their origins - are perfectly capable of collaborating closely for the benefit of the entire community to which they belong.

Despite the extent to which Abriachan has altered in recent decades, Katharine Stewart comments towards the close of this book, 'the feeling of solidarity can still be real.' Mrs Stewart continues: 'The old sense of community expressed in shared effort is growing steadily and leading to a renewed appreciation of all that working in close partnership with the environment really means.'

As someone who's long been convinced that the Highlands can have a good future, and as someone who's equally been convinced that incomers to our area have a very positive part to play in that future, I welcome those statements. More to the point, I welcome the book in which they've been included. A new Highlands - peopled partly by new Highlanders - is presently emerging. And the Highlands now taking shape, I believe, will be superior in many respects to the Highlands of earlier times. But all of us, no matter whence we came, are the better for knowing something of what's gone before in the places where we've chosen to settle. Often it's all too difficult to gain access to local history. But that, thanks to this book, certainly can't be said about Abriachan. What's presented here is an easily accessible, and highly readable, insight into Abriachan's development over many, many centuries. Everyone involved in this book's production, then, deserves congratulation.

But for all that lots of folk - as you'll see on turning this book's pages - have contributed to it, this book is essentially the work of one remarkable woman. 'My own writing,' Katharine Stewart observes at one point, 'owes everything to my experience of living and working in the community that was, and now still is, Abriachan.' But such debts as Katharine Stewart feels she owes Abriachan are debts which she has amply repaid with this account of the locality's history. Her book is one of which Abriachan people should, and will, be proud.

Dr James Hunter,
Kiltarlity.
April, 2000

1

THE ROCKS REMAIN

Westward from Inverness the way leads along the fault-line of the Great Glen, Glen Albyn as it is known to its older inhabitants. On one side lie the deep waters of Loch Ness, on the other birch and pine rise above giant slabs of rose-red granite. Before the road-widening operations of the 1930s there were caves with stalactites and stalagmites, where the travelling people used to shelter. Now there are lay-bys for the ever-increasing numbers of car-bound tourists come to spy out the elusive creatures of the loch. The loch might well be a refuge for a species of another age, its origin securely hidden in impenetrable clefts and fissures in the rock.

This is three-dimensional country, deep, wide and tall. Everywhere there is rock. Perhaps best seen from a point on the other side of Loch Ness is the huge outcrop, at over 1250 feet, known as the Red Rock. Beside it is the deep water-cut cleft named Slochd am Famhair, the Pit of the Giant. There is Creag nan Uamh, the Rock of the Caves, which is 16 feet high and 31 feet long. The cave here was said to be of a size to *'shelter forty sheep or goats on a stormy night.'* Outside is a large boulder called Clach nam Fiann, Stone of the Fingalians. This is certainly a place for heroes, though no legend concerning it has survived.

These are rocks on a gigantic scale. Beyond them, in the grey schist on the lower slopes of the upper hills, are pockets of blue clay. This can be made into attractive pottery but it has not been exploited commercially. In certain hidden places a blue mineral is found, at one time thought to be unique to the place, and named accordingly. There is also the shine of pegmatite. The area has for some time attracted the attention of many eminent geologists, including that of Professor Heddle of St Andrews.

'Westward from Inverness ......' an eighteenth century view by Alexander Nasmyth

'great slabs of rose-red granite..' the Pit of the Giant

The granite has provided a valuable source of building materials. Polished, it was known as 'marble' and was much in demand for gravestones. Quarries everywhere are evidence of the hewing and shaping of the stone that went on through the years. Many local men became skilled masons, working on buildings all over the area.

The rocks remain, but the underlying movement of the earth is never quite stilled. Between 1768 and 1906 more than 56 quakes were recorded in the Great Glen area. In recent times some minor ones have been felt. These serve, perhaps, as healthy reminders of our own small place in the huge scheme of things.

2

THE EARLY SETTLERS

Some eight miles from Inverness, along the Great Glen Way, a sign points to a minor road on the right, rising steeply to a destination named Abriachan. Some native woodland borders this road, scattered birch, hazel, alder, hawthorn and rowan, with undergrowth of whin and broom. From one of the first bends on the narrow, twisting ascent there is a glimpse of gold-brown water, as it roars and rushes from the hills above to join the waters of the big loch below. The name Abriachan is thought to have been derived from this great natural feature, which cascades in dramatic falls on its way down, 'aber' meaning confluence and 'riachan' beautiful, or speckled. Etymologists differ in their opinions.

At this point, crossing the burn by a substantial bridge, the road diverges as the water runs through a deep gorge, flanked by large oaks and other trees, to reach, at a height of about 800 feet, some level ground and the surprise of houses and fenced fields. Sheep are grazing but there is little sign of cultivation, now, beyond a potato patch and some gardens. These were the croft lands of former times. Their hill grazings have been planted with conifers.

To the right, the old corn mill still stands, now converted to a dwelling, but protected by Historic Scotland and still recognisable as a mill. Further up the road, past side turnings to the left and the right, and past the old Schoolhouse, the landscape opens out to vast vistas of Ben Wyvis, the hills of Strathfarrar and peaks further west. This area, known as Caiplich, the place of horses - from the vulgar Latin, caballus, a horse - bears distinct traces of some of the oldest settlements in the place.

Revealed after a drastic burning of the heather in the 1950s are the footings of eleven hut circles, one larger oval enclosure and several dividing walls. The place has now been scheduled as an ancient monument and is considered to be a small Bronze or Iron Age farming settlement. Farming indicates a certain degree of settled life, probably the growing of small patches of bere, a primitive form of barley. The field system consisted of lynchets, small terraces, walls and clearance heaps of stones. Sheep, cattle, goats and horses had been brought into the country by incomers of earlier times. Heather and wild grasses would have provided fairly adequate grazing.

For people of some several thousand years ago this would have been an attractive place for a settlement. Well above the dense woodland of lower levels which could harbour fierce beasts - bear, wolf, boar - it made a vantage point from which all comers, friendly or unfriendly, could be easily seen. The west-facing slope had been terraced to give level places for the foundations of the dwellings. There would have been an ample supply of materials for their construction - stone and turf for the low walls, some sturdy branches to support the roof and heather or rushes for thatching.

With small game in abundance and fish in the nearby small hill loch the people's larder would have been well stocked. Cows, goats, even sheep, would have produced milk. In summer and autumn there were ample crops of berries - raspberries, blaeberries, cranberries, rowan berries, brambles. Infusions would have been made of heather and thyme and other herbs. Heather ale also made a stimulating drink. The women would weave woollen fabrics for clothing. Deer skins could provide extra protection in the worst winter weather.

When a new road was being made through the area in the late nineteenth century, the workmen picked up flints which they used to light their pipes. Flint arrow heads and scrapers have since been found. This probably indicates earlier occupation and is also evidence of trading, since flint is not found in the area. There must have been a certain amount of travelling by wandering packmen coming to barter their wares. A large boulder, at a point which is still a crossroads not far from the settlement, may well have been a marker-stone pointing to the lie of the long road south.

As technology progressed - the amalgamating of copper and tin to make bronze, the extracting and smelting of iron ore - some of the earlier artefacts remained in their pristine form. A sharp stone implement cut better and was longer-lived than a similar one of bronze. Iron, even down to last century, was a commodity to be highly prized, not squandered on tools of minor use.

So we have some evidence that people of what we call the Stone, the Bronze and the Iron Ages lived here and must have found conditions congenial enough since the place remained in occupation for several thousand years. How exactly they lived, what were their thoughts and observances regarding death and the hereafter we can only surmise. Cupmarked stones have been found in the area, their significance remaining a mystery. Burial sites at a little distance from this settlement and of the same period, show delicacy in the ritual of interment, objects to help the passing to another world being buried with the corpse.

A cache of blackened stones in a hollow at the foot of a slope towards the hill loch seems to indicate a place where water was poured over heated stones to produce steam for the cooking of meat, perhaps a communal cooking after a successful hunt. A primitive 'steamie'! Could it have been an original sauna?

It seems clear that the people worshipped the sun, the prime source of life. The entrance to many of these houses faced east, so that the inhabitants stepped out to greet the morning sun. Today we commemorate the renewal of warmth on May the first and boost our morale with song and dance at the dying of the light!

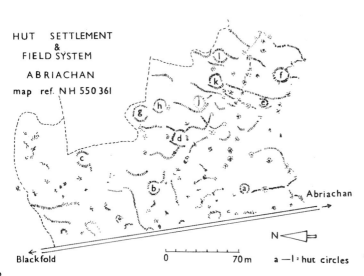

HUT SETTLEMENT
&
FIELD SYSTEM

ABRIACHAN

map ref. NH 550 361

Abriachan

Blackfold

0   70m   a —l : hut circles

N

There are no signs of fortification in the immediate area. Perhaps the people had no assets worth risking a fight to plunder. Probably they did not stir very far from their home ground, the tasks involved in keeping alive - getting food, making clothing, keeping warm - filling up most of their time. They would have been happy to welcome the occasional arrival of some men of peace, bringing goods for barter and news of happenings in other parts. When the winter wind blew straight from the slopes of Ben Wyvis, they would be glad to keep in the shelter of their small dwellings.

As the centuries passed, things outwith the control of such small communities - climate change, the incursion of new peoples - various factors tended to make life difficult in the sparse uplands. Some people would move on, looking for more congenial surroundings. Those who remained, better equipped, better fed, clothed and shod than their predecessors - would have made forays further outwith the confines of their settlements. They would have exchanged ideas and the learning of skills in the making of ornamentation in bronze and other more precious metals, silver and gold. They would have heard of the armed incursions of the Romans in the south and of people fleeing north to escape them. Fear led to the manufacture of weapons - swords, spears and targes for protection. Refuge would have been sought in fortified places, even those at a distance from peaceful settlements.

The people still living in Caiplich, when they ventured down through the wooded slopes where there was abundance of fruit, nuts and berries, down to the groves

above: 'vast vistas of Strathfarrar and the peaks further west...'   23

*the slopes of Abriachan and the route taken by the missionaries to the east coast.
Kilianan can be seen on the near shore, its dark cypress trees a clear marker*

on the shore of the big loch which we now call Ness, would have found people living under the guidance and also in the fear of one man who had risen above his peers by virtue of superior intellect or strength, to become their high priest or Druid. Perhaps crouched in the shelter of the rocks they would watch, in amazement, the processes of worship, of punishment for wrong-doing and so on. They might have heard the agonised cries of the victims of human sacrifice. They would have returned quickly to their upland fastness. There, word would reach them later on, that these magical men, the Druids, had power over life as well as death, that they could cure illness and could prophesy, seeing into the future as well as into the past, that they kept the story of the race deep in the recesses of their minds. They knew the properties of plants and could read signs in the pattern of the stars. Out of fear of these supermen would grow a certain admiration for their skills. A story still lingers today that a crofter in Caiplich, in comparatively recent times, consulted the Christian minister on his visit to the uplands and the so-called Druid who still lived in the oak groves on the loch shore below about the likelihood of good weather for the harvest. Whose advice he took is not recorded, even in oral history.

3

THE VALLEY OF THE SAINTS

By the latter part of the first millennium of the modern era news would have reached the hill people of other happenings on the low ground. A strange man, speaking a strange tongue, with a band of followers, had sailed up the loch in a small boat, on his way, it was said, to the big settlement on the coast, further east. He was reputed to have strange powers, could foretell the future, heal sickness. Was he a kind of Druid?

His followers found the patch of greensward by the loch, with the clear water of the burn flowing past, a congenial place to stop overnight and, eventually, to settle. As more of them came from the little island in the west - Hy, or Iona as we call it today - they built their small dwellings there and a tiny chapel and began to live a fruitful life, cultivating the ground, teaching the people to grow different food crops and healing herbs, as the leader of their community on the island, their Abbot Columba, had shown them.

To this day a heart-shaped stone, with a hole in the centre, which is always, miraculously, full of water, is known as Columba's Font Stone.

Eona MacNicol (née Fraser) whose forebears on both sides came from Abriachan, says:

'Kilianan means the cell of Fianan, (some say Adamnan), a monk of the sixth or seventh centuries. The point at which the Abriachan brae crosses the course of the stream above the graveyard was known by the name meaning the 'Crossing (Ford) to the Mass.' Above the graveyard is a beautiful old stone. Large and flat and almost heart-shaped, it has in it a round man-made hole. This has been thought to be the foundation-stone of Fianan's house-cell, the hole supporting the central wooden pole for the roof. The sanctity of the worship cell has, I believe, become transferred to the house-cell. And this stone is called a Font Stone. It is even called by a name greater than Fianan's - St Columba's. Its connection

'large and flat and almost heart-shaped..' Saint Columba's Font Stone

with him seems reasonable, since it is known that he approached King Brude's Dun at Inverness via the Great Glen. The power attributed to the stone agrees with what is known of St Columba, a special interest in women in childbirth. It was believed up to a generation ago that the water held in the round hole was of benefit to women in childbirth. My parents remembered also that infants had a few drops of the water put into their baptismal bowl. There is mystery about the water. It is present even in dry weather and if the hole empties it fills quickly, though there would seem to be no inlet to allow the entry of spring water. Birth and death the forgotten saints preside over; marriage too, or rather betrothal, which in the old Highlands was almost equivalent. A little higher up the hill slope, no doubt part still of the holy ground, its site known now to few, if any, in Abriachan, stands the handfasting stone. This bears hollows capable of accommodating the hand in three different positions.

The stream is called Allt Kilianan at its entry to the Loch, above it was fitly called the Eas (waterfall). Between the falls are deep pools. In my childhood days there was a lingering fear of this place and tales told of water sprites who resented intrusion and were ready to punish it.'

As the settlement grew the monks attracted many to their way of life. They were able to teach boys the rudiments of Greek and Latin, so that they could join fully in the forms of worship of their God. They also passed on their skills in working wood and metal, as well as agricultural skills and the art of illuminating manuscripts. The settlement became known as Kilianan, a name which suggests dedication of the chapel either to Adamnan or to St Fianan.

Missionaries from the west were to travel either through the dense and dangerous forests and along the rough tracks of the Great Glen or by the succession of waterways which we now call the Caledonian Canal, on their way to preach to the peoples of the north and the east. These people, and among them those who would by that time be living in the uplands of Abriachan, were known to the Romans as Picti, painted ones, on account of their habit of daubing paint on their

bodies in times of tribal conflict. The presence of the Romans in the south would no doubt have been reported by word of mouth by the travelling traders or other itinerants. It is thought that a legion, perhaps lost in the fastnesses of the hills, may have penetrated almost to the shores of the big loch. A naval squadron was certainly seen in the Moray Firth. But they had offered no real threat to the people of the uplands.

the cypress trees at Kilianan growing as one

So many missionaries, bringing messages of peace, passed along this route from the west that the way they took became known as the 'Valley of the Saints'. Ninian, who worked mostly among the Picts further south, is thought to have travelled north. A well near Loch Ness is dedicated to him. Erchard preached in neighbouring Glen Urquhart, as also did Drostan. These three preceded Columba. A cousin of his was his companion in missionary work and founded a cell at Kilvean, near Inverness. St Donnan, who later worked in the isle of Eigg, had a cell at Glengarry. Perhaps one of the most beloved missionaries was Moluac, or Luac, the prefix 'mo', meaning 'my', being a sign of affection and respect in the Gaelic tradition. He was known as the 'pure and brilliant son of Lismore of Alba' and was something of a rival to Columba. 'Croit mo Luaic', near Inverfarigaig, on the south shore of Loch Ness was his croft. He founded the famous cathedral of Lismore.

Cummine, seventh Abbot of Iona, founded 'Cill Chuimein,' the settlement now known as Fort Augustus. It is thought that Adamnan, Abbot of Iona from 679 to 701, may have been linked to the foundation at Kilianan. Curadan, a contemporary of Adamnan and later Bishop and Abbot of Rosemarkie, certainly founded a church at Bona, at the eastern end of Loch Ness, known as 'Cladh Churadain.' On the ridge between this point and the area of Caiplich, where the early iron age settlements were, is a large stone known as 'Suidh Churadain,' which it is thought was the place where he rested on his way over to preach to the people.

The occupation of this area was clearly continuing. The hard, dedicated lives of these spiritual messengers led the way to improved conditions for the people. Settlements such as that at Kilianan would have been established in many parts and good practices in husbandry, the rudiments of technology and literacy would have been taught and encouraged.

Following in the wake of the Christian missionaries many Gaels came over from Ireland, some settling in the colony already established at Dalriada in Argyll, others moving east and north. Many of them intermarried with the Pictish

above: 'recumbent grave-slab' at Kilianan

people and handed on to them as well as their unique skills in metalworking, their gifts in the arts of storytelling and of composing poetry. The bardic tradition was an old and venerable one among the Gaels. Columba himself is said to have taken a bardic training and composed twenty-five 'lays.'

The artistic expression of the Pictish people had lain in the sculpting of symbols, of creatures, of people and, later, of Christian designs on the huge slabs of rock which must have inspired them. The men of Abriachan, some of them their descendants, were happy to work in stone.

Intercourse with Ireland was steadily maintained. Just visible from one of the higher points in Abriachan, across Loch Ness, is Dun Deardail, the place where, it is thought, Deirdre (Deirdre of the Sorrows) took refuge with her lover. Soon every Pictish leader had a bard in his train, as well as a Druidical teacher, the latter declining in importance as more reliance was being placed on Christian doctrine and teaching.

In the ninth century A.D. the coming of the Norsemen disrupted much of the new peaceful way of life. They were after good land to cultivate, land being in short supply in their mountainous country, and they did not scruple to pillage material goods, gold and silver being the chief objects of their desire. This they sometimes found in the larger settlements, where more ornate churches had been built, with precious ornaments in celebration of the God of Christ. Iona suffered badly from their depredations.

As time went by many of the Norsemen settled down to farming and were accepted by the native peoples. In the old burial ground at Kilianan a sculptured grave-slab is said, in local legend, to mark the resting place of a 'Norwegian Princess.' It is certain that many of her compatriots did convert to Christianity. In her case it is believed that she was the sister of a Norse chieftain and was well-liked by the people.

In the Proceedings of the Society of Antiquaries, vol. XXXVI, a detailed description of the stone is given. It concludes: *'In this case there is no sword on the slab, but a pair of shears is incised on the calvary below.'* The shears were taken to indicate the burial of a woman. In a 'Notice of sepulchral slabs at Kilmore and Kilianan, Glenurquhart, Inverness-shire, by Angus Grant, Drumallan, Drumnadrochit (1892)' we read: *'This ground is very old and Gaelic scholars aver that its name indicates its having been dedicated to St Columba. There is a tradition that these stones and many others now lost, all originally belonged to Kilianan, but that, in the absence of any surveillance, they were taken away by anybody who chose to engage in such sacrilege. It is said that a boat loaded with sculptured stones in the course of removal from Kilianan was wrecked on Loch Ness, and that within living memory the stones could be seen on a clear day at the bottom of the loch.'*

Those living in upland Abriachan would have had little or no contact with the Norse invaders. Their land was poor and they had no possessions worth pillaging. From what we can glean from oral tradition and from reading between the lines of some early written material their lives would have been hard but not without enjoyment. For the men there was the thrill of the chase. For all there was the pleasure of welcoming the arrival of wandering bards, harpists, with evenings spent listening to the stories of mythical heroes and mythical beasts, of the exploits of daring warriors. And there must have been song. The children would learn from the storytellers all the history of their race and thus acquire a sense of their own identity. The storytelling habit, along with a passionate interest in genealogy, was kept alive until quite recently among Highland people. It is being revived today as its value is being rediscovered.

above: 'a pair of shears incised on the calvary below...' the sculptured grave slab at Kilianan

4

THE CLANS EMERGE

As we enter the period of recorded history it is clear that power struggles were bound to have taken place among people now growing more numerous and competing for the occupation of territory. The land was the one great asset on which life depended. Housing, clothing, food, all came directly from the land.

In the year 843 Kenneth Macalpine, a Scot, as the Gaels from Ireland were called, established his rule over the southern Picts, in an attempt to unify the country which we now know as Scotland. This may well have been in order to present a front against the invasion of the Vikings. The men of the north, however, were always inclined to resist amalgamation. Many fierce battles took place between rivals ruling small areas. The people joined in the fighting willingly enough. No doubt there was the hope of acquiring booty to take home to their families. Soldiering was ever thus.

Over the next couple of hundred years there was an almost constant state of warfare, on a lesser or a greater scale. After the Norman invasion of England in 1066, colonisation of the north began to make an insidious advance. Norman nobles were given large grants of northern land to keep them from troubling the powers in the south and in the hope that they would pacify the rebellious highlanders. What happened, eventually, was that they became themselves, in many cases, the leaders of the highlanders, adapting to the country, assuming later the status of chiefs.

It was just about this time that the clans came into being. The word itself (clann in the Gaelic) means children. That fact is the key to the understanding of the system. A group of people living in one area, separated from a neighbouring group by a range of high hills or impenetrable forest, would naturally form a close association and look to one of their number to protect them in the danger-

31

ous conditions prevailing. The chief they regarded as their father, they themselves as members of an extended family. He held the land in trust for them and they respected his rights of jurisdiction and fought alongside him in contests with another clan. Cattle raiding was often a cause of fighting. The sense of kinship was a very close one, the chief often having his sons fostered by a member of the clan. He saw to it that every clansman had the right to take *'a stag from the hill, a salmon from the pool and a tree from the wood.'* Though the clan system has long vanished yet the old feeling of kinship with one's peers and of closeness to the land remains.

The clans varied in size. The chiefs of some of the larger ones - the Macdonalds who were known as the Lords of the Isles, the Mackenzies, the Campbells - acquired high status, though their followers still called them by their first names as a sign of devotion. They kept a retinue of retainers, among them a harper and most importantly, a bard, who composed praise poems in their honour and satires against the enemies. Evenings would be spent listening to storytellers recounting the exploits of the old heroes and the legends of the Fiann, a band of warriors chosen for their chivalry in the defence of Ireland. The Irish connection remained strong. The Fiann were also active in Scotland and even in other parts of Europe. They maintained a tradition of fair play and boundless hospitality. Entry to their ranks was testing. I quote:

'No man was taken until he were a prime poet, versed in the twelve books of poetry. No one was taken unless he could ward off nine spears thrown at him all at once. Not a man of them was taken till his hair had been put into plaits and he had run through the woods followed by the other Fianna, his start being only the width of one branch. Unless he could, at full speed, jump a stick level with his brow, and pass under one level with his knee, and unless he could, without slackening his pace, extract a thorn from his foot, he was not taken into Fianship'.

The oft-repeated recital of these heroic doings would have inspired the generations to emulate their ways.

Abriachan had for long been church land and had come under the jurisdiction of the powerful Bishops. It is recorded that, in the early thirteenth century, a *'group of vassals called 'Bisset's Barons' were in Obriachan.'* This is the Bysset who was to found the Priory at Beauly. Such records were kept in the ecclesiastical establishments and are a valuable source of information about the past, though the scribes' spelling is sometimes erratic. Later, adherents of clan Fraser from the Lovat lands nearby and of clan Macdonald further west were by far the most numerous. At one time, very much later, when the Fraser chief was anxious to strengthen the clan, he persuaded people with other loyalties to switch allegiance to him, offering a boll of meal as inducement. These people were known as *'boll o' meal Frasers.'*

5

THE IMPACT OF FEUDALISM

The colonists from England had brought in their wake many new ideas consistent with the running of a country under the rule of a king, including the setting up of Royal Burghs as well as the granting of charters for the occupation of land. They had also brought a consolidation of the Christian establishment. Monasteries were set up at Pluscarden and Kinloss to the east and at Beauly, some ten miles from Abriachan. John Bysset, an incomer, known as lord of the Aird, a hilly district to the west, had set up a priory at Beauly in 1230. The monks were of the Vallascaulian order and were great agriculturists and gardeners. Their orchards produced phenomenal amounts of apples and pears. They were also teachers. It is likely that some privileged boys from Abriachan would have gone there for their schooling.

In 1233 an establishment of Dominican preaching friars, was set up in Inverness and later a teaching order of Benedictines arrived. Young men from Abriachan could well have gone there, too, to be educated, as they do today. Though the monks taught mostly the sons of chiefs, the democratic setup was such that many young clansmen were accepted as students. Again, this custom still prevails. The 'lad o' pairts' was never refused tuition because he maybe had no shoes to his name!

Attachment to the church is evident in the life of the people of Abriachan. The settlement at Kilianan, with the Columban connection, had been central, the whole area being considered a sanctuary. It is likely that men outlawed or landless on account of clan feuds would have sought refuge there and been hospitably accepted. A stone in the old graveyard marks the bounds of the sanctuary. There is a tradition that, in later times, some of the Macdonalds who escaped the slaughter in Glencoe made their way to the sanctuary at Kilianan.

The strengthening of religious establishments was a great furtherance of the work started centuries before by Columba and his monks, but the movement from the south was primarily one of military aggression. In fact it was the start of the Wars of Independence which were to continue for nearly one hundred years. The men of the north, ever of independent mind, were quick to take action against what they saw was a threat to their whole way of life. Leaders soon emerged. One, Andrew de Moray, son of a longtime incomer family, with Alexander Pilche, a burgess of Inverness, led a strong force of men determined to liberate the north. The Constable of Inverness, Sir Reginald le Chen, worried by the activity of this force, called Sir William Fitzwarine, Constable of the Castle of Urquhart on Loch Ness, to a conference on the Sunday before Ascension Day in 1297. In his 'Scottish Wars of Independence,' E.M. Barron takes up the story:

'Sir Reginald le Chen despatched an appeal to Edward for help, and a little later summoned his subordinates to take counsel with him at Inverness. Thither, accordingly, Sir William Fitzwarine, the Constable of Urquhart Castle, betook himself on the morning of Sunday, 25th May. But Andrew de Moray was well advised of the movements of his foes, and when the English knights were sitting in close conference in the Castle of Inverness, the object of their deliberations was hurrying with his men to prepare a surprise for Fitzwarine.

The conference ended, Fitzwarine got to horse. The times were troubled, so a strong escort rode with him, but he anticipated no danger, least of all from those

above: Urquhart Castle - a nineteenth century view of how it might have looked
- Alexander Ross, the Inverness architect

rogues whose fate he had just been deciding. So by the old hill road which wound over the shoulder of Dunain and thence by the way of the Caiplich, where the burgesses of Inverness were wont to cut their peats, he took his way, a rough, uneven way no better than the hill tracks which abound to this day. His escort was strong, well-armed and mounted, and a brave sight they made as they rode along the parlous path, expecting no danger and discussing, perhaps, the chances of an onfall on the rebels at Avoch before they fled in fear. For how could they hope to stand against the knights and men-at-arms of England? And so, armour clanking, accoutrements jingling, they cantered on.

On a sudden came a slight sound, a faint whir-r-r, a flight of arrows, a rush of armed men. The spot, be sure, was well chosen, for well did Alexander Pilche and the burgesses of Inverness know every turn, every evil brae, every treacherous, boggy bit, every likely spot for an ambush, on that weary road. Horses and men went down before the wild onset, the air was full of shouts and cries, the ringing of arms and armour and the groans of wounded men, in one brief moment the whole aspect of the day was changed, and where before there had been the quiet of a May evening, there was now the noise of battle and a fierce confused mêlée. For a little it looked as if not a man of all the English force would escape. But they had two great advantages over their foes. They were mounted, and they were clad at least in part in armour of proof. And in right good stead did these stand them now, for Fitzwarine and some of his men were able presently to break clear of the mêlée and driving their spurs deep into their horses flanks, gained in safety the shelter of Urquhart Castle. But they left behind two of Fitzwarine's principal followers, who fell sore wounded into de Moray's hands and a number of lesser men whose fate is not recorded. They lost, too, eighteen horses, a grievous loss in a country where horses accustomed to carry knights or men-at-arms were difficult to obtain, and they had been compelled to flee before the foe they despised. It was a great day for de Moray and his little army. They had struck a strong blow for freedom and they had won.'

King Edward, hearing of this skirmish, ordered forces from Aberdeen to relieve Urquhart. His proclamation said: '*We learn that certain malefactors and disturbers of the peace, roaming about, have killed some of our servants...and are maliciously laying ambushes for our beloved and faithful William Fitzwarine...*' The men of Caiplich would have been amongst those who caused Edward to reconsider his position in the north.

The very names of the protagonists in these struggles, le Chen, Fitzwarine, show how the feudalism from the south was penetrating the northern regions. But the men of the north did not give in easily. Andrew de Moray later that year joined William Wallace at the battle of Stirling Bridge, where he was badly wounded and later died.

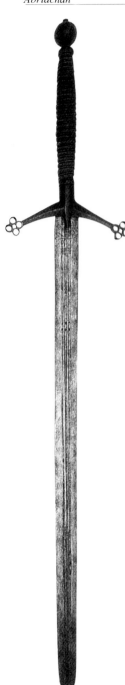

Feudalism meant government by the king and his appointed functionaries. He was lord of all the land and he could grant parts of it to favoured lieges. For this favour he was entitled to military service and to fines incurred by malefactors. The granting of land by charter involved the taking of an oath of fealty. This - the personal loyalty of man to chief - was a custom well understood by the people of the highlands, so they rallied to the incomer lord as they had to their chief. This lord had, in fact, become leader of a clan. He might, as in the case of the Frasers, have come originally from France and reached the north by way of England and the Border country, but he was lord of their land and they were obliged to help him defend it.

For the people living under the introduced régime in the countryside, there was, in fact, little change. They continued in the ways of their forefathers, growing small crops of barley and oats, which provided their staple food, along with milk and cheese and the produce of the chase. Their houses were simply constructed of stone and turf, perhaps lined with wickerwork, with roofs of thatch. Being well used to the possibility of attack by raiders of other clans, they had little to fear of any new authority. It is recorded that one family, at least, on spying the approach of an unwelcome visitor, drove their livestock into hiding up the hill and, returning home, set about the task of rebuilding their dwelling, which took them only one day to accomplish.

There is no doubt that the new enterprises - the building of new castles, the tending of large flocks of sheep - would have involved the employment of bonded labour. However, as the number of incoming lords was limited, this would have happened only on a small scale. Some men of Abriachan could well have been employed on the building and rebuilding of the ancient castle of Dounie, a stronghold of the incomer Fenton family, which was later to pass through marriage to the Frasers of Lovat and to become for many years their principal residence. When eventually Dounie became Beaufort, the stone-working skills of Abriachan men were called on for building and repairing the great walls.

a two-handed sword, said to be that of William Wallace

6

BARONS AND BISHOPS

The first mention of Abriachan in written history occurs about the beginning of the thirteenth century when it is described as being in the possession of the Byssets of Lovat. These Byssets were the great benefactors of the Church, who had founded Beauly Priory. The power of the Church grew under Bricius, Bishop of Moray, and among the lands gifted to it in the early part of the century was the Barony of Kinmylies 'including Easter and Wester Abriachan.' For about a hundred years the district remained in ecclesiastical care. Then, in 1334, John, Bishop of Moray, gave to Sir Robert Lauder, Governor of Urquhart Castle *'for his manifold services to our said church a half davoch of land at Aberbreachy'* for payment of an annual fee of 4 merks sterling. A davoch was an old Pictish term for an assessment of the value of a piece of land.

The deed was worded thus:

'John, by divine permission the humble minister of the Church of Moray, to all sons of Holy Mother Church to whom these present letters shall come, Greeting in the Lord everlasting; know all that we by the advice and with the approbation of our Dean and Chapter, having regard to the common advantage of our Church aforesaid, and having moreover its more careful management in view, have given, granted and in feu farm demitted to the noble person Sir Robert Lawadyr, Knight, for his manifold services to our said Church, a half davoch of our land of Aberbreachy, lying between the Barony of Bonach on the East on one side and the Barony of Urchard on the West on the other....To be held and had by the said Sir Robert and his heirs of us and our successors for ever with their right marches and divisions freely, quietly, fully, peacefully and honourably in pleas, courts, malt-kilns, mills and multures and with all other liberties, commodities, easements

and just pertinents belonging to said lands...Rendering therefore annually to us and our successors the said Sir Robert and his heirs four merks sterling at the two accustomed terms of the year by equal portions in lieu of every other exaction, service and demand and giving therefore to us and our successors and to the Church of Moray the said Sir Robert and his heirs fidelity and homage. In testimony whereof we have publicly caused these our letters to be sealed for him with our seal along with the common seal of our chapter aforesaid. Given at Elgyn on the feast of St Nicholas (6th December), Bishop and Confessor, in the year of Grace 1334.'

Sir Robert's successors resigned the lands and on 3rd February 1386 Bishop Alexander granted them to Alexander Stewart, brother of King Robert III. The terms couched in language similar to that used by Bishop John some forty years earlier, state:

'The Bishop, having regard to its common advantage and with its more careful treatment, bestows on that great and potent lord, lord Alexander, the Seneschal, Earl of Buchan, Lord of Ross and Badenach, Lieutenant of our Lord the King and Justiciar of the part North of the water of Forth, because of his many serviceable benefits and protection bestowed and faithfully in future to be bestowed upon us and our Church a half davoch of our land at Abireachy...which lands with the pertinents Sir Robert de Chisholme [son-in-law of Sir Robert Lauder] Knight, Lord of that Ilk, held of us in chief and he, induced neither by force nor fear, nor deceived by error, but by pure and spontaneous free will, did give up and purely and simply resign into our hands by staff and baton, the foresaid lands, with the pertinents....... Giving the said Lord Alexander and his heirs to us and our successors and Church fidelity and three attendances at our three Head Courts at Brennach annually. Paying therefor yearly the said Lord Alexander and his heirs to us and our successors four merks sterling.....Sealed...at Elgyn the third day of the month of February, in the year of the Lord 1386.'

This Alexander Stewart became known as the Wolf of Badenoch. He was a man of wild disposition and became a great enemy of the Church when he was refused certain dispensations. He burned down the great cathedral of Elgin and committed many other depredations.

The lands at Abriachan clearly had a certain value. Though at a height of some seven to eight hundred feet they benefited from a certain amount of alluvial deposit and the configuration of the ground gave some shelter from the prevailing winds. There was also good pasture on the higher slopes. In 1398 a Macdonald from the west, one of a clan always on the lookout for good land, seized possession. In 1429, Hugh, Lord Lovat, sent Donald of the Isles packing after pursuing him to the moor ground of Caiplich. In 1451, the lands were returned to the Church. In that year James II confirms to John, Bishop of Moray, the Barony of

Spynie with '*the two Abriachans,*' reddendo being a red rose to be paid at Inverness on the feast of the nativity of John the Baptist, with intercession and devout prayers.

The lands of Abriachan remained with the Church till 1544, when Bishop Hepburn granted a charter to Hugh Fraser, Lord Lovat, whose clan territory was nearby. The granting of charters was feudal. Some clan chiefs acquired land in this way, thus making large increases in territory. In 1589 Maclellans and Mackilroys were said to be in possession of land in Abriachan. In what circumstances they came there is not known. No doubt Lord Lovat would have been happy to have plenty of help in organising and carrying out the great deer hunts, or rather deer slaughters, which took place in Caiplich. The modus operandi is still remembered today. A large body of men would be sent out to scour the highest ground, as beaters at a grouse shoot do today, and drive the deer into a hollow, where they would be trapped and slaughtered by the swords of the huntsmen waiting there. Hounds, well leashed, would be eager for their share of the prey. A slope in the area is known as Meall na h-eileirg, the hill of the deer-trap. And a place nearby is called Tom a' Choin, the hillock of the hounds. Hounds were an essential part of life, so important that they were said to have the power of speech.

Caiplich was good ground for a deer hunt. The west side, Lovat territory, was in the parish of Kiltarlity, the east in the parish of Inverness and Bona. In 1646, during the Covenanting Wars, Montrose, having abandoned his attack on Inverness Castle, made across Caiplich on his retreat to the west and south. According to the Wardlaw Manuscript, an account written by the Reverend James Fraser of Kirkhill, he '*managed his retreat so well that with little loss he came to the Capplach and so marched with his few forces over the Stock Foorde of Rosse and leagured two miles above Beauly in the wood of Farley.*' An old lady who lived until the 1960s on the west side of the strath would point out what she called her 'battlefield.'

On some flat ground over which Montrose must have marched after the ascent from the Ness and on the way to Beauly, several mounds are clearly seen. This could well have been the site of a skirmish between the people and a marauding band of hungry soldiery. One contemporary writes: '*Between the bridge-end of Inverness and Guisachan, 16 miles distant, there was not left in my country a sheep to bleat or a cock to crow day nor a house unruffled, so severe were the depredations.*' It is not surprising that the memory of happenings such as these have lingered. Caiplich was often the site of contests and disputes. In 1737 another Lord Lovat was to fight a duel there with the Chamberlain of Urquhart.

Since 1591 when a 'Charter to Inverness Burrough' had granted '*power and liberty of pasture, peats, foggage, turf...on Capulach Muir,*' disputes had arisen

'pasture, peats, foggage on Capulach Muir...' four hundred years later

between neighbouring chiefs wishing to contest the terms of this charter. The right to acquire peats and turf was a very valuable one, for these were building materials for houses as well as fuel. The grazing was essential for the well-being of the cattle on which the people depended for their livelihood. The power of the burghs was resented by those trying to make a living off the land.

7

BUYING AND SELLING

In 1647 the lands of Abriachan were sold to Colonel Hugh Fraser of Kinnaries whose son resold them to Ludovic Grant. In 1704 they were put under wadset (mortgage) for 1000 merks to James and Alexander Fraser of Reelig, who conveyed the wadset in 1730 to Evan Baillie of Dochfour.

The frequent buying and selling of lands in the seventeenth and eighteenth centuries was probably a sign that the clan chiefs were beginning to feel the onerous nature of their position. They had inherited the burden of responsibility for the basic welfare of their clansmen, supporting widows, cancelling dues in bad seasons and so on. Also with the growing improvement in communication, the building of roads, there was more contact with other parts of the country and they were beginning to emulate the customs of their counterparts in the south.

Their own lifestyle had always been as lavish as their means allowed, with a well stocked table open at all times to kinsfolk and guests. As people of Celtic descent they liked to dress well, with appropriate ornamentation, fine brooches for the women, decorated dirks for the men. Hospitality was a rule of life. Calls for help from beleaguered clansmen, often in far-off places, were speedily answered.

The way into the wider world was not going to be easy. Ordinances from the south - demands for the provision of educational facilities, as a 'civilising' measure, and so on - these things were going to make further inroads into their fortunes. As time went by, the clansmen no longer needed as warriors in a private army, the chiefs began slowly to assume the rôle of landlords. The clansmen became tenants, but the rents they could pay on the produce of their meagre holdings was minimal. Many of the chiefs, with growing burdens of debt, were compelled to borrow and to deal in wadsets.

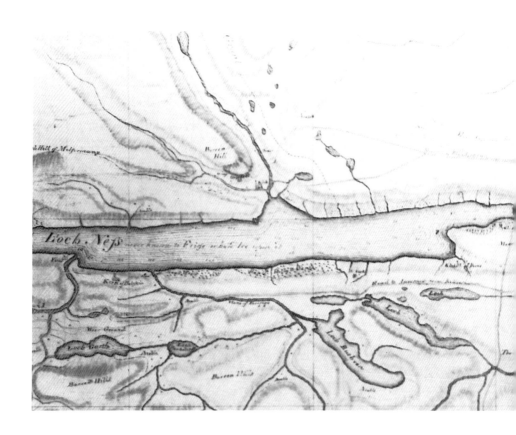

The wadset on Abriachan was eventually redeemed by Sir James Grant in the nineteenth century. The Grants, Norman by descent, had come up from Speyside to the Glenmoriston area, some centuries previously. They were 'king's men' and had been intended as a buffer against the wilder clans, in particular the Macdonalds from the west. Like other powerful clans they had extended their territory by conquest and by marriage and were later established in Glen Urquhart. Their tenantry was, on the whole, treated fairly.

In a survey map made between 1725 and 1730 by Joseph Avery for the York Building Company, which was interested in the purchase of woodlands for the 'Iron Manufactury,' this part of Caiplich is described thus: *'Moor ground for about 12 miles long and three broad.'* This map also shows very clearly the *'road from Urquhart and Glen Moriston to Inverness'* which passed though Caiplich and is still regarded, by the older people, as a right of way. Flora Macdonald is known to have taken this road travelling from Inverness to Skye. The road appears to branch a few miles from Loch Laide, one part going through the lands of Abriachan to the present-day Drumnadrochit probably by Achpopuli, the other making for the road from Urquhart to the west. The old drove road from

above: a section of the m

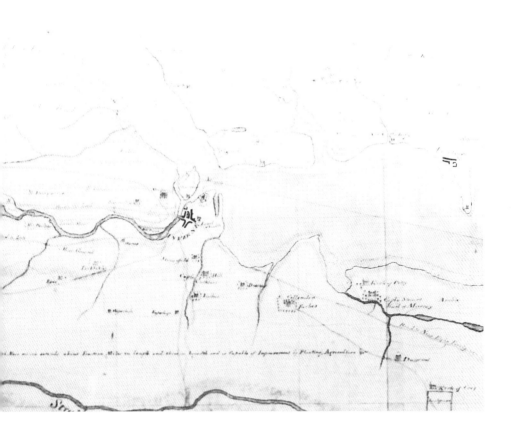

the Aird is also clearly marked. It crosses Caiplich, goes over the hill by Dunain to the ferry at Bona and so on to the big markets in Perthshire or further south. Parts of it can still be walked.

Some chiefs/landlords were starting to make efforts to bring in previously un-cultivated land. Charles Fraser-Mackintosh, a historian of the nineteenth century, tells us in his book 'Antiquarian Notes' of an instance of Simon Lord Lovat attempting an 'improvement' a century before it became common. He says that the land to be improved is situated *'on the high ridge of the Caiplich, and even if, at present* [writing in the 1880s] *a cold, bare, exposed place, what must it have been like in 1732?'*

Lord Lovat agreed to lease to three men - John McHucheon, Clunes, Andrew McCommish and Roderick Barron, Knockbain, *'as much ground of that place commonly called Caiplich (lying in the parish of Kiltarlity and sheriffdom of Inverness) as they are able to take in and improve during the currency of this present tack (lease) together with the houses, biggings, yards and other easements that they shall happen to make out of the same, and that for the space of seven years.'*

During the seven years no rent was demanded of the three men, but at the *'expiration of this tack,'* they were to *'leave the said possession void and redd'* so that *'Lord Lovat...may enter thereto and enjoy the same.'*

In a footnote Mr Mackintosh says: *'The lease deserves the writer's commendation as a piece of conveyancing; but a seven years' tenancy of a barren muir or hill, without the least improvement, on the heights of Caiplich, with an implied obligation to remove at the end of seven years without compensation would not now be thought strikingly liberal.'*

But this was the way in which much of the Highlands was reclaimed. The Caiplich here described is on the opposite side of the wide strath to the 'Caiplich' which was part of Grant territory. It is now known as 'Street' since the houses and their holdings are in the linear development which was adopted later. The ground has been well worked over the years and is now productive.

In his 'Antiquarian Notes' Fraser-Mackintosh also has a description of what he calls:

'Mount Caploch...that great ridge from which, on either side, waters are drained off into the estuaries of the Ness and Beauly respectively, the name being found in many charters. The town of Inverness had the right to cut peats in the mosses of Caploch which right having been challenged by the Lairds of Dunean and Reelick gave rise to considerable litigation 200 years ago in the Supreme Courts. Through the valley of Caploch was the old Urquhart road, and its tracks may yet be traced from Kinmylies to Gartallie. It is a pity that this track is not fit for carriages, for once the ascent of the Leachkin is completed, the ground for the whole journey is

almost level land, though destitute of wood beyond Dochgarroch far from uninteresting...long ago there were, it is said, hazels. One of the pleasantest rambles I ever had in the Highlands was the ascent from Lochend of the steep hill of Dochnacraig or the Red Rock, the descent into the valley of Caploch and on to Urquhart, having in the journey tasted of the famous mineral Fuaran Dearg (red Well), seen Cairn na Baintearn (the Lady's Cairn) and heard the pitiful story of the abducted lady, accidentally killed by one of the rescuing party; also seen the hamlet of Bal-na-greasich (the town of the shoemakers) where it is said no fewer than three shoemakers at one time found employment; Tomcon (the hillock of the dogs) where dogs met to deliberate in those days when they had the power of speech; and the mysterious Loch Lait with its occasionally floating islet.'

Fraser-Mackintosh's spelling of Gaelic words is his own, also the story of the lady's cairn. With territories changing hands on monetary terms, 'improvements' such as those in Lovat's Caiplich adding to their value and with the heritors demanding increased rents for 'improved' holdings, the people were beginning to lose their sense of allegiance to an ideal of community. Nevertheless, when Jacobitism took to the field in 1745, many clansmen answered the call of their chief and embarked, willingly or unwillingly, on a perilous time of bloodshed and hardship.

8

CULLODEN AND ITS AFTERMATH

It was on bleak moor ground to the east of Inverness, on the 16th of April, 1746, that the contest took place which was to mark a sort of watershed in the already apparent abandonment of the traditional concept of community in the Highlands. The story of the battle is well known. The 'wild Highlanders' were defeated, their charge with broadsword and pike overcome by the power of disciplined musketry. It is said that the sound of the gunfire was heard in Abriachan, carried on the strong easterly wind. The roar of the Highland charge would not have carried so clearly. The women from Glenurquhart joined the Abriachan women and took the Caiplich road to meet those of their men who survived the fighting and to hear news of those who perished.

In the ensuing days unimaginably wild behaviour was indulged in by the victorious Government troops. The harrying of the countryside was as atrocious as the slaughter on the field. The Redcoats came thundering west, where, they were told, the barbarians lived, barbarians who were to be exterminated once and for all.

They would have taken the same route through Caiplich, burning and pillaging as they went. The houses, with walls of turf and roofs of thatch, would have been easily destroyed, the few cattle beasts, sheep and poultry taken for food. One place, in a hidden hollow off the direct way west, Corriefoyness, was, according to tradition, mercifully bypassed. Five families lived there at that time, with small, well-tended fields, water in abundance and the shelter of the surrounding forest. They survived to shelter the less fortunate. As the soldiers moved on to Glen Urquhart they found richer pickings. Resistance was overcome by killing and rape. No-one was spared. Men, women and children were put to the sword.

In his book, 'Urquhart and Glen Moriston' William Mackay has a *'Report of the Cattle and other Effects taken by the Army from the country of Glenurquhart in 1746'* (Kingston's Light Horse). He quotes:

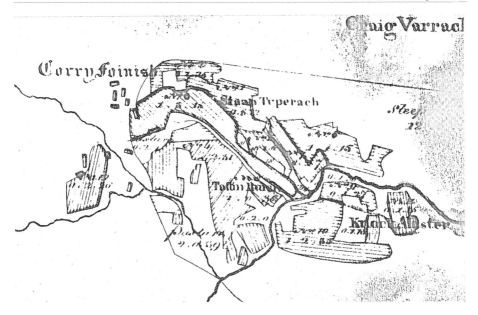

Estate map of 1830. At this time there were five small holdings at Corriefoyness, occupied by Macdonalds from Glenurqhart, said to have escaped from Glencoe, after the Massacre. The road through to Abriachan was not made until the 1830s. Corriefoyness remains isolated.

'John Fraser in Divach had taken from him:

28 cows at 28 merks Scotch money each	*£43:11:1*
2 mares and 2 foals at 100 merks	*5:11:1*
100 sheep at 4 sh sterling each	*20*
50 goats at 4 sh sterling each	*10*
Household furniture value 30 merks	*16:13:4'*

Subsequently the estates of clan chiefs who had taken part in the rebellion were made forfeit to the crown. Most of them were sold. Some chiefs were forced into exile, many of the clansmen banished to the emerging colonies. For those who died in the horrendous conditions of the prison-ships at Tilbury while awaiting transportation a memorial has now been erected. Those remaining were forbidden to carry arms, to wear traditional dress or to play the pipes, which were considered an instrument of war. Needless to say, many a gun was hidden securely in the thatch, the material of the plaid was made into trews. The pipes were hushed, but there was always the mouth-music, 'port-a-beul.' The Act of 1747 forbidding the wearing of Highland dress read: *'From and after 1st August 1747 no man or boy within Scotland, other than such as shall be employed as officers or soldiers in the King's forces, shall on any pretext whatsoever wear or put on the cloaths commonly called Highland cloaths.'* The penalty for the first offence was 6 months in prison, a further offence meant transportation for 7 years. In 1752, in terms of an 'Annexing Act' fourteen estates were made over to the Crown 'for ever.' The application of rents and profits was to be solely *'for the better civilising and improving the Highlands of Scotland and to preventing disorder there in the future. The Protestant religion, good government, industry and manufactures, principles of duty and loyalty to his Majesty'* were to be promoted. In 1755 a Board of Commissioners for the Annexed Estates was set up. The members were drawn from the ranks of the nobility and the legal profession. The Lovat estate became forfeit under this Act, but in 1774 it was restored after the young lord had distinguished himself in the American War. The Inspectors working in the field for the Commission were required to submit reports under as many as 30 headings. One injunction reads: *'As all Highland clans live generally in clustures* (sic) *together which enables them to be so troublesome, it will be necessary to chequer them by introducing some strangers, who may sett a good example of industry...'*

Great emphasis was laid on the importance of new schools and churches. Teaching and preaching was to be in English. No person who could not speak English was to get a farm. Detailed reports on each family were required - the number of children - under 10, those of 10-17 - those over 17, the numbers speaking English, the numbers who could spin, the kind of stock kept, the kind of crops grown. Other information required included the distance to the nearest J.P., the nearest prison, the nearest church, the nearest schools and *'what is taught in them,'* also whether the laws prohibiting the wearing of Highland dress and the carrying of weapons have taken full effect and *'what progress the English language has made'* in the area. The discomfiture of people living under this type of scrutiny, their independent and interdependent way of life disrupted at every turn, can be imagined. In 1784 the Disannexing Act was passed. Estates were returned to their owners. By then other developments were beginning to disrupt the lives of many Highland people. Other agencies had been at work. In 1727 a Board of Trustees for Manufactures and Fisheries had begun work. Coastal villages had been established to develop the fishing. In 1760 a thread-making factory was established in Inverness. By 1765 there was a tannery, using local oak bark. Brick-making, soap and paper-making were also tried. Many efforts were made to train skilled boys. The idea of the Highlander as a Jack-of-all-trades, having all the skills needed to work the ground, provide for all his family's needs, make his own tools and equipment - sleds, harness, creels, furnishings - this idea was anathema to the 'improvers.' They must have him, no longer simply minding his own business, but out there in the world of industry and commerce. And they wished *'to induce the second sons of Highland gentlemen...to abandon their dogs, guns and idleness'* for work in profitable industries. The end of an era was looming.

9

'MR LACHLAN'

That there must have been a lively population in the Abriachan area in post-Culloden times is shown by the fact that in 1766 the name of James Rhind appears in the annals of the Scottish Society for the Propagation of Christian Knowledge as a teacher in Abriachan.

The S.S.P.C.K. was a society which had been set up in Edinburgh in 1709 by a group of professional men who were anxious to further the means of education for the people of the highlands and islands. Knox's old ideal of a 'school in every parish' had not fully materialised. The parishes were enormous and many of the heritors, as the landlords were now known, were not keen to provide schools, schoolhouses or salaries for teachers.

In the Letters Patent granted to the Society it was stated that it was to: '*erect and maintain schools in such parts of the highlands and islands as should be thought to need them most; in which schools the children of Popish as well as Protestant parents should be taught the English language, reading and writing and especially the principles of true religion.*' A second Patent, in 1738, gave the Society powers to set up schools '*for the instruction of children in some of the most necessary and useful arts of life.*' Woodwork, metalwork and other crafts were to be taught.

The teaching was to be in English and the teacher was to be '*a person of piety, loyalty, prudence, gravity, competent knowledge and literature and endowed with other Christian qualifications suited to that station.*'

By 1715 the Society had established 25 schools, though one of the earliest, at Kilchuimein, now known as Fort Augustus, had to be closed, as the children, whose first language was Gaelic, could not follow the English teaching. By 1795 there were 323 Society schools.

Accommodation for the early S.S.P.C.K. schools was often extremely primitive. Sometimes a barn, possibly part of the mill, a derelict house, would be brought into use for the pupils, the teacher lodging with a family. In some cases the school would have to be closed early when a leaking roof made work impossible.

When James Rhind was appointed there is no mention of a school building. His salary was £6 a year, which was roughly the equivalent of a labourer's wage. There were 9 girls and 25 boys on the register. Ten years later, the name of a teacher of whom there is a full record appears - Lachlan Maclauchlan. His salary was £10 a year and he had a small schoolhouse and school building provided by the heritor, the 'good Sir James' Grant. There were 40 scholars on the roll.

Lachlan Maclauchlan was born in 1729, at Kinmylies, near Inverness. As a young man he witnessed some of the atrocities of the aftermath of the battle of Culloden, including the massacre of fugitives by the Government soldiery. Described as 'pious and energetic' he was engaged by the S.S.P.C.K. to teach in various schools in the neighbourhood of Inverness. Then, at the age of 46, he was selected to teach in Abriachan. Being reluctant to take up this post, as he had heard that the people were wild and addicted to distilling whisky and indulging in gambling, he had to be persuaded by *'a peremptory letter'* and the threat of a withdrawal of salary, before he eventually acceded to the demand.

He soon settled, carried out all his duties, which included catechising and sometimes preaching. His wife taught the girls sewing and knitting. He went warily at first, and wisely, among the people, even agreeing to join in their Sabbath games of shinty, provided they agreed to come to his service afterwards. And they did.

In his book: 'Metrical Reliques of the Men of the Highlands' published in Inverness in 1851, John Rose in his Memoir on Lachlan Maclauchlan says: *'He came soon to be deeply prized by the people and before many years passed over, the meeting house of Abriachan was the rendez-vous of all the godly of the neighbourhood. There were not a few who walked every Lord's Day ten, even twenty miles to hear Lachlan Maclauchlan exhort. He had more than one kind of weapon with which to assail evil; no doubt one was prominent - the word of God...but he was also a true poet, and many who defied his exhortations..trembled when they became exposed to the lash of his satire.'*

Card-playing, which was much practised throughout the Highlands, he especially abhorred and this he satirised in a Gaelic poem *(translated by Norman MacMillan)*:

> *'I fear the act of playing cards*
> *Seems so far to be in fashion,*
> *A better trend for local lads*
> *Would be to tend a diverse passion.'*

In religion the law of patronage he found particularly abhorrent. On the death of his eminent friend, Hector MacPhail, minister of Resolis, he wrote an elegy, which is one of the few poems committed to writing which has survived. It begins:

> *'We will prepare a poem of sorrow*
> *As we weep, still steeped in mourning*
> *For the district of Resolis*
> *As will many more who know it.*
>
> *But the reason for this poem,*
> *Though we may be sad and sombre,*
> *Often we have felt elated*
> *By sounds of tuneful, golden trumpet.'*

To a people with an innate respect for the bardic tradition this was more effective than direct homily. It was said of him that *'he was all things to all men, that by any means he might gain some.'* So eventually he won the people's trust and even affection, becoming known as 'Mr Lachlan' and leaving a memory which lingered for many years. His daughter Helen married into a nearby family of Macdonalds, another daughter, Janet, married a later teacher in Abriachan, and their son also became a teacher. His son, James, became a minister, Moy being one of his charges. In a letter to this son an aspect of Lachlan's character is revealed when he says *'with regard to the love of God, you do well to put that before hating sin. I fear the going through our time empty-handed of this love.'*

That he was a scholar is shown in the entry that occurs often against his name in S.S.P.C.K. records: *'wants* (i.e. needs) *books.'* As a man of sensitivity he must have been gladdened, when, in 1767, the S.S.P.C.K. decreed that some teaching could be in Gaelic, the only language clearly understood by the children. He was much opposed to the law of patronage which enabled landowners to appoint the minister of their choice. His grandson (James' son) was the Reverend Dr. Thomas Maclauchlan (1816-86), who became Moderator of the Free Church, having inherited his grandfather's outlook on the ministry. By the eighth annual dinner of the Gaelic Society of Inverness he was its chief, and is remembered as a distinguished Gaelic scholar who translated the 'Book of the Dean of Lismore' in 1862, and wrote a history of the early church.

'Mr Lachlan', though a poet of considerable ability, shortly before his death burned most of his manuscripts, considering his work inadequate. Some fragments only have been handed down, transcribed from oral recitation. He died in 1801, three years after retiral, and is buried in the graveyard at Kirkhill.

'a seat, with a plaque bearing his name, where people could rest...'

The schooling started so many hundreds of years previously by the monks at Kilianan would have continued safely in hands such as those of Lachlan Maclauchlan. A descendant of his, a young scientist from Aberdeen University, came, a few years ago, to see the place where her forebear had lived and worked. In his memory she provided a seat, with a plaque bearing his name, where people could rest and look at the hills he knew so well as he walked among his flock.

10

THE GOOD SIR JAMES : 1738-1811

The 'good' Sir James Grant it was who redeemed the wadset on the Abriachan lands held since 1730 by Evan Baillie of Dochfour, thus making them, eventually, part of the estate of the Earls of Seafield. Born in 1738 he was too young to have known of the aftermath of Culloden, when many of the men of Glen Urquhart and probably some from Abriachan, were betrayed and exiled. He was educated in England and lived mostly at Castle Grant on Speyside. At an early age he took over the management of his lands, becoming Member of Parliament for Moray. By 1773 he had succeeded to the title and in 1776 founded the village

the 'good' Sir James Grant and his wife at the signing of the deed founding Grantown-on-Spey

of Grantown, where, he hoped, people would find employment and settle, work-ing at trades and crafts. He also planned a village in Urquhart, known as Lewiston, after his son. This consisted of a row of houses, many of which still stand, each with a small acreage of ground for the growing of potatoes and vegetables and the keeping of poultry, perhaps a pig, the villagers to find employment on the estate, later in the building of the Caledonian Canal, and other works. The nearby village of Milton was also established, each house having a small plot of land and water providing power for several mills - a meal mill, a tweed mill, a bobbin mill, a sawmill.

Many Highlanders did not take kindly to settlement in villages, with industrial employment. As Mrs Grant of Laggan, writing at about this time, said *'to put a Highlander to the loom is like putting a deer to the plough.'* He would work on his own, at his own pace, but not to set hours and wages. Nevertheless the vil-lages did provide a refuge for many of the dispossessed.

Sir James was opposed to emigration. He employed many people in bridge-building, tree-planting, the construction of river embankments (to prevent flood-ing) and of roads. He turned the track along the north side of Loch Ness into a road suitable for wheeled vehicles. He established lime kilns at Gartallie and made the use of lime on his ground compulsory. He introduced turnips and rye grass, insisted on the rotation of crops and encouraged the growing of potatoes and flax. When the potato was first introduced it had been thought that the green top was to be the edible portion. The people protested until they were shown that the tuber was nutritious, as well as providing seed for future crops. Thereafter, from the early nineteenth century onwards, the potato became a very important item in the diet. It took up less ground than other crops and was easily stored. When it failed, through blight, much hunger ensued. The flax, it was hoped, would provide employment for the women. In 1764 a flax mill had been built, as part of the remit of the Forfeited Estates Commission which was pursuing meas-ures to develop the Highlands along industrial lines. It is recorded that Elspet Maclauchlan and Janet Fraser, both of Obriachan (the spelling with initial 'O' quite often occurs) *'got a reel.'* They were probably members of the schoolmas-ter's family and it is likely that the work could be done at home.

In the mid-eighteenth century the people's houses were built mostly of turf, rough branches supporting a roof of turf covered in thatch of heather or even bracken, the walls lined inside with wickerwork. It is known that wickerwork dates back to very early times and may have been at the origin of many Celtic art forms of interlacing designs. Sir James encouraged the people to build in stone. He also advocated the modernisation of much farming equipment. With the im-provement of roads the sleds used to pull loads over rough ground or the 'lobans,' small carts with wicker sides, could be replaced with larger wheeled vehicles.

For the 'withies' used for reins and traces stronger material, leather, would be substituted. Some of these reforms were considered irksome by people accustomed to making their own devices from material ready to hand.

There is a story that one Duncan Grant, Sir James' factor, coming home one night, stopped to water his horse at the Kilianan burn. As he stood watching the horse drink he was suddenly attacked by an unseen force. There was a struggle. He eventually got home, took to his bed and never rose again. Tradition has it that this *'worthy but exacting'* factor received *'chastisement from the devil in Kilianan burn.'*

Sir James had an uphill struggle in his modernisation programme and he had, of course, to cope with the unpredictability of the occurrence of natural disasters. By 1780 Urquhart was in a turbulent state, rents not being paid punctually, some emigration taking place, new ways causing disturbances and frustration, especially with the new concept of tenant and landlord.

Then, in 1783, after crop failure, there was a state of near-famine. Sir James, reverting to the rôle of chief, when the clan people were regarded as family, did his utmost to relieve suffering. However, his resources were not limitless and the estate ran into debt. He made many economies, took on a post as Cashier of Excise, and lived for a time, quite modestly, in Edinburgh. Returning north in 1793, he raised a regiment of 'Fencibles,' some of whom saw service in Ireland. Local volunteers formed a kind of Home Guard for protection against possible invasion in the war with France. In 1794 he was made Lord Lieutenant of Inverness-shire. In 1811, after a long and painful illness, he died. His son, Sir Lewis, was to succeed to the title, Earl of Seafield, after the death of a cousin. So the good Sir James' lands, including Abriachan, became part of the Seafield Estates.

above: traditional building in Abriachan: 'rough branches supporting a roof of turf'

overleaf: survey for the Caledonian Canal: note the spelling with initial 'O'

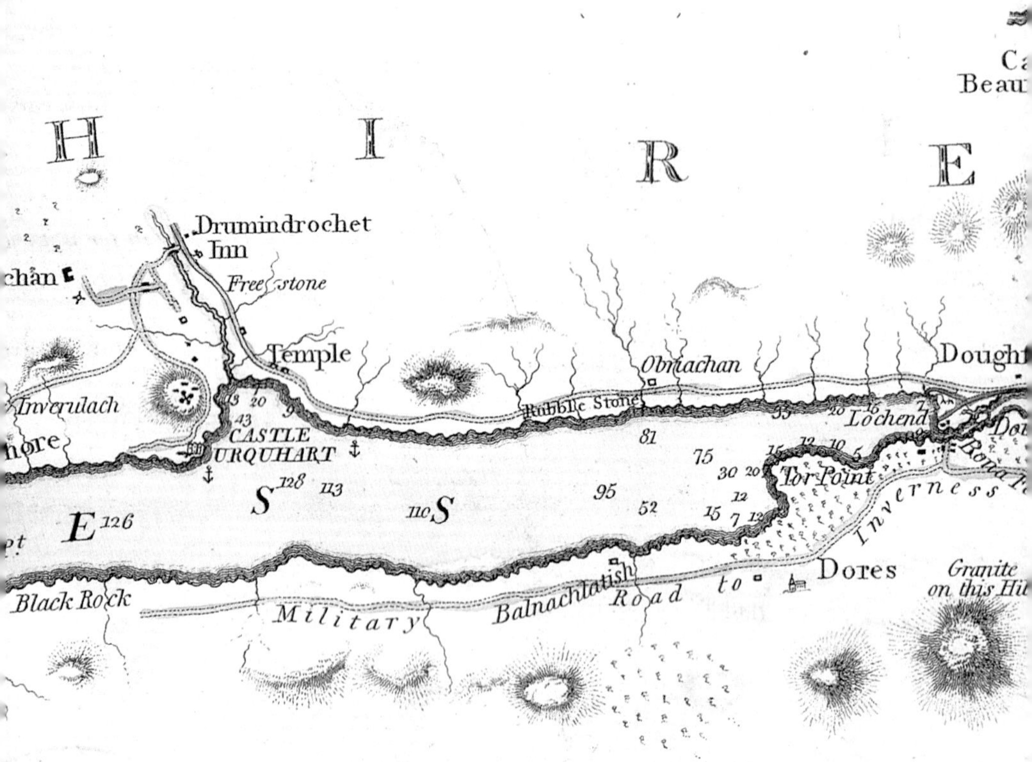

H I R E

Drumindrochet
Inn

chàn

Free stone

Temple

Obriachan

Dough

Inverulach
hore

43 20 9
13
CASTLE
URQUHART

Rubble Stone

Lochend

Do

S 128 113

81

75 30 20

33 40

12

Tor Point

Inverness

E 126

110 S

95 52

15 7 12

Black Rock

Military

Balnachlatish

Road to

Dores

Granite
on this Hill

Ca
Beau

GENERAL P

INLAND

From the EASTER

INVERNES

By

SEA,

Reduced from the original Surveys, by John Howell,

Kirk
Torradell
Kirk
Free Stone Quarry
Red Castle
Kirk Kirk hill
L O C H   B E A U L Y

Lime Stone
Quarry
for Water works
Lime Stone
Rubble Stone
Quarry
Clachnacary Bason
Doughgarrouch
Muirtown
KESSACH
Castle
Fort George
Holme Bught
TOWN of
INVERNESS
Castle Hill

Kilmuir

MUNLOCHY BAY

KESSACH FERRY

Rough Pt
Longman's

Carse
Road

In this space there
is from 15 to 18 feet
Water at Spring ebbs
all the way across.

Along the
on the S

Lime Stone

N of the INTENDED

NAVIGATION,

to the WESTERN SEA,

ND FORT WILLIAM.

ro Telford & Downie.

Engraved by J. Barlow Blackfriars Road.

Clachnacar

Clachnacar
Papen

Don
Ferr

94 Feet
50

11

OPENING UP THE HIGHLANDS

Sir James' modernisation of his estate and the work of his successors was part, of course, of a process which was going on all over the Highlands, with greater or lesser degrees of benefit to the people living there. During his lifetime the gradual introduction of bigger numbers of sheep had led to the displacement of tenants and attempts to provide alternative sources of livelihood for them. The planned villages of Grantown, Lewiston and Milton would, it was hoped, help the people to settle to a different way of life.

Conditions in the Highlands were causing disquiet country-wide, with fears of further uprisings. In 1784 the Highland Society of Scotland had been founded and had acquired a Royal Charter. Its aims were to promote the establishment of industries and also to further the modernisation of agriculture and to encourage enlistment in the armed forces for service in wars overseas.

Then, in 1801, Thomas Telford, a brilliant engineer, was asked by the government to prepare a survey on the state of communications in the Highland area. Telford, a countryman by birth, set out on this task with enthusiasm and by 1802 had produced his report. The main consideration was to *'render the intercourse of the country more perfect by means of bridges and roads.'* In its wider context it sought to provide means of preventing emigration by promoting fisheries on the coasts and by creating employment in public works.

The greatest single enterprise was to be the building of the Caledonian Canal, which was to form a route from the east to the west coast by linking a series of lochs. This would ensure a safe passage for shipping, cutting out the dangers of the route through the Pentland Firth, where the weather often kept ships storm-bound and where they were subject to attack by French privateers. It was also to have a strategic value in the Napoleonic Wars. The Brahan Seer, that Highland prophet, had predicted: *'Strange as it may seem to you this day, the time will come, and it is not far off, when full-rigged ships will be seen sailing eastward and westward by the back of Tomnahurich at Inverness.'*

The building of the canal was to form a source of employment easily accessible to the men of Abriachan, as it was to those of many loch-side communities. The work was incredibly hard and the living conditions primitive. Pick, shovel and wheelbarrow were the implements in general use. Pay was barely adequate and often did not arrive on time. The labourers were housed in wretched huts. Skilled men, such as masons, were treated better. They came from towns - Forres and Elgin, in particular.

Joseph Mitchell, engineer, in his 'Reminiscences of My Life in the Highlands' wrote: *'I lodged with about thirty masons in a house built for the lockkeeper at Cullochy. The men slept in temporary beds, one above the other like the berths on a ship. The men began work at 6 a.m., one being told off to cook about half an hour before meals. The breakfast was at nine o'clock, the fare consisting of porridge and milk and thick oaten bannocks. They dined at two on the same fare and at eight had supper. The fare varied when the new potatoes came in and fresh herring were brought in from Loch Hourn in the autumn. On Sundays they luxuriated in tea, oaten bannocks and butter for breakfast.'*

The Highland labourers lived chiefly on brose, that is *'meal in a bowl, a little salt and hot water mixed into a mess.'* There is no mention of tea, potatoes or herring in their diet and when the all important oatmeal failed to arrive, as sometimes happened, they must have been extremely badly off. The only concession was *'whisky for those working in the water.'*

It is no wonder that, from time to time, they rebelled. As people with their own independent way of life, they were not accustomed to obeying orders, to strict timekeeping and to working outside in hard winter conditions. Normally, indoor jobs were done then - barn-milling, rope-making, repairing of implements, and so on. At seed-time and harvest they were compelled to return home for a while. Peat-cutting to provide winter warmth for their families, days at the herring fishing, as well as ploughing in spring and harvesting in autumn - these were the things of basic importance in their lives. They had not been really accustomed to the feel of money in their hands. So, as a work force they were not ideal in their employers' estimation. Some Irish labourers were brought in.

In spite of troubles, the Canal was built, although it exceeded the original estimates of cost and of time needed for its completion. In later years it provided employment of another kind for the men of Abriachan who worked as crew and stewards on the steamers which plied up and down Loch Ness and were, until the 1930s, the main means of transport for people and goods going to market in Inverness.

overleaf: the lands of Caiplich from the estate map of 1856

LOT. I.

LOT. II.

Ballnagriaskin

The paddle steamer 'the Gondolier' called regularly at the pier at Abriachan from 1866 and an amusing anecdote concerning the Loch Ness Monster is recounted in Nicholas Witchell's 'The Loch Ness Story':

'As we move nearer to the present day, greater reliance can be placed on the eye-witness accounts, since they are more specific in their details and less uncertain as to their sources. In 1802, Alexander Macdonald, a crofter in the village of Abriachan, told one of the ancestors of the former Loch Ness water bailiff, Alexander Campbell, that he had several times seen a strange animal in the loch. On one occasion he was rescuing a lamb that had fallen down the hill when a creature surfaced and swam to within fifty yards of him. He could see that it had short appendages with which it was propelling itself. Then it turned and proceeded into the open loch until it submerged with a great commotion at a range of about five hundred yards. Mr Macdonald said the animal appeared to be about twenty feet long and reminded him of a salamander. It is said that until he died he often referred to the animal as the 'great salamander.'

Meanwhile, of course, Telford had supervised a vast construction of roads and bridges all over the Highlands. The building of these also provided employment for many Highlanders, as it has done in more recent times. As well as the work of construction there was also the maintenance and upgrading of roads to be undertaken. This was to be a valued source of employment for many years to come. Towards the end of the century, we find the words 'roads contractor' against certain names in the census records. This type of employment, which allowed the participants to remain at home, in their own locality, and so to continue to work their holdings, was of the greatest value in crofting communities.

Some thirty years after the completion of the Canal, in 1854, the Countess of Seafield, armed with a spade and a mahogany barrow, cut the first turf for the construction of the Highland Railway. This was to provide labouring work, often in dangerous conditions, for many crofters. Later, the bright scholars, including some from Abriachan, were to find clerical and supervisory jobs in this great enterprise.

12

CHANGING TIMES

In the years after the Rebellion of 1745, when the clans were adrift, many erst while chiefs finding solace in the fleshpots of the south, when new roads for the military to travel were intruding into the fastnesses of the north, life everywhere was changing. A money economy meant that any enterprise must pay and the managing of clan lands was now an enterprise. Some of the former clansmen were, of course, sucked into this enterprise culture. We have seen how some of them found paid employment on the estates. The opening of communications also gave them work on the roads and on the building of the Canal and so on. Yet many of them were struggling to subsist on very small places.

In 1819 a *'Measurement and Estimate of the lands of Abriachan'* was made by a surveyor on the Seafield Estate. We find that at Tom a' Choin there were 2 tenants on 12 acres of arable ground worth £9.19.10. At Rinudin there were four acres of *'poor thin land.'* At 'Auchbuie' 2 tenants had fourteen acres and *'an improvement at Donald Fraser's house'* was noted. At 'Leahault' the schoolmaster had two acres of arable and two of pasture. John Macdonald (father of the Bard) at Tyeantore had five acres. Other places were assessed in like manner. 'Auchpopuly' is described as a *'shealing'* with 32 acres of pasture and 8 of arable ground. Hill pastures possessed in common amounted to 3003 acres. The total area consisted of 168 acres of arable and 3389 of pasture.

The Summary of the Report runs as follows: *'28 different tenants. From this number of people, the lying of the ground, it being much cut and intersected with burns and gullies and with very steep sides, no division could be made with any sort of regularity and it was thought as well to allow them remain and to progress as formerly.'*

The lands were valued at £87 12/- *'not near its value, but by the mode of possession by those numerous poor people is fully equal to what they can pay....Could the numerous people here be removed and otherwise provided for the whole of Abriachan would make a famous farm and in my opinion more valuable than that of Shewglie* [up Glen Urquhart] *worth fully more yearly rent from the local situation and climate being so much preferable.'*

From this it appears that there was some idea of turning the place into a sheep-run, but this was not carried out. The tone of the report would seem to indicate a generally sympathetic attitude to the tenants on the part of Sir Lewis Grant, via his factor. In spite of some emigration, the population was increasing, the people becoming 'numerous' as the report puts it. This was perhaps due to some improvement in agricultural practices, such as those advocated by the 'good Sir James,' better health measures and the hope of further consideration of their circumstances.

Many tenants were anxious to increase their holdings, if at all possible. In 1820 there was a request from the widow Anne Macdonald of Achcullin to let her have the whole farm as she understands that *'Donald Macdonald the piper is giving up his half of the farm...'* Donald Macdonald was hereditary piper to the laird of Grant and had been settled at Achcullin as reward for his services.

Any tenant who had difficulty paying his rent was likely to be ousted by someone doing better. Thus, in 1820, Hugh Munro of Dores, on the other side of Loch Ness, put in an offer for part of the land at Balchraggan tenanted by John Mackenzie, who could not pay his rent.

In 1826 consideration was given to the improvement of the road through the settlement, the existing access being not much more than a track, in fact three separate tracks, two leading to the area of Balchraggan, the other a 'sunk road' to Achcullin and Balmore. There were of course various other footpaths and a track leading to the Mill. The cost of an improved road was quoted as £7 3/-. The people were to provide the labour.

The demand for land was constant. In a letter to an Inverness-shire solicitor from the Rev James Maclauchlan, the son of the schoolmaster, Lachlan Maclauchlan, a request was made on behalf of Archibald Macdonald, *'tenant in Achabuie married to a niece of mine,'* that land should be given to his father-in-law *'who is married to my sister.'*

In 1828 three *'Birleymen of Urquhart'* Alexander Ross, Donald Macdonald and William Macdonald - the latter two could not write their names - were appointed to make a 'comprisement' of the 'black houses,' dykes, kilns and other appurtenances in Abriachan. The Birleymen's task was, acting as an independent body, to assess situations in cases of dispute, to make, as in this case, valuations of property, perhaps for incoming tenants, and so on.

Typical is the valuation of the property of Farquhar Fraser of Balchraggan:

Dwelling house including three windows, four doors, three thumbsnecks and three partitions........	7	15	-
Barn with two doors, lock and key.............................	3	15	-
Sheep cote..		8	-
Cart shed..		10	-
Little barn and door..	1	5	-
Byre with door and cowstalls......................................		16	
	£ 14	9	-

249 Ells, dyke below the arable lands at 10½d per ell..	£10	17	10½
40 Ells garden dyke at 10d per ell..............................	1	13	4
	£ 27	0	2½

We, the above designed Alexander Ross, Donald Macdonald and William Macdonald, Birleymen of Urquhart, have valued the above black houses and dykes at the sum of twenty-seven pounds and two pence half-penny, using our best skill and judgement witness our hands place and date above written

James Kerr   *Alexr Ross*
witness   *their marks*
                                      Donald X McDonald
                                      William X Macdonald

Many other places were assessed in like manner. The black houses of John Macdonald of Balbeg were valued at £6 10s, a kiln at Balbeg at £2 10s. John Fraser's black houses in Balbeg were meticulously assessed. Thus:

Dwelling house with 4 doors, 3 partitions, 3 windows............	£5
Barn with 2 doors	10s
Byre and door.. .	10s

Duncan Macdonald, the miller at Balbeg, had houses valued at £8 17s. It was reported that widow Catherine Macdonald of Balchraggan had a peat house at her place. Thumb snecks and locks and keys were all duly recorded. The value of Donald Macdonald's place at Balchraggan was put at £73 14s, this extremely high value being due to the fact that he had built *'many dykes'*. These can still be seen today.

It is not recorded to what these meticulous assessments were due. It could have been disagreements about rents, the people being unwilling to make improvements on their places, if it meant an increase in payment to the landlord. To meet even the minimum amount of rent was becoming increasingly difficult.

In 1836 Donald Macdonald of Balmore petitioned against any increase in rent pointing out the dangerous nature of his place, where horses were liable to *'go over the precipice'* into the depths of the Balmore burn. Janet Fraser in Caiplich complained that Donald Mackenzie, the joint tenant of her pasture, had *'put the plough'* to it. William Fraser of Balnagreisachan also complained about Donald Mackenzie. He was clearly a man desperate for more ground. All the troubles of the world, it seems, stem from disputed territory. In April 1837 a petition in favour of Archibald Macdonald, tenant in Achbuie, was drawn up, signed by Donald Tolmie, the schoolmaster, and ten inhabitants of Abriachan, six Frasers and four Macdonalds. Praise is lavished on Archibald Macdonald, who has been working the land inherited from his father for the last 15 years, as an *'honest, sober and peaceable good neighbour.'* The petition was raised against an intended rise in rent.

During the nineteenth century there were protests throughout the Highlands against increases in rents and against the forced evictions of those who could not pay. They had other troubles to contend with, too. In 1832 and again in 1849 there were outbreaks of cholera in Inverness, which spread to the surrounding areas. One young woman in Abriachan died of the disease. There must have been others. One cause was thought to be the overcrowding in the town by people evicted from their holdings and looking for shelter and work. The people dreaded infectious illness. Then the Disruption in the church caused the loss of Mr Tolmie,

above: traditional building in Abriachan: cruck beams and thumbsnecks

their respected teacher, who had seceded and could no longer work under S.S.P.C.K. terms. The people pleaded for his return, without success. For several years no regular teacher was in charge.

The Grants, at least since the time of the 'good Sir James,' were reputedly good to their tenants and had discouraged emigration. Only Ludovic had besmirched their reputation by sending to Bardados, without trial, 16 men of Glenurquhart and 68 of neighbouring Glen Moriston, after accepting their surrender, following defeat at the battle of Culloden. Sir James' successors, who had inherited the title Earl of Seafield after a cousin's death, were mostly men interested in developing their estates. The seventh Earl, in particular, who lived from 1815 to 1881, and who was known as 'the Good Earl' encouraged tree-planting, the building of new houses and steadings, the reclaiming of waste land. He wore the kilt and held Highland Games. It was in his time and in that of his son, Ian Charles, that ground in the Caiplich area was brought in, and five 'new lots' appeared on the map.

Mapping in the Highland area had been actively pursued during the latter part of the eighteenth century, mainly in order to facilitate the movement of troops over the new military roads, troops sent to quell the unruly population. General Roy's map appeared at this time.

The lairds then employed surveyors to map their estates and many beautiful maps were produced. Those of Abriachan include: *'Plan of the lands of Abriachan lying in the Parish and County of Inverness. The Property of Sir James Grant of Grant Bart. Surveyed by Geo Brown, 1808, copied by G Campbell Smith, Banff, 1850.'* There is a list of possessions, with amount of arable and of pasture moor, the total given in Scots acres. There are descriptive notes, e.g. *'steep face, with long heath, yields pretty good pasture in some places,'* or *'flat, stony, bare moor ground, yields little pasture.'* The houses and other buildings are clearly seen, also the acreage of each field, the heights of some of the hills are given. The scale is in Scots chains. The Gaelic spelling is erratic.

The next survey made in 1856-62 by George G. Mackay produced a *'Map of the Low Grounds of the Estate of Glenurquhart, the property of the Right Honourable the Earl of Seafield.'* In the section called *'Part 3, from Drumnadrochit to March of Dunain'* the holdings in Abriachan are clearly delineated. The 'new lots' in Caiplich are seen, marked out in straight lines, as was the custom at the time. There is less descriptive detail, but this is a most beautiful, coloured map.

Then in 1870, the Government, in the form of the Ordnance Survey, stepped in to produce official maps, the first in 1870-71, the next edition in 1904, and thereafter at regular intervals, on different scales. In 1870, the surveyors published a 'Name Book' for the Abriachan area, that is, a 'List of Names as written on the Plan, with various modes of spelling the same names.' One can imagine the difficulties for English-speaking officials encountering Gaelic place-names. Great

care was taken to ensure accuracy. Knowledgeable local people were brought in for consultation - the schoolmaster, the minister, the estate factor, the tenant. The name of Thomas Macdonald, the Bard, appears in this context several times. The various headings for the description of each place included *'Authority for the modes of spelling', 'Situation', 'Descriptive Remarks or other General Observations which may be considered of interest.'*

For instance: *'Easter Altourie:*

Authority for spelling: James Mollison, factor, Samuel Ian Ferguson, schoolmaster at Dochgarroch, Mr Alexander Mackenzie, tenant. This name is applied to a farmhouse one storey high, with suitable offices attached, the whole are thatched and in good repair. E Baillie, Esq, Dochfour, Proprietor.'

At Lady's Cairn, Charles Fraser-Mackintosh, the noted historian, the Rev Allan Macpherson from Dores and Mr MacGillivray, schoolmaster of Abriachan, were called in to provide the 'Descriptive Remarks' which were that this is a *'cairn to commemorate the resting of Lady Grant's coffin on its way to burial in Inverness.'* The croft at Ladycairn was noted as the property of Sir John Ramsden of Invereshie Lodge. Every feature in the area, natural or man-made, was recorded and described. Thus *'Fuaran Dearg'*, the Red Well, the water much prized for its medicinal qualities, *'Creag nan Sithean'*, Hill of the Fairies, *'Glac na Greighe'*, hollow of the herd of deer. Many names show the close observation and poetic gifts of the people who knew and loved these places. *'Glac Ossian'* is described as *'a large hollow to the north of Doire Mhor.'*

'*Cnoc na h-Eachdraidhe*' is called the hill of history and has now been identified as the site of a prehistoric settlement. The school is noted as a '*small parish
school, thatched, in fair condition.*' Leault is '*occupied by the schoolmaster, slated,
offices thatched, good repair.*' At Balnagriaschan there are '*four one-storey
thatched houses in bad repair.*' At Achbuie there are '*four or five thatched houses.*'
At Achcullin '*three or four thatched houses in bad condition*'. Balmore is described as a '*cluster of houses.*' Balchraggan is also called '*a cluster of houses*'
and described as '*middling.*' Balbeg and Tyeantore are '*very small places.*' At
Corriefoyness there are two small thatched houses, uninhabited: in very bad repair. At Kilianan there is '*a small croft house in good condition.*' Also noted is
the graveyard with sculptured gravestone and holed stone. Caiplich is described
as an area '*covered with heath*'.

The area was well visited by the authorities during the century, with Census
returns being made every ten years from 1841. These give a fair picture of the
times. The figures themselves are revealing and the information regarding 'occupation' shows how, with the changing times, paid employment was being taken
up.

In 1841 there were 104 houses with a population of 213 men and 253 women.
People were asked to state whether they were born in the county, whether they
were a 'foreigner' or born in England or Ireland. The number of windows in the

above: the nineteenth century 'sunk' road winding up through Abriachan

house had also to be entered. Regarding occupations, as well as the schoolmaster, there was the miller, three shoemakers, one blacksmith, one mason, three sawyers, one tailor, one 'meal dealer,' one wright, seven labourers.

These men would all, of course, work their small crofts part of the time. Many others would depend entirely on the produce of their holdings. There were also, at this time, eight people described as 'cottars,' that is people having no land, and depending on spells of work here and there, paid in money or kind. The houses would be small, easily destructible and very overcrowded. Lives were spent largely out-of-doors, with the roof for shelter at night or in times of storm. Little sign of many of them remains.

In 1871, in addition to names, ages and relationships, people were required to note their 'rank, profession or occupation,' whether any in the household were 'deaf, dumb, blind or imbecile,' the number of children attending school and the number of rooms 'with one or more windows'. Filling up the forms must have been a daunting task for the many whose English was extremely limited.

By 1881 the Census returns show 70 houses with 149 men and 163 women. There are now five shepherds listed and a gamekeeper, who has a 'white house,' that is one built of stone and lime. These are signs of the farming of sheep and the development of 'sporting' activity on the estate. There are also three masons, a carpenter and a 'road contractor,' two shoemakers and six people listed as 'paupers.' Though some of these occupations might well have been full-time, yet many families were largely dependent on many small crofts for a living. How did James Macdonald, in Blackfold, bring up 5 children on 10 acres, one wonders, or Alexander Fraser rear 7 on 15...?

From the notebook of John Fraser, Balmore, then a pupil in Abriachan School, in 1882:

'Abriachan since ten years
Abriachan 20th Feb. 1882
Dear Sir,

> *there is no doubt that Abriachan has greatly improved since the last ten years. Perhaps the most important of these improvements is the new road which was constructed several years ago. This road is a great benediction to the place and serves for the purpose of carrying on traffic. A few years ago a new schoolhouse was erected where daily instructions are given.*

We have a new mill also built, which saves considerable trouble from going elsewhere to grind our meal.

There was a wood planted three or four years ago, above Balmore, and we hope when old enough it will supply us partially with fire etc., as well as protect us from the severe northern winds laden with keen frost from the Polar regions.

John Fraser'

In 1891 the returns record the number of houses falling to 58, the number of people likewise, to 110 men and 150 women. There had been some emigration, to towns and overseas. We now find women's employment noted, with three wool-spinners, a dairymaid and a dressmaker, also an important new job - that of postmaster (in 1882) as well, of course, as the schoolmaster, the miller and a 'road contractor'. There is also mention of three boarded-out children. This was the beginning of the system of boarding orphaned or deprived children on the crofts, a system which was to be developed over the years. People were also asked to state whether they spoke Gaelic or English or both.

Meantime the Crofters' Act of 1886 had been passed, so that tenants could not be arbitrarily evicted from their holdings, but they still found difficulty in producing money for payment of rent. By the late 1880s most of the tenants on the Seafield Estates were in arrears with their rents. In December 1887 and January 1888 the area was surveyed and a *'Report and Valuation Urquhart and Abriachan 1888, by Robert Black and William Mackay'* was drawn up. As a result of this report many rents were brought down. The Grants of Seafield, like their predecessors, had always been understanding of their tenants' difficulties. In a 'General Description' of the district the Report states:

'It is for the most part very high, the highest reaching over 1000 feet. Soil on south side overlooking Loch Ness of fair quality but steep and heavy to labour. Higher portion of face poor and moorish. The Loch Lait (sic), *Achpopuli and Caiplich subjects are poor holdings, high moorland situation and crops seldom fill or ripen. Early frosts prevalent and potato crops frequently destroyed. Land poor, scattered and steep.'*

At Achpopuli which is described as *'reclaimed by tenant'* the rental of £25 is reduced to £6, with the addendum: *'tenants to make road and to be allowed £64.3.7 for arrears.'* The *'new lots'* in Caiplich are all described as *'reclaimed by tenant'* or *'reclaimed from heather.'* John Macdonald at Tye-an-Tore (another spelling of the Bard's place) is to *'get timbers sawn for barn'.* His house is 'fair.' He has 10 acres of arable, his rent to be reduced from £10 to £7.5/- Barnabas Stuart, at 2 Balchraggan, is to get *'manufactured wood and slate and start leader,'* that is a drain. His house is new. *'This is an improving tenant.'* John Fraser at Balbeg has a slated house and steading. He works the mill which was *'erected some years ago in response to petition of tenants.'* He wishes to be relieved of the mill as he *'loses considerably by it.'* In return for milling he would receive a proportion of the meal, but he lost a considerable amount of time, which held up his work on the croft.

Roderick Mackay, at new lot no 4 in Caiplich has 12 acres of arable reclaimed from moor, his rent to be reduced from £4 to £3. Donald Macdonald, also in Caiplich, has five acres of arable, his rent to be reduced from £2 to £1.10/-. His place is described as a *'very poor subject'* and himself as *'tenant poor - one arm.'* He is to get £4 off (arrears) for a new house.

Rebates on arrears were given for many reasons. As in this last case, for building a new house, also for making drains, for planting trees, for making roads, for using 'sawn timber' for roofing instead of rough branches, in fact for anything regarded as an 'improvement'. By the end of the century standards in housing were rising. Soon they would be built of stone with fine slate roofs.

from the Inverness Courier, 1889:

'On Monday last week, Thomas Fraser, Caiplich, was evicted, along with his wife and children. Some time ago Fraser became bankrupt, and, at the instance of his creditors, a trustee was appointed. His effects were realised at the Whitsunday term and his farm let to another tenant. Fraser however continued to occupy the farmhouse after the term and refused to quit, on the grounds that he did not get timeous warning. On Wednesday Mr Alex Macdonald, messenger-at-arms, Inverness, with a staff of assistants, proceeded to Caiplich, and after explaining to Fraser the object of their visit he proceeded to carry out his warrant. Fraser offered no active resistance, but his wife gave the officer and his men some trouble. When they came to the cradle which contained an infant a few months old, the officers asked Mrs Fraser to remove her child, but this she stoutly refused to do. In a short time, however, she thought better of it, and walked away with the infant in her arms to a neighbour's house, and the other child piteously crying in Gaelic for a piece of bread. The mother had none to give, and the pleading tones of the infant moved to compassion even the heart of the officer, who handed the child a shilling. Shortly thereafter the officer, having completed his work, left, leaving Fraser sitting on a hillock with his faithful collie beside him, and whittling a stick.'

Abriachan, by this time, was very much part of the 'sporting' side of the estate, providing grouse shooting, some stalking and trout fishing in Loch Laide for the wealthy sportsmen who rented Balmacaan Lodge for the season. A full-time gamekeeper was installed and there was part-time work for ghillies and stalkers. The building of dykes also provided some off-season employment for tenants.

Further afield, but not too far, that great enterprise, the building of the Highland Railway, was creating work at all levels - labouring, clerical, administrative. As had the building of the canal, this provided a 'boom' in job prospects, almost equivalent to that of the oil industry today. Abriachan was becoming part of the world of enterprise.

13

MORE SCHOOLMASTERS : 1798-1872

After the death of the much-loved 'Mr Lachlan' in 1801, and through the vicissitudes of the ensuing years, the people never lost their belief in the value of education. They were beginning to have more contact with the outside world, some of the men being employed in the building of the Caledonian Canal, and, later on, the construction of the Highland Railway, and having some sort of wage, however small. Soon the Census records would be showing a man's occupation, no longer as a 'farmer' (crofter), but as a 'labourer,' that is someone working for another, no longer mostly for himself. Word would be circulating of events in other places, of changing circumstances. The people were acquiring confidence in their ability to express their wishes.

In 1825, after the death of the highly respected teacher John Fraser, who had succeeded 'Mr Lachlan', in fear of not getting another teacher, through their spokesman they demanded, and soon got, repairs done to the school which was said to be in *'a ruinous state.'* They also begged for £40 to build a new house for the schoolmaster and this was done.

Abriachan was no longer the *'detached and isolated place,'* as it had been described in a report by an Inspector of the S.S.P.C.K. in 1803. In this report the Inspectors (a minister, an elder, a tenant and some parents) had commented favourably on the children's progress, particularly in religious knowledge. The number of scholars was 41. The first class could read the Old Testament in English and Gaelic, and also translate English into Gaelic. The youngest scholars are *'joining and spelling words of one or two syllables and can repeat the Lord's Prayer, Creed and Ten Commandments in Gaelic.'* There is a request for religious books, not only to *'forward the progress of the scholars'* but also so that *'the Scriptures would be more generally read by the young people to their Parents in their respective houses, especially during the winter season, when they*

can seldom go to the Church which is ten miles distant.'

Shortly after this visit of inspection a letter was sent to Sir James Grant asking him to put in a request for books. An Inspector's report in 1824 finds the schoolmaster ill and confined to bed, the school taught by his son. The people express their concern over his illness as they value his teaching and particularly his encouragement of their learning to read the Bible in Gaelic, as *'they hardly understand any other language.'* The report states *'53 scholars attend during winter. The house and schoolhouse are in good repair and thatched by the inhabitants, garden and cow's grazing are attached and the people supply the teacher with fuel.'*

The Inspector's report on the condition of the school does not seem to tally with that of the community who, as we have seen, were demanding, the very next year, that serious repairs be done. The Report continues: *'The teacher reads and explains and catechises in the schoolhouse where all the neighbourhood assemble on those Sabbaths on which they cannot venture to hear sermon in Inverness, more than ten miles distant and partly the road excessively bad .. he has been in this respect as well as in his regular school, extremely useful to the neighbourhood.'*

This report contains the first mention of a school in Caiplich. It says: *'there is an Inverness Society school at Caplach, a mile distant from this station, but*

separated by a hill unpassable in winter. About 40 scholars attended this school last winter. It is taught by a young man of apparently serious disposition.'

A report in 1826 describes Abriachan as *'a station singularly and romantically situated on the top of a hill to which there is access only by a narrow road lately made.'* The newly arrived schoolmaster, Neil Maclean, from Coll, was considered *'an excellent teacher.'* The report continues: *'the schoolroom is about 36 feet in length and 16 feet wide. The windows are too small. It is furnished with forms, but wants desks and accommodation for writing.'* Improvements are still needed.

The report goes on: *'In the schoolroom the teacher reads on Sundays to the people when there is no sermon in the neighbourhood. The teacher's dwelling-house is at a little distance from the school. It is a new house only finished this summer. Colonel Grant, upon whose property the school is, contributed liberally to the expense of the building. The rest was done by the inhabitants...The teacher has also a good garden and a large croft, which, however is not yet enclosed, and he has also the right of pasturage on the common'*. House, garden, croft and pasturage are still in place today, the property now known as Leault, or sometimes, the School Croft.

Mrs Fraser, the widow of the former teacher, was in charge of a *'school of industry'* for the girls, teaching them sewing, spinning and knitting. She would make one girl read while the others were sewing or knitting, an arrangement much approved of by the Inspectors. The population of the time is recorded as 300, with 84 scholars attending. Though things seemed promising, Neil Maclean stayed only seven years in Abriachan before going to teach in Lewis. He was, after all, an islander.

above: 'it is a new house only finished this summer....' 1826
the School Croft, Leault

In 1833, when Mr Donald Tolmie, who came from Laggan, was in charge, on the day of inspection the scholars had been competing with four other schools for awards given by the Celtic Society and *'had carried off the greater number of prizes.'*

Two years later the Inspectors examined *'such of the classes as understand English.'* Gaelic was clearly very much in evidence in the school, as it was in the children's homes. Nevertheless, they performed well in English and the examiners were impressed by the general intelligence they displayed.

In this report, Abriachan is described as *'situated at the top of a hill the access to which is by a very steep, narrow road about two miles in length. As you ascend the hill there is no appearance of any habitation but on getting near the summit you all at once come upon a great number of cottages, with well cultivated fields.'*

Smuggling is said, in this report, to be on the way out. This was probably not quite so, though great efforts were being made to suppress it. The people of Abriachan are described as being *'quite insulated and separated from all others.'* They *'keep themselves quite secluded and have little intercourse with the rest of the parish.'*

This, no doubt, is how it must have seemed to men coming from the town for a brief visit. Geographically speaking, still today the area is comparatively isolated and liable to be cut off for short spells by hard frost or deep snow. But mid-nineteenth century hill people thought nothing of walking or riding horseback for miles to 'ceilidh' with friends or relatives. News was circulating in the old oral tradition. Abriachan was becoming part of the worlds of politics and religion.

After the Disruption in the Church in 1843 Mr Tolmie seceded to the Free Church. Dissatisfaction with the system of patronage had been simmering for many years.

> 2, Attendance very irregular. Children kept at home working on peats and herding. All present prepared lessons very well. And made ordinary progress.

> 9 Attendance decreasing. On Thursday and Friday examined all present on work required by Ro. Code. Very well done. Rest went through the usual course and made ordinary progress.

Inspector's report

Under the rules of the S.S.P.C.K. Mr Tolmie had to leave his post as teacher, seceders being considered to have disruptive tendencies. He had been well liked and his services to the community much appreciated. The people had petitioned for his return but to no avail. Many followed him into the Free Church.

For several years the register of teachers is blank, the school probably taught by students or other volunteers. One name, that of Mr Duncan Ferguson, is recorded in 1859-60. Then, in 1861, Mr Angus MacGillivray was appointed and was to remain in his post for 13 years. He is still remembered by the very old as 'bodach bheag' - the wee man. He had 45 pupils on the roll and was to be the last man to teach in the original building, which was described in a report of this time as being *'neither suitable nor quite safe.'* Nevertheless, the Inspector comments that *'it is creditable to the teacher that he has a pupil at present who has gone through Euclid (6 books) and a certain amount of applied mathematics.'*

The next report describes the schoolroom as *'sound but very rough.'* Reading and spelling are said to be *'good,'* meaning only *'fair.'* Copybooks are *'clean and carefully written.'* Against *'grammar'* and *'singing'* is the word *'none.'* In a further report (undated) there is mention of the childrens' difficulty in expressing themselves in English and it says *'Reading is fluent and careful. The Gaelic accent, which is marked, renders it less intelligible than it might otherwise be.'* So it would have sounded to the English-speaking Inspectors. Old ways of speech are long in dying.

The general report states that the school is conducted with very fair intelligence and efficiency and is evidently very popular and useful in the place. The discipline is good. But by now, the late 1860s, it is also stated: *'the present school accommodations are in a state of great dilapidation. I got Mr Craig, Lord Seafield's factor, to accompany me to the school today and he has given me to expect that the present buildings will be replaced by new ones before my next visit takes place.'* This was to happen.

At about this time - 1867 - there is further mention of a school in the Caiplich area, when Mr Lewis Robertson is named as teacher, with 25 pupils on the roll. Religious knowledge was highly commended. Gaelic was often used in teaching as the children did not understand English. There is no mention of a schoolhouse. Most probably the teacher, a young man, would lodge with a family.

The hours of attendance were long. From 1st February to 1st October the school was open every weekday from 7-11 a.m. and 1-5 p.m. For the rest of the year the hours were 8-12 a.m. and 1-3 or 4 p.m. In late summer there were three weeks of holiday, known as the *'harvest play.'*

At Christmas and Easter there were only a few days off. Attendance at school often depended on whether the children were needed at home for fieldwork, peat-cutting, herding and so on. The year was divided into four quarters - Lammas, Hallowmass, Candlemass and Beltane. School fees were paid by the quarter. They varied from place to place. Approximately thus:

1s 6d a quarter for reading
2s   a quarter for reading and writing
2s 6d a quarter for the three Rs
2s 6d a quarter extra for Latin

Some parents sent their children to school in turn, a quarter at a time. The teacher received a salary, perhaps ten pounds a year, plus a small sum from the 'heritor' or landlord and small emoluments for extra duties such as acting as Registrar, choir master and so on.

In Caiplich in 1868 and 1869 Mr Robertson is still on the register as teacher, then Mr Archibald Maclean's name appears and is there from 1870-73. He is still remembered as a character of legend by the few remaining native people in Caiplich. After this it seems that the school may have been discontinued for a time, as it is next mentioned in the Minutes of the School Board of the 11th April, 1902, thus: *'the inhabitants of Caiplich and Alturlie wanted a school as they are 4 miles from Abriachan school and 3 miles from Dochgarroch.'* On the 6th May of that year the Minutes record: *'a school is to be built. It is to have two rooms.'* It is ruined now, but the outline of the playground, on the edge of the moor, is still clearly seen and the well flows abundantly. A new house has lately been built on the site.

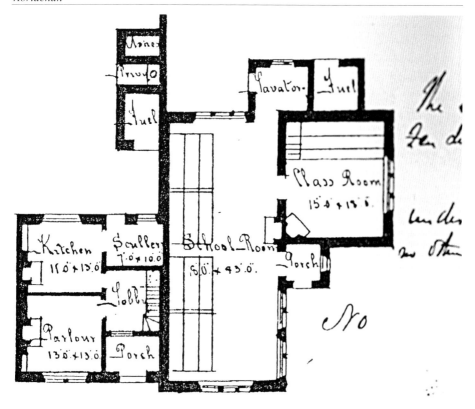

'the great new edifice taking shape....' plan of the school, 1875, the rooms with tiered seating

Soon after the passage of the Education Act of 1872 new school buildings were erected all over the Highlands. Mr MacGillivray, in Abriachan, must have watched in amazement as the great new edifice took shape just over the road from his 'dilapidated' schoolroom. He was soon to retire to his schoolhouse, a comfortable enough place, with its garden and its croft. His little old schoolroom is now a rickle of stones, but he and his wife are remembered still in the hearsay of the oldest people.

14

THE BIG SHEEP

With the final breakdown of the clan system, towards the end of the eight eenth century, territories changing hands on monetary terms, former chiefs becoming landlords and demanding increased rents to fund their improving life-styles, the people lost the sense of allegiance to an ideal of community. Many young men joined the regiments which were being recruited for service overseas. The landlords were busy making improvements on their lands, introducing new crops, draining, planting trees. The biggest 'improvement,' one which would bring in a substantial income, was that of the coming of the 'big sheep.'

The people had for long been in the habit of keeping a few small, hardy sheep to provide the wool needed for spinning and weaving, the making of warm gar-ments. The ewes' milk was often made into cheese. The 'big sheep' were to provide wool for the factories in the south which were busy turning out uniforms for the soldiery engaged in foreign wars. The Highland landlords were happy to accommodate the lowland flock-masters with huge acreages of grazing for their sheep and substantial houses for them and their families. Some of these, built of stone with slated roofs, can still be seen in the glens, along with the remains of huge sheep fanks.

The landlords, faced with non-payment of rent from their impoverished ten-ants, were well pleased with their vastly 'improved' financial situation. But what of those tenants whose cattle were driven from their hill grazings to make way for these 'big sheep'? Their derisive hatred of the uncouth, greedy, white-faced beasts found its way into satire, and, in a place not many miles from Abriachan, into violent action. The year 1792 became known as the 'year of the sheep' when thousands of animals were driven from their grazings by enraged tenants. The army was brought in to quell the rioting and the ringleaders were eventually caught and imprisoned in Inverness, subsequently, with the help of sympathetic jailers, making their escape. Later there were to be riots in many parts of the Highlands, as the people protested against their loss of grazing.

Soon, they were to lose more than their grazing. On some estates they were evicted from their holdings, sometimes by force, with their houses burnt before their eyes, sometimes with an allocation of a few acres of marginal land on the moor, or on the coast, where they were to work at the kelp industry, the burning of seaweed to produce an alkaline substance used in the manufacture of glass. This was to provide a substantial income for the landlords. The people were also to work at the development of the fishing, though many of them had never seen the sea. It was at this time that many people were forced to emigrate, packed into unseaworthy ships, to help in the development of the emerging colonies in America and other parts of the world.

Those who remained were expected to eke out a living on the small parcels of land allocated to them, known as crofts, from the Gaelic 'croit', meaning a small area of enclosed ground. Supplementary sources of income were to be found at the kelping, the fishing or other paid employment on the estates. Henceforth the people were to be known as 'crofters.'

Formerly they had lived in 'townships,' in small houses clustered companion-ably together and had worked the ground in common, on the 'run-rig' system, that is, with the crops grown in strips, allocated fairly from year to year. Their main means of subsistence lay in their cattle, which grazed the 'out-by' land and, in summer, at the high hill pastures of the 'shielings.'

Now, they were to build themselves houses scattered over a wide area, each with its own small, individual allocation of land - and with no access to hill pasture. The disruption to their way of life can be imagined.

As one bard, John MacLachlan put it:

> *'On an April morning, I no longer hear*
> *Bird songs or the lowing of the cattle on the moor,*
> *I hear the unpleasant noise of sheep*
> *And the English language, dogs barking*
> *And frightening the deer.'*

Mrs Anne Grant of Laggan, a minister's wife who was living at about this time among Highland people saw the effect on their lives by what she called the *'rage for sheep farming.'* Her love for and admiration of the people she often expressed in poems and in her well-known 'Letters from the Mountains'. In one of these, written to a friend, she says of the people: *'there is a musician in every house and a poet in every hamlet.'* These were a people who would survive.

implements of the crofters - from the former Abriachan crofting museum

Rioting continued all over the Highlands and in the islands, crofters refusing to pay rents unless their grazings were restored, destroying walls, burning ricks. One cold spring day in 1882, at Braes in the Isle of Skye, when the people ignored warnings to take their cattle off the hill needed for the laird's sheep, a body of police and Marines was sent in to force the issue. Most of the men were away at the fishing at the time but the women and children stood up to the attack, throwing stones and brandishing sticks, their only weapons. This skirmish became known as the 'Battle of the Braes' and is commemorated today by a cairn and a plaque at the roadside. It was fully reported in the 'Illustrated London News' of the time. It was to be one of the many contributory reasons for the eventual setting up of a Royal Commission to investigate the causes of what had become known as the Highland 'Land Wars.'

15

THE ROYAL COMMISSION OF 1883

The various 'civilising' agencies which had been at work in the north from the eighteenth century - the S.S.P.C.K. and other educational enterprises, the Forfeited Estates Commission, the surveys and reports by Telford with the subsequent vast improvement in communications, the founding of the Highland Society of Scotland - all this activity, much of it undertaken out of fear of future rebellion had resulted in the emergence of a population much more fully aware of the larger issues in the world around them.

Previously, some 'heritors,' as the landlords were known, had been reluctant to provide schools on the grounds that educated tenantry might be difficult to manipulate. By the late nineteenth century, as we have seen in Abriachan, the people were making demands, via their M.P.s. In 1882 they had a post office established. John Murdoch, an Excise officer, who travelled widely in the Highland area, and who had worked in Ireland and had seen the troubles there, did much to encourage the people to defend their rights.

In former times small tenants had security of tenure subject to the payment of rent and/or services. It was held that this claim to security had been transmitted in what was known as a 'kindness', a right of permanent occupation by one's kin. This right had never been codified in law, but was widely felt to be valid. In any case, as Lord Selkirk is quoted as saying: 'how little avail was a piece of sheepskin and a lump of wax.'

Sadly the established church did little to help the people in their struggle to resist eviction, the preaching being that the laird's word must be obeyed. After the Disruption, however, in 1843, the ministers of the Free Church came out firmly on the side of the people.

At fireside ceilidhs, at meetings in barns or schools, in bardic utterances circulating in the communities as well as in rioting and desperate acts of destruction, the people were finding ways of expressing their discontent. The Gaelic Society of Inverness was in the forefront of those demanding that action be taken to tackle the plight of the Highland people.

At last, in 1883, a Royal Commission was set up to enquire into the situation. In the chair was Lord Napier, K.T., a Lowlander. Other members were Sir Kenneth S. Mackenzie, Donald Cameron of Lochiel, M.P., Charles Fraser Mackintosh M.P., Sheriff Officer Nicolson, and Professor Mackinnon, M.A. These members were all of Highland origin; several were Gaelic speakers. A notice announcing a forthcoming meeting of the Commissioners with delegates was to be posted on the church door of each area to be visited. Men chosen to appear were to state their grievances to the members of the Commission. Most of them spoke only Gaelic and had to depend on interpreters to convey the meaning of their statements. Many were afraid that if they spoke out too bluntly they would incur reprisal. Typical of the situation is this encounter of Angus Stewart, a crofter in Braes, Skye - where a famous skirmish with police had taken place - with the members of the Commission, as recorded in the published proceedings.

He was asked to state his occupation, where he was born, whether he was freely elected. Then he was told: *'Now will you have the goodness to state to me what are the hardships or grievances of which the people complain who have elected you?'* - *'Yes, but it is in Gaelic that I prefer to speak. I want the assurance that I shall not be evicted from my holding ....I would not have a fire at my house at Whitsunday.'* It is clear that intimidation was a factor. Another crofter from the area of Braes said: *'The principal hardship I see is that the people cannot take a crop out of the ground. And the rent is heavy.'* The ground was wet, boggy and overcrowded with tenants evicted from elsewhere.

Angus Mackay from Farr, in Sutherland, said: *'We and our fathers have been cruelly burnt out of Strathnaver, like wasps and forced down to the barren sea shore, where we had, in many cases, to carry earth on our backs to form a patch of land.'* Murdo Maclean, a crofter from Uig on the island of Lewis, stated: *'The crofters cannot do without heather ropes in order to fasten the thatch upon the houses. There is one day set apart by the game keeper upon which you are allowed to go and pull heather to make ropes...you cannot attend on another day...or you are liable to be fined for it.'*

At a sitting of the Commission in Inverness on October 11th, 1883, it was stated: *'After getting the people to trench and drain their crofts, to insist upon a rotation of crops, sow grasses - clover and rye grass - turnips, carrots, cabbage, Jerusalem artichokes and numerous other vegetables of which they never heard before...seeds were forced upon them, without any instructions as to how they were to use them and they had to pay for them.'* This is clearly an example of the new 'improving' ideas, being in some places forced upon the tenants regardless of suitability.

Glenurquhart, on the Grants' estate, was a fertile glen where it was acknowledged that the people were *'comfortable and happy.'* In other parts things were different. Alexander Ross, aged 63, had lived on the Novar estate till 1882. He was well-known as 'the Bard' and gave his evidence in Gaelic, with Sheriff Nicolson as his interpreter. He said: *'My rent was £8 and I kept two cows and a heifer and a mare and a foal. I gave no offence to the proprietor except that I was not present at the time of the paying of the rent and was a little behind with it afterwards. As soon as I was able, I paid the rent, all except £2, and would have paid that, too if only they had given me time. I was removed a year from Whitsunday last. They knocked down the house, and we were two nights obliged to live on the hillside...yes I've often written Gaelic verses and poetry. I never wrote a satire against anybody but I may have said some sharp things when I told the people the truth that people didn't like!'*

A Colin Chisholm, speaking of Strathglass, said: *'A Mr Winans, an American, bought land for deer forests. I don't like his butchering style of killing game at all. Gathering the poor animals together and driving them before the muzzle of the gun.'-* *'Does he not stalk them?'-* he was asked. *'You might as well send an elephant after them to stalk them.'* This Mr Winans became notorious in the area.

In an appendix to the Report, Alexander Carmichael, an Excise officer, who knew the Highlands, and particularly the Islands well, made the following statement :

'...the crofters meet during the day probably at Cnoc na Comhairle, the Council Hill, or Clach na Combairle, the Council stone. If they meet at night, it is in some central house ... These meetings are held at night to avoid losing time during the day. To me these meetings of the crofters were highly interesting as showing the ability of the people, their logical and legal acumen, their readiness of resource, and, I am happy to add, their invariable courtesy to one another. In seeing these respectable, industrious crofters quietly, friendly and judiciously thus arranging their farming affairs, often wet, weary and hungry, without food, without rest....I have felt that they are cruelly maligned.

When a crofter is elected Constable of his Townland, he takes off his shoes and stockings and taking his bonnet in his hand and bowing low and reverently, he declares on honour, in presence of earth and heaven, in presence of God and men - that he shall be faithful to his trust.'

The duties of the constable were to allocate peat-banks, to see to the repairing of roads and dykes, to regulate the 'souming' or number of livestock allowed on the common grazing. His reward was in kind, in free grazing and tillage.

the souming dyke at Achbuie, separating the cultivated fields from the higher common grazings

The Commissioners spent many months listening to evidence from crofters in all parts of the Highland area. They were considered to have carried out their remit fairly and conscientiously, even putting themselves at some risk on their journeys, particularly from shipwreck on the way to the islands. The people responded in like manner. When at last the hearings came to an end and their deliberations were concluded, the Commissioners' Report was published in 1884. Two years later, after much deliberation by a Government not unsympathetic to the situation in the Highlands, the 'Crofters Act' was passed. This gave security of tenure to the people in their crofts, the assurance of fair rent, the establishment of a Crofters Commission, but it still did not restore to them an adequate amount of land.

16

AFTER THE SHEEP - THE DEER

Inevitably, as in every market-led enterprise, there were fluctuations in the wool trade. Also, lands became overgrazed and soured. There were losses among the stock. The lairds began to look for other ways to make their estates pay.

They themselves had always enjoyed the pleasures of the chase. Those who could still afford to maintain a fairly lavish lifestyle would entertain large parties of guests during the shooting season. This provided welcome employment for some of the tenants, who acted as gamekeepers, stalkers, ghillies. Lodges were built in the more remote parts of the estate. Good stone houses were provided for the keepers. On the larger places these employees were made to wear suits of specially designed tweed. As the nineteenth century wore on and people were looking for an escape from the ever more crowded parts of the south country, the appeal of the Highlands, which Queen Victoria and the Prince seemed so enthusiastically to enjoy, attracted many travellers and visitors. The image of the 'wild' Highlanders was becoming, perhaps, less daunting. Some of the more impoverished lairds began then to develop the sporting sides of their estates, with a view to attracting shooting tenants who would pay handsomely for the privilege of enjoying the chase. Deer and grouse were plentiful on the high hills, the rivers were stocked with salmon, the lochs with trout. Pheasants were reared by keepers, hand-fed, then released for a shoot. Ducks could be shot at dawn by the younger, more active members of the party.

Signs of these activities began to appear in Abriachan. The Grants had a large house, built as a shooting lodge, at Balmacaan, at the eastern end of Glen Urquhart. This could be let, along with the shooting rights over miles of hill and moor. These hills and moors included those of Abriachan. A local gamekeeper was appointed and given a house and croft. He was to inspire as much fear as the ground-officers of earlier times. A sitting tenant was displaced to make room for

him and his family. There was no longer to be any question of *'a deer from the hill, a fish from the pool, a tree from the forest...'* The crofters, those who dared, had to sneak a fish from the high hill lochs, using a device known as an 'otter' to snare them, with a lookout keeping watch. Even rabbits were prohibited game.

Butts were built, where the privileged stood at ease to shoot, their guns loaded by their ghillies. Loch Laide, the small loch which had fed the people over the ages, with its fish, its ducks, its little island where the black-headed gulls laid their eggs, this loch was now to be stocked with trout and to become notable for famous fishing contests.

The development of the estate, for sport, though it provided employment for some of the people, perhaps the younger sons of tenants, yet meant disaster for many. Large areas of ground were fenced off with high wire, to become known as deer-forests, where deer were to graze and breed, thus depriving the people of grazing for their cattle. In some parts, the rapidly increasing deer, allowed to roam indiscriminately, made depredations on the crofters' small crops of oats and hay. In spite of protests, no compensation was granted for these losses.

Many places in the vicinity of the hunting lodge at Balmacaan were taken over to enlarge and increase the productivity of the Home Farm, which supplied food for the hungry shooters. The people displaced were allowed ground in remote

above: bringing in the deer from the high tops   89

areas. Over the whole of the Highlands, these lucrative times of shooting went on, day after day, till it seemed that nothing that moved could survive. It is interesting to note the numbers of creatures shot in one season in this extract from a typical game-book of that time.

A game-book of 1884-85

Stag	208	Brown hare	865
Hind	130	White hare	648
Fallow deer	40	Rabbit	2,111
Grouse (brace)	7,475	Trapped rabbit	7,467
Black grouse	238	Fox	117
Ptarmigan	103	Weasel	376
Capercaillie	7	Hoodie Crow	147
Partridge	993	Hawk	137
Pheasant	766	Peregrine Falcon	2
Woodcock	60	Raven	15
Snipe	125	Owl	21
Wildfow	187	Magpie	21
Plover	50	Jay	46
Wood pigeon	18	Cat	159
Hedgehog	209	Squirrel	70

With slaughter on that scale going on, year after year, it is a wonder that wild life in the Highlands today has not suffered total extinction.

A surreptitious shot or the setting of a snare by a crofter meant 'one for the pot', a meal for a hungry family. To his mind the only real predator, the one he could see and smell, the one who preyed on his few domesticated creatures round the door - the lamb or the chicken - was the red fox. Hoodie-crows could be a menace too, stabbing the eyes of new-born lambs. Other creatures he respected, studying their ways as his forebears had done, killing out of necessity. Trees and plants he regarded as valued parts of his world, providers of nourishment and healing.

The 'keepers,' the men who 'kept' the game for the delight of the sportsmen, who laid the corpses of birds and animals out in rows at the end of the day's shooting, these men had to see a predator in any creature which might damage the prospects of the favoured prey. The crofter himself, of course, came into this category.

In times of fear or sorrow resort was always had to the rallying call of the bards. One of these, in Morvern, where the clearance of the people to make way for sheep and deer was particularly harsh, wrote (translated from Gaelic):

'Is it not a great change, in every respect, that has come over our native land, since we received a message from the court that caused us a sad awakening; that every delightful home should be without smoke, every field and corner under moss since the son of the deer has put us in disarray and banished us to a distant land..the customs of our forebears have undergone a change....old laws were set aside.' But *'the deer forests will be done away with and the ground will be cultivated and everyone will set to work with plough and harrow as of old...Wake up, do not be negligent.......there will be freedom on land and peace on the sea and you will have a written title to it, but there will be harsh strife around Scotland before the debts are settled.'*

Another bard wrote:

'A new song about the destruction of the crofters: the many glens they have made desolate, with deer in the place of people - the poor crofter is left unpitied in a house in which they would not lodge their dogs. It is their desire to stock the glens for themselves with deer and grouse: a land of blood and destruction and treachery for those who were once proudly in possession. The rights accruing from their service - a red rusty sword - today it is worth no more for rent or tax than its price in hard steel. Once again lift up your noble mighty spirit...it is a reproach upon you to be dumb and inactive when your help is in your own hands, to be enslaved by the landlord when you have been so valorous in battles.'

Poems such as these, many of which were published in the Oban Times, and many of which would have been said or sung at the fireside ceilidhs and public meetings of the remaining tenants must have inspired the new insurrections which were taking place.

Druim

17

ANOTHER ROYAL COMMISSION

Though the Crofters' Act of 1886 had given the people security of tenure in their holdings, it still had not allowed them enough land to work nor restored most of their hill grazings. The continuing development of the 'sporting' side of many estates now meant the loss of even more land to husbandry. 'Tha moran ri dheanamh fhathast' - 'there is still much to do,' people were saying. So it was that in 1892 another Royal Commission was set up to look into the state of the crofting communities.

Of the eight members of the Commission, one, David Brand, was Chairman of the Crofters' Commission, one was a land valuer, two were M.P.s, two others were 'from Inverness,' one not identified, and only one, the Rev John Malcolm MacCallum, a minister from Argyll, appeared to have real understanding of the problems of small tenants. Many people appearing before the Board to testify were estate factors, valuers, other agents, some speaking at great, and tedious, length. Crofters were in a minority. The changeover from large scale sheep farming to the creation of deer forests meant changes in the type of employment available for tenants. On the estate of Glen Urquhart at this time 13 shepherds were displaced and 4 or 5 men employed as gamekeepers. Some ghillies found work in pheasant rearing and so on.

At the 14th sitting of the Commission at Drumnadrochit, at the east end of Glen Urquhart and some 5 miles from Abriachan, on July 4th 1893, Hugh Macdougall, a blacksmith and crofter, stated: *'Gentlemen, in my opinion, there is a considerable amount of land in Glen Urquhart suitable for new holdings, and for the enlargement of existing holdings, that comes within the scope of your remit, and there is also among the people of the glen a strong desire for such land. In the deer forest of Balmacaan, there are many acres of arable land. Some have been planted. Much arable land has been added to the home farm. ...there were a number of families..the ruins of some of the houses are still standing and much of the old arable land is still under heather.'*

Crofters from Balmacaan had been removed to high places, some at close on 1000 feet above sea-level. One man testified: *'Small tenants that were put on the hills between this and Abriachan, they only got the barren hill-grazing there.'* Some 20 families had been evicted from land in the vicinity of the Lodge at Balmacaan, their crofts being added to the home farm.

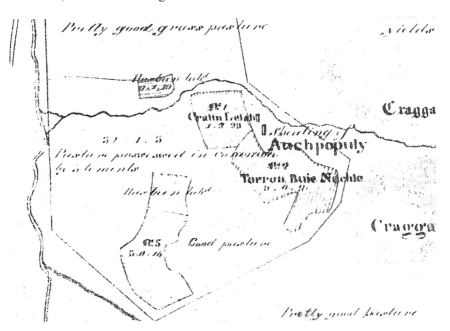

One of the families was that of the Macleans who were allocated ground at Achpopuli; 1000 feet above sea-level, near the old road through Caiplich to the Glen. There they were left to fend for themselves. Stone was to hand for the building of house-walls and heather for thatching. They were allowed to bring the cabers (roof-beams) from their former dwelling, as timber was scarce. Some fifty years ago a descendant of the family would recount how, after sheltering for the first night as best they could, they set to, at first light, at the building. The story goes that, by the following morning, they were supping their brose from dishes placed on top of the wall and that by that night they had a roof over their heads. That was the reality of the evictions. Eventually, several other houses were built in the vicinity. The original house was rebuilt to modern standards, and, after years of hardship and work, the place became a good hill holding. The boys would labour, before and after school, at the access road which now carries lorries, vans and the post bus up to the farm.

One other place in the heights - Rhivoulich - was also developed. The whole area had previously been shieling ground, where the people from Caiplich brought their cattle for summer grazing. Traces of the small shelters they used can still be seen.

The Balmacaan forest was let at this time to a Mr Bradley Martin of New York. He entertained lavishly at the Lodge, feeding his guests on the produce of the chase and on the good food provided by the home farm, from land taken from the crofters. The sight of his horse-drawn vehicles labouring up the steep road to the Abriachan hills has passed into legend. His memorial is in the village hall in Drumnadrochit which he had built as a token of appreciation of the benefits the tenancy had brought him. These benefits, of course, were at the cost of the inflictions imposed by the proprietor of the estate on his small tenants.

They were scattered, as we have seen, to the most barren parts. Some were given paid employment, to be at the beck and call of their employer. Every household was to receive the gift of a portrait of the young laird as he came of age.

In an addendum to the report of the Royal Commission, the Rev Malcolm MacCallum, the man most likely to understand the people whose views were being heard, stated: *'The unanimous Report of this Commission and the evidence led before it, in my opinion conclusively prove that there is urgent need for the settlement of the land question in the highlands...The joint right of the Highland clansmen with the landlords to the land has, so far as existing crofters are concerned been recognised, and to some extent been given effect to, by the Crofters' Act. But with respect to the land cleared for sheep and deer, and constituting an area much more extensive, valuable and fertile than that presently in the occupation of crofters, the landlords have appropriated the clansmens' rights and interests in it without payment or compensation of any kind. The solution of the Highland problem is not land purchase but resumption of the clansmens' right to occupy the Fatherland. It is an inexpensive solution and one that would not impoverish, but might ultimately benefit, the landlords, seeing that the return from the large grazings is a constantly diminishing quantity and many of them, well suited for crofters' holdings, are admittedly unlettable.*

In any case, the demand that the cleared lands, now lying almost wholly waste, should be made available for the enlargement of present holdings..is a call for simple justice and a wider and more consistent application of the main principle of the Crofters' Act.'

More than a hundred years later, the land question in the Highlands has still not been settled, but at least it is in the forefront of political thinking and, more importantly, within the grasp of activists on the ground.

18

DISTILLING

By the mid-eighteenth century the brewing of ale had been largely given up and wine from the continent was penalised by heavy duties, so that whisky was the principal drink in the Highlands and was not unduly costly. Then, the Government seeing a chance to obtain much-needed revenue, passed various acts imposing licences on a growing distilling industry. In the Highlands, where distilling had been on a modest scale, this meant that the business could not profitably be carried on.

In the 'Statistical Account of Scotland', published in 1796, we read: *'Distilling is almost the only method of converting our victual (barley) into cash for the payment of rent.....and whisky may, in fact, be called our staple commodity.'* The harsh measures imposed by the Government meant that the business of distilling had to go, quite literally, underground. The bothies where the craft was carried on were often in caves or dug-outs.

Fraser-Mackintosh, in his 'Antiquarian Notes', says: *'in no place in the Highlands was smuggling carried on with greater vigour than in Abriachan, which, from the fine water, its unapproachableness in some parts, its natural hiding-places in others, rendered the pursuit of the business a secure one.'* There were also ample supplies of peat and of juniper which gave a smokeless fire.

It was a skilled affair, but it was also a ploy which intrigued the men as a challenge to authority, and, of course, it had its economic necessity. Times were hard, rents never got any less, and there was always a customer for a good dram. Whisky - 'uisge beatha,' the water of life - was, and still is, prized as a health-giving drink in the cold, damp climate of the country. 'Toddy' -whisky with hot water and a spoonful of honey, taken at bedtime - is still considered the best cure for a cold. Of course, the tasting of the brew sometimes led to tragedy. A story still told in Abriachan today is that of the two men who were lost on their way home

from the bothy at the Red Rock. The body of one was found in the burn, the other vanished, leaving an intriguing unsolved mystery.

There are many good tales, too, of Excisemen exasperated and outwitted, of kegs of whisky flung at the last minute into the peat-bog and searched for in vain for years. Duncan Fraser was known as the King of the Smugglers. The remains of one of his bothies, built into the slope of the hill on the far side of Loch Laide are still discernible. One day a neighbour, coming down the hill after looking for lost sheep, stumbled through the camouflaged roof of the bothy, where he spent a pleasant night!

This same Duncan Fraser once disguised his old father as a corpse, laid him out on the kitchen table, covered with a sheet, and put the tell-tale cask in his hand. No-one would dare to interfere with a corpse. A grand-mother's skirts, plumped up as she sat warming herself at the fire, would also make a suitable hiding-place.

Sometimes the Excisemen would stay for several weeks in the schoolhouse so as to be quick off the mark for arrests. They would also sail up and down Loch Ness looking for tell-tale smokes rising from the wooded hillside. But the look-outs were keen-eyed and by the time the officers of the law were ashore all the smokes were extinguished and a hail of stones would come down in greeting.

Substantial bribes were offered to the people to inform on the smugglers but,

above: the 'Swapper's' house in Caiplich, home of the last of the stillers

though some may have disapproved of the business, it is not recorded that a single bribe was accepted. The one exception - unrecorded - is that of a man, who, when the worm was worn out, reported his own still to the authorities, and, with the reward for giving the information, bought himself some new equipment and set up a still in another place. A smuggler caught red-handed in his bothy could, and often did, receive a prison sentence. His friends would see to his work while he was away.

In the 'Inverness Courier' it is recorded that on April 2nd, 1818: *'Abriachan again figures as a notorious place of smuggling. The Excise officers found a number of illicit utensils in a cavern and two stills in an adjoining birch wood. They were attacked by the people rolling down stones from the rocks and a party of armed men had to be sent to the top for their protection.'* On January 29th of that year, the Inverness Courier records that: *'Mr Lewis Bayne, officer of Excise, lately discovered a private still in Abriachan under very singular circumstances. It was in a vault excavated in a rock which formed the foundation of a house. The floor of the apartment above it was paved and likewise covered with a bed of clay to the depth of 18 inches, to prevent noise. The entrance was from the stank or gutter of an adjoining byre. The smoke was conveyed into the common chimney of the house.'* Mr Bayne made his way to the spot by digging and boring and among other utensils found a tun capable of holding 400 gallons.

In 1823, when vigorous measures to stamp out smuggling were being adopted, it is recorded that 400 people in a wide area including Abriachan were fined 20 shillings for illicit distilling and 4 guineas for selling without licence. Yet still, in January 1873, the 'Nairnshire Telegraph' records thus the *'Seizure of an Illicit Still'*:

'It appears that smuggling still goes on in certain districts of the Highlands. Early on Saturday morning, acting on information, Messrs Fraser and McLeod, preventive officers, Nairn, proceeded to a remote part of country at the head of Loch Ness, and discovered in the woods of Abriachan an illicit still-head in perfect working order. The still was an uncommon one, being what is known as a double horned still, having two worms and capable of containing 40 gallons. The still was brought to the Seizure Store, Inverness.' It is not recorded who the distiller was or whether he was found or arrested. He must certainly have been a skilled and enterprising operator.

It must be remembered that the distilling of whisky and its subsequent sale to many townspeople eager to buy was an important factor in enabling tenants to pay their rents. For that reason many landlords would close their eyes to it.

In 1836 John Macdonald of Corriefoyness and his neighbour Donald Macdonald were given summons of removal. Earlier that year he had asked the estate to provide a road to his croft so that he could transport lime. His rental was £16 per annum, a considerable sum. Apparently he avoided being removed for in 1843 we find him requesting a reduction of rent. His letter of 23rd November reads thus:

'That your petitioner's father and forefathers occupied the farm of Corryfoinish for a period of upwards of 100 years maintaining themselves in comfort and independence, till within the last twelve years, when the source from which their competence flowed was suddenly dried up in the suppression of smuggling, which was carried on to a considerable extent in these parts, the tenants generally distilling their own barley and finding a ready sale for the produce were in a condition to regularly pay up their rents independent or otherwise of the failure of their crops.'

That is a masterly letter! The result of it is not recorded but it is certain there were Macdonalds at Corriefoyness till well after 1843.

With the coming of the twentieth century, many younger men emigrating to the towns or abroad, the inherited skills of their forefathers were lost. Their equipment has mostly disappeared without trace, though occasionally a long-buried worm is turned up by a mechanical digger or a tree-planter on the old hill grazings.

Today, wine-making, on a non-commercial basis, is carried out in many homes. Sap is extracted from the birches, berries of many kinds are used, rowan and elder in particular, sloes are added to gin. Until comparatively recently juniper berries from bushes growing along Loch Ness were exported to Holland for use in the gin trade. Heather ale, that old drink favoured by the Picts, is on sale in the pubs again!

above:Corriefoyness

19

EMIGRANTS AND IMMIGRANTS

The 'good Sir James' had always, in the late eighteenth to early nineteenth century, discouraged emigration from his lands. He was, as we have seen, a great 'improver', and needed his tenants to help him with his improvements. Who else than the people on the ground would be so adept at draining, ditching, walling, road-building, tree-planting, even cutting peats for his fire? It was likewise with his counterparts in the west who needed a labour force to work at the profitable kelp industry.

By the time the wadset on the lands of Abriachan had been redeemed from the Baillies of Dochfour and Sir James' son had inherited the title of Earl of Seafield, tenants all over the Highlands were being displaced to make room for sheep-runs or deer-forests. There was a rumour that Abriachan was to be turned over to sheep, but this did not happen.

In spite of the efforts of two Royal Commissions and the passing of the Crofters' Act in 1886, there was discontent among the people as, although they had been granted security of tenure, yet their holdings were still too small to provide an adequate living. The Seafields who were rapidly developing the sporting side of the estate, did offer a certain amount of paid employment for men to work as stalkers, ghillies, gamekeepers, rearers of pheasants and so on. But the Highlander is never entirely satisfied with paid labour. There was still a desire for independence. So the lure of Canada, America, Australia, New Zealand, if they could get there on their own terms, grew stronger.

Mail services were improving and letters home from former emigrants were eagerly read. Sometimes they spoke of the advantages, sometimes they warned of the disadvantages, particularly from Canada, of the intense cold. Advice about what to take for those intending to emigrate and about the importance of encouraging teachers and ministers of religion to accompany them, was of great importance. In 1809 a book called 'An Emigrants Guide to N. America' written in Gaelic by Robert MacDougall had been published. It contained much information about the country, gleaned at first hand, and much good advice for those intending to emigrate.

Many of the emerging colonies were, of course, appealing for emigrants. In the 'Inverness Courier' of 20th May, 1851, there had appeared an article entitled *'Why not send them to the Falkland Islands?'* - *'them'* being the *'surplus population of the Shetlands and other Scotch isles.'* Some thirty years later, a crofter from Caiplich, whose name has not been recorded, went out to work as a shepherd in the Falklands and was welcomed despite the fact that he had lost a leg, very likely as a soldier. He was a brave man! The agent who arranged these emigrations and the shipping companies who carried them out often dealt dishonestly with the people involved, causing much heartbreak and distress. Promises were not fulfilled and conditions at sea were often appalling.

In the early 1900s, in crofting families, most of the sons would learn a trade. Inverness being only ten miles distant, young men from Abriachan could travel there on a daily basis, taking shortcuts through the hills or could lodge with relatives or friends established there, to serve their apprenticeships. Abriachan became thus well provided with skilled craftsmen of many kinds - stonemasons, joiners, slaters as well as the self-taught weavers, tailors and shoemakers. These skills were much valued in the building of improved houses of stone and slate which was taking place at this time. The eldest son would expect to inherit the tenancy of the croft but for most of the others a different life would beckon. So it was that emigrants from Abriachan tended to take their skills with them to their adopted countries. Donald Macdonald, a skilled carpenter, who had made himself an attractive dwelling at Achcullin, went to South Africa, initially to find paid employment in the hope of acquiring land or setting up a business later. The Boer War upset his plans and he returned to work on his croft and on his house and at his trade, his sisters keeping house for him. He soon acquired the affectionate nickname of 'Kruger.'

Donald Fraser, from Balchraggan, also a skilled joiner, went off to Canada and plied his trade successfully. He returned home more than once, for the pull of the homeland was strong. His brother Alexander remained at home looking after his widowed mother Seonaid, who kept a small 'shop,' just a stock of groceries, in her house, to sell on to neighbours. There were several such small 'shops' in the area. A young lad would fetch the stock from the steamer. Once in wintertime, when he had taken a sled for smooth passage through the snow, the vehicle capsized and the load was dispersed in the drifts.

Alexander, who was a skilled worker in stone, perhaps inherited from ancient Pictish forebears, inscribed a large slab of granite with the names of his family and a decorative edging, to form part of the kitchen floor. This stone is now in safekeeping, protected from weathering. After his mother's death he went out to join his brother in British Columbia. Seonaid's house no longer stands but her garden still puts out growth in spring and in summer the gooseberries are sweet. James Macdonald from Achbuie, a master mason, went to Egypt and died from typhoid at the building of the Aswan Dam. James Maclean from Achpopuli went to Australia, also Kenny Maclennan from Balmore and Donald John Matheson, an orphan from Caiplich. Two brothers from Benlee, Donald Fraser, a joiner from Balchraggan and Duncan Macdonald from Achcullin all went to Canada. They all did quite well in their adopted countries, some acquiring farms.

Most years descendants of emigrants such as the Frasers and of others of whom we have little record but hearsay come to look for the places where their forebears lived. Some arrive equipped with information gleaned from our Highland genealogist in Inverness. A Highlander himself, he gives sympathetic guidance to many wanderers from overseas. Their eyes light up at the sight even of the skeletal outline of a house, its walls depleted maybe to build a barn or a wall elsewhere. For some, not even the skeleton remains, everything is mounded in grass, with perhaps a bank of nettles nearby. But the sense of ancestry is strong. A hardheaded accountant, trader, lawyer will stoop to gather a handful of earth or a small stone from a crevice to stash away and place in a cabinet back home.

For the people of Abriachan emigration was not the only solution to the problems they may have had. One, starting in a very small way selling wares locally set up a successful business in Inverness and reared a family of teachers, doctors, writers and other professionals. Many seem to have been contented enough to continue in their traditional ways, making what they could of their pitifully small

above: James Macdonald from Achbuie

101

holdings, taking seasonal jobs on bigger farms, sons and daughters who had moved away sending contributions to the family purse.

The disastrous famines which followed the failures of the potato-crop, the food source which could most profitably be grown on their small acreages, in so many parts of the Highlands in the 1840s, did not appear to have occurred in Abriachan. Crops could be lost or diminished for reasons other than blight - frost, drought and so on. Perhaps the height at which they were grown kept them healthy. In fact, potatoes, both ware and seed, were to become a notable export from Abriachan. People would be crowding the dockside in Inverness awaiting the arrival of the 'tattie-boat' and scrambling to lay hands on stocks. The trade enabled several tenants to acquire a considerable income.

Those who had not enough land to benefit from this trade managed to subsist when times were really bad, using ways and means handed down through the generations. Nettles went into the broth, providing a ready source of iron, the leaves of willow-herb made an infusion as good as that of tea, the roots of silverweed could be ground into meal, coltsfoot would give a fill to the pipe-smoker. All these customs were followed until well into living memory.

By 1881, census records show that some paid employment was available on the estate. Ten years later John Mackenzie is postmaster, Catherine Stewart in Balchraggan is a dressmaker and Elizabeth Shaw is a wool-spinner. The crofts on which these people lived were exceedingly small, very few exceeding 20 acres, some as small as 2. Yet they probably considered themselves fortunate not to have been evicted as had been so many of their contemporaries in other parts. Their landowners had been fair-minded men.

It was at about the end of the nineteenth century that certain immigrants began to arrive in the community. These were orphan children, subsequently known as 'boarded-outs,' who were to be lodged with crofting families and were to be brought up with the children of the house. Fostering was no new concept in the Highlands. In ages past the chief would have his sons fostered by a member of the clan so as to affirm the closeness of the unit.

Originally the children to be boarded came from Inverness or other nearby towns, but latterly from further afield, notably Greenock or Glasgow. Some were indeed orphans, others came from unsuitable backgrounds or homes. In most cases the system worked well. The children's health improved greatly, their help was welcome in the work which all crofter children were expected to do - herding, cutting peats, harvesting, gathering firewood and so on. The allowance paid for their keep was a small addition to their guardians' income.

Some families took in older people, known as "patients," that is, those who were mentally disturbed, for whom a slightly larger allowance was given. With these people, as can be imagined, certain problems would arrive. Careful supervision was needed. Inspectors came regularly to see that conditions were proving suitable for the fostered. Occasionally, instances of alleged cruelty occurred, but overall the scheme was of benefit to those involved. Many "boarded-out" children kept in touch, as adults, with their guardians and returned on visits. Fostering continued until increasing age debarred prospective carers from taking children into their homes. The fostered children kept the school roll in a healthy state. In 1948, out of a register of 28, boarded-out pupils numbered 23. Ten years later, when there was one local pupil and one boarded-out, the school had to close.

In 1970 came a letter from John Graham, who had been boarded out at Achcullin in the 1920s. Addressed to 'the present occupier, Achcullin,' he wrote:

'This letter out of the blue so to speak will come no doubt with considerable surprise, so please forgive me for writing it, but of late I've had a notion in my head to write. Please don't be offended, but the facts are these, you see, I was brought up from being a little boy in that lovely house and know every inch of it and the surrounding countryside, you see I was an orphan and brought up by the good people who lived there, their name, by the way was Annie, Mary and Donald

Macdonald and I spent a wonderful childhood there, oh how I long to see it again. Myself and another boy shared the little room at the top of the stairs and his sister shared the old ladies' room. Donald had the room on the right hand side of the front door, there was also a little room right in front of the main door which a friend of the Macdonalds always slept in when she came visiting as she lived in town somewhere. Her name was Annie Johnstone and I remember her very well although it's going back 60 years. If you look in the little bookcase that was there at the time you may come across a Bible with my name on it, which I won at school. I was so proud of it, perhaps it is still there.

above: the 'hanging chimney' at Achcullin

Achcullin - the place of holly

As children we had to carry water from the well not the burn water, but we enjoyed it. I also remember the hut being built where the coal and the firewood were kept, but we used a lot of peat in those days. We would spend all day cutting and stacking it, taking mashed potatoes and fresh milk with us. My mind goes flying back in time as I write this and I'm afraid the odd tear is not far away. Are the rose bushes on either side of the door still there (red and white) - they were beautiful in summer and the view over Loch Ness was out of this world. I'm afraid I'm getting carried away with my memories, oh how I long to see it once more before I die. I do hope it hasn't changed. If I were an artist I could paint it all from memory. I do hope you will forgive my forwardness in writing, but, like they say 'memories live longer than dreams.' I will say goodbye now and go back to my dreams. God bless you all who live there now.'

Sadly, the old folk who had brought up Mr Graham were now all dead, and the houses at Achcullin which he remembered so well had become ruinous. This was explained to him and a reply came:

'Dear Mrs Stewart, here is an answer to your most welcome letter, although I feel a little sad about the house as I hold so many fond memories of the place, 'God but I would like to die there' and be buried up on the hills at the back overlooking Loch Ness. I am indeed very sorry I have no photos of the old place. How the years have passed and memory is not so good any more, only the most

important parts of ones life seem to stick in the memory. Does the grocer's van still come once a week like it used to? That was the highlight of us children's week, the driver would give us a handful of sweets, 'Batchelors Buttons' they were called and maybe some broken biscuits. In winter we children used to pull a sledge to meet the van as we had to get enough bread for the week, eight loaves and other goods and it was too heavy for any of us to carry.

corn in stook, Abriachan, 1920s

We had about a dozen hens but we would only get one egg on Sunday morning, the rest of the week we got porridge which I love to this day. I used to catch enough rabbits to keep a hotel in stew for a month, the old people never complained, every little helped in those days. We (the dog and I) once caught a hare. It was a monster, I had to drag it home, I can't remember exactly how long it lasted us but believe me we never bothered catching any more in a hurry. Funny I could certainly eat one now but they are so expensive here, no pensioner could afford one, not even a rabbit, I do miss all the Scots food here, Scots bread was beautiful, well, I can't change things by thinking about them.

Well I must thank you for answering my letter I will write to you later, in the meantime, 'God bless you all' and thanks again.

John Graham'

20

SOLDIERING

For the Highlander combat had always been a part of life. The call-to-arms had been instinctively obeyed when it was a question of clan loyalty. With the dissipation of the clans in the late eighteenth century and with the ensuing disruptions to the traditional ways of living, many young men took to soldiering as a means of subsistence. There was also the hope that their eventual reward might be some land in the new world across the water, where much of the fighting was. They were at least assured of food and clothing and, perhaps best, the feel of a weapon in their hands again, after the time of deprivation. Even the playing of the pipes was now encouraged. Some, it is said, found the musket and muzzle-loader clumsy. In older times the bow was favoured, as it could be abandoned when a final charge was made, and easily replaced thereafter. The axe and sword had always proved adequate.

Though fighting was in the blood of the Highlander, yet to be recruited into a regiment was obeying an alien compulsion. Some accepted the 'king's shilling' with a grudge, when home-based going absent when the call of the old croft-life was strong, particularly at harvest time. Round the coast young men were being carried off from their frail fishing craft by members of the Press Gang, to serve in the King's Navy. The Highland regiments were to be the making of the British Empire, as their bravery won lands in many parts of the world.

Meantime, as threats of invasion by Napoleon became alarming, many landlords recruited special local forces for the defence of the home territory. A contingent raised by Sir James Grant of Glen Urquhart threatened mutiny if they were to be sent to serve outwith the country, even to England. The pull of the homeland and its traditional life was always strong.

By the end of the nineteenth century the eyes of Victoria's politicians were on South Africa. Dutch farmers, the Boers, were disputing the intrusion of the British. Hostilities were breaking out and things going badly for the British. One battle in particular, at Maggersfontein, in 1899, had resulted in a vast defeat, with huge losses. It seemed that the British command had not got the measure of the enemy, was not acquainted with his ways of warfare.

At this point, Simon Joseph Fraser, Lord Lovat, suggested to the War Office that a body of Highlanders could be assembled, given some basic training and deployed in South Africa, to defeat the Boers at their own game. The men's natural ability in stalking, shooting, spying, he argued, would make them adept at guerilla tactics. The War Office people were inclined to agree.

In a letter dated January 4th, 1900 and sent to all Highland landowners, Lord Lovat says:

'I have been asked by the War Office to raise a corps of 150 stalkers, ghillies and picked men for primarily scouting service in South Africa.... As it is essential to secure the best stamp of man with all possible dispatch, I would be much obliged if you could see your way to send for some of the most likely men in your district and acquaint them with the scheme, in order that they may have both an opportunity of judging for themselves, and also of acquainting others of what is on foot.'

The men were to enlist for one year, with pay, allowances and bounties the same as for troops on active service. The corps was to be attached to the Black Watch, to be commanded by Highland officers and to be sent out to the front as

---

above: 'a corps of stalkers, ghillies and picked men......' the pipers at Brodie Camp, 1906   107

Johnny Finlay, Leault, a Scout from Abriachan

soon as possible. Several men from the Abriachan area joined up. In a matter of weeks a body of recruits was mobilised at nearby Beaufort. The men were billeted in the home farm, the officers, all local landowners, in the castle. As in former times, when clansmen and chiefs were close, there were bonds of respect and friendship, rather than a hierarchy between officers and men.

The Scouts, 'Lovat's Scouts', as they became known, formed the last of the old clan regiments. These were the days of the cavalry. Many men supplied their own mount, a garron, that hardy workhorse found on all the crofts. There were shoeing-smiths and other craftsmen among the contingent. They were kitted out in sturdy tweed, with slouch hats sporting a red Fraser tartan flash. The old Fraser clan motto, 'Je suis prest', Norman French for 'I am ready', was much in evidence.

Though, in the press, there was some adverse criticism of the project, in the field the men's skills were soon recognised. Only four were lost in the first action. The following year, 1901, a second contingent was sent out, six of its members shepherds, who took their dogs, with the idea of rounding up the Boers' cattle and sheep. There were problems, of course. Some of the horses sickened and died. There was a shortage of telescopes which the men were accustomed to use rather than field-glasses. Highland landowners, particularly the Brodies, were generous in supplying both these needs - horses and telescopes. And their wives worked hard at supplying extra food and clothing.

Sometimes communication was difficult. For most of the men English was a second language, only acquired painfully at school and subsequently much of it forgotten. Their thinking and most of their speaking was in Gaelic. The tactics they were to employ - scouting, observing, stalking, signalling - suited them well, but the transmission of information to their English-speaking officers sometimes presented problems. A certain amount of unorthodoxy was smiled upon as their sterling worth and bravery were recognised. General Hector Macdonald, under whose command they came, said of them: *'As scouts or guides, on pony or on foot, as individual marksmen or as a collective body in the fighting line, they are all specialists and picked men. They are a splendid band of Scotsmen, which is the highest compliment I can pay them.'*

During the years of peace between 1903 and 1914 recruiting to the 'Scouts' continued. Training camps were organised, a mileage allowance paid to men coming from a distance and £5 for the hire of a pony. Pipers were welcome and wore kilts of hunting Fraser tartan.

above: Donnie Riddell, Pipe Major of the Lovat Scouts

With the outbreak of war in 1914, a third contingent of Scouts, about 1200 men, was mobilised and was soon in action. Several men from Abriachan were involved. At Gallipoli they suffered indescribable hardship, with dysentery and frostbite. Along with the Gurkhas, with whom they felt much affinity, they provided the rearguard to cover the successful withdrawal from Suvla Bay. Later, having become infantrymen - many of them loath to part from their mounts - they had to adapt to conditions in Egypt, fighting the Bedouin. For two years, 1916-18, their skills in field craft were used in operations in Macedonia, and in the last months of the War they joined up with a group known as sharpshooters in France. These sharpshooters, with their gifts for spying and reconnaissance, were of inestimable value in the conduct of operations.

After the War these skills were further honed with training camps attended regularly. In 1939 the 'Scouts' were mounted again and were given rigorous training in orthodox riding and horse management. Many young men, some from Abriachan, suffered and even died, from infectious diseases contracted in the training camps, some of which were held in England, where facilities for shooting practice were available. These young men, brought up in clean hill air, had not acquired immunity to infections.

The Scouts' first assignment was to Norway, where Donald Riddell, from Abriachan, a piper of note, became Pipe Major of the band which was to become the pride and joy of the Lovat Scouts. Donald was a splendid leader, maintaining the highest standards of smartness and military efficiency while exercising his great gifts of musicianship.

From 1940-42 the Scouts were in the Faroe Islands. These were of strategic importance in the north Atlantic, Thorshaven having to be defended against possible invasion. The Scouts did useful work as observers and signallers. The Faroese called them '*the best foreigners we have ever met.*' Some married Faroese girls and many contacts have been maintained. In the summers of 1942 and 1943 the Scouts provided the royal guard at Balmoral. After this comparatively quiet time in the Faroes the Scouts were sent to Canada to undertake training in mountain warfare, including the use of skis. Avalanches and severe frostbite were par for the course. To their delight they came across some Canadians who still spoke the old Gaelic of their forebears - one can imagine the ceilidhs that were held!

In 1944, as real 'mountain men,' they were despatched to the Appenines, where their newly acquired skills, allied to their traditional 'nous' made them exceptionally adept at the kind of tactics employed there. And they again found extremely compatible allies in the Gurkhas. An article in the Inverness Courier of the time describes the Scouts as the 'McGurkhas!'

In the immediate post war months the Scouts saw service in Austria and Greece, arresting prisoners escaping through the hills and supervising the surrender of weapons. Simon Fraser, Lord Lovat, the son of their founder, had done sterling work, training the troops known as the 'Commandos' and had led them in person in the invasion of occupied Europe.

The Pipe Band, under Donald Riddell, had continued to delight and inspire, the members doing guard duty and acting as stretcher bearers, often in conditions of extreme danger. After demobilising, Donald Riddell taught piping and fiddle-playing, inspiring many young players who were to make names for themselves in later years. He also made fiddles which are now much prized. And his name is remembered wherever Highland music is played. One of his compositions, dedicated to 'Johnny Finlay' of Leault, Abriachan, himself a fiddler of note, is often heard today.

The Scouts continued to attend training camps. In 1947 they became part of the Territorial Army, linked to The Scottish Horse, a Tank Regiment, then in 1949, they were redesignated a mountain regiment, and later served in anti-aircraft. After the reorganisation of the Territorial Army in 1967, the Lovat Scouts, as such, were disbanded. Their legend lives on.

In these later wars, as in the previous colonial fighting, many Highlanders, including some from Abriachan, had joined forces other than the Scouts, notably the Camerons and the Seaforths. In the Big Room in Abriachan School, there is a brass plaque *'to commemorate the self-sacrificing spirit of the men from Abriachan and district who joined His Majesty's forces during the Great War, 1914-1918.'* On it are listed 76 names, an asterisk denoting those who were killed. There is no indication of the regiment in which they served.

above: commemorative plaque in Abriachan School

Between 1941 and 1945 a valuable contribution to the war effort was made by the so-called 'Sawdust Fusiliers,' the Canadian Forestry Corps. Camps were set up for them by the Royal Engineers and the Pioneer Corps. One contingent, lodged at Dochfour, worked at timber extraction in the Abriachan area, along Loch Ness. They also did valuable work in road-building - one access road in Abriachan is still known as the 'Canadian road' - and helped in fire-fighting after muir-burn, the burning of the heather in spring. Only occasionally was there a fracas, over deer-shooting by hungry men!

The Canadians quickly made friendships with other units, in particular with the Lovat Scouts and established good relations with the civilian population, attending parties and dances and entertaining the children. There were many good pipers among them. Several married local girls and some stayed on in the Highlands.

During the Second World War several men from Abriachan were called up to serve in the Royal Engineers, where their special skills were valued, or in other regiments. Among the older men an active unit of the Home Guard was formed. They were issued with kit, had instruction in the use of firearms and held regular parades. A local piper, Willy Maclean, led them on route marches. Though they never, of course, actually had to deal with the enemy, even in the form of agents, a minister visiting an outlying place was nevertheless challenged by a keen Home Guarder in case he was an agent in disguise! Yet they were not unaware of enemy activity.

One night a German pilot, making for home across the North Sea, after seeking out the aluminium works at Foyers on the other side of Loch Ness, let loose his cargo of bombs on the moor ground high up above the school. One likes to think he was avoiding human habitation. The only victim was a mountain hare. Soon Abriachan became known as 'the place that was bombed'.

Loch Ness claimed one of our planes in December 1940, when a Wellington on a training flight came to grief in a severe storm, over the water. Some of the crew survived. The wreckage was brought to the surface a few years ago, the peat preserving some of its identity, and it has since been restored and put on display in an R.A.F. Museum in England. Another 'one of ours' crashed into rocks just beyond Corriefoyness on a reconnaissance flight. The navigator escaped injury and came back within the last few years to visit the scene of the misadventure. Pieces of rusted wreckage are still to be seen by those who venture up the pine-clad rocks. Images of war are found in the most unlikely places.

21

SCHOOLING SINCE 1872

On the first of February, 1875, Alexander Maclean, a young man of 25, was appointed headmaster in the new school. He had trained in the College in Moray House, Edinburgh and had taught for four years at nearby Glenconvinth School. There were about 70 pupils on the roll. His salary was £85 a year and he had an assistant who was paid £20 a year.

In terms of the Education Act of 1872 schooling was to be compulsory between the ages of 5 and 13. School Boards were set up to see to the running of schools and Attendance Officers were employed. The headmaster was to keep a record of progress and attendance in school. This Log Book was to be *'stoutly bound and consisting of not less than 500 pages.'* It was stipulated that no entries of a personal or critical nature be made. From the entries a picture emerges, not only of the life of the school, but of the life and times of the whole community. There are records of storms, of illness, of death, of the problems of bilingualism and absentees. The character of the headmaster is also reflected in the entries. Some of them show a clear understanding of the problems of parents, others are repetitious and dull.

The first entry made by Alex Maclean, in February 1875, states that attendance was irregular owing to illness and storms. By the end of April of that year the children were being kept at home to help with the potato-planting. The summer vacation was from 20th August to 2nd October, then came the potato-lifting which continued until the middle of November. For a young keen schoolmaster these enforced absences of the scholars must have been frustrating in the extreme. The first Inspector's Report since the 1872 Act was issued on 25th July 1876. It states that: *'the school is taught with great ability and very good results, most creditable in the circumstances.'* It then says *'all should have slates....and slate-racks*

and pen holders in the desks should be provided.' The Inspector reports well on Dictation, Arithmetic, Notation and Industrial Work, then adds: *'arrangements should be made to have Music taught.'* By the time of his next visit, the following year, the Inspector is pleased to see that *'Music was begun this year.'* He also says that the discipline is *'good, but might be more genial,'* and that *'the books are still too advanced.'*

The standard of teaching and learning is indicated in entries made in a note-book by a pupil, John Fraser, in 1882. There we find, in beautiful handwriting, a Latin vocabulary, parsing of the sentence, 'How do you do?' and an essay on the life of Cromwell. There is also a letter to an imaginary recipient entitled *'Abriachan since ten years'* in which is mentioned a new road, the new school, a new mill and the planting of a wood. From such notes is history made! There is also evidence of this pupil's ability to write Gaelic, as the words of several songs are included.

Mr Maclean, perhaps discouraged by the frequent absences of the pupils, stayed only a short time. Attendance was poor, the weather was appalling with snow-storms in October and April, making it impossible for children who had several miles to walk to reach school safely. Nevertheless, in a report of February 1881 we read *'Latin class making considerable progress.'* Imagine Virgil's lines echoing round a bleak classroom, with gales battering the high windows!

above: the school and school-house in Abriachan

In April of that year the Log Book records the *'children kept at home to assist in farm work and in planting a young wood in Caiplich.'* In 1882 many severe snowstorms were recorded followed by several funerals. In 1883, on March 17th, the entry reads: *'owing to a severe snowstorm and the funeral of Thomas Macdonald, Balintore, there were no scholars present on Friday.'* This Thomas Macdonald was the Bard. In April of that year most of the children were ill with measles. Measles was a serious epidemic among children who had little natural immunity and, of course, no preventative injections. In June the entry reads: *'Lessons not so well prepared as most of the children required to herd before and after school hours.'* Keen as the parents were for their children to be educated, yet maintaining life had to be the first priority. Cattle had to be kept out of the growing crops by human means when fencing was almost non-existent.

On November 3rd, perhaps in desperation, Mr Munro writes: *'The Default Officer went through the district. The people, however, will not send their children to school until the potatoes are lifted.'* In 1884, on April 11th, the school was closed for the funeral of the Earl of Seafield. In the autumn of that year Mr Munro departed. November 6th saw the arrival of Mr Donald Mackay. He was a man who really understood the situation in which he found himself and he was to remain in office for 22 years. He is still remembered with affection by the descendants of the pupils he cared for.

In his first years we read of a child having to walk over three miles to school, of a *'want of English'* in the children from Caiplich, of twins from the Poorhouse in Inverness being lodged with a family from Caiplich. On December 11th 1885 he notes that attendance is good, but *'those who have been away since the end of spring forgot a good deal of what they acquired previously.'*

In 1886 the Act which gave the crofters security of tenure in their holdings encouraged them to keep the land in good heart. It also meant that the childrens' help was even more essential. On April 16th the children and their parents had a *'social entertainment of tea etc. in the schoolrooms. There were about 200 present. Mr MacIver, Inverness, showed a great variety of views by the magic lantern which interested the children immensely.'* That same year, we hear that Donald Fraser, monitor, went to Caithness as clerk in the employment of the Highland Railway. In the winter of 1887 there was an outbreak of diphtheria, several small children dying. The sight of the small coffins was to remain in the memory of the community for many years. By autumn the Queen's Jubilee was, nevertheless, to be celebrated by a steamer trip for scholars and parents to Fort Augustus.

Two years later, on January 25th, a night school for *'grown-up boys and girls'* was opened. *'The attendance is good'* we read and *'they are very diligent at their work, which is reading, writing, arithmetic, spelling and singing by the notes at the close. Hours from 7 to 9.'*

In March 1890 it is recorded that a child's absence is *'due to lack of boots. She lives at a very high and cold place, in the direction of Glen Urquhart.'* There were still infectious diseases about. In February 1893 *'by order of the County Council Dr MacFadyan, Inverness, today vaccinated 30 of the scholars in the classroom.'* Things were progressing. Books as prizes were donated by the London, Inverness, Ross and Tain Association, a scheme for Gaelic as a specific subject was introduced and Mrs Baillie of Dochfour started a knitting class for grown-up girls to make stockings for the Highland Industries Society.

In 1896, after outbreaks of infectious illness - whooping cough, measles, scarlet fever - the school was closed for several weeks while it was *'thoroughly disinfected, whitewashed and the wood all varnished.'* 1897 was another Jubilee year which saw the children *'taken to Inverness in four carriages'* for a 'Jubilee Play.' Next year each scholar was presented with a copy of 'The Pilgrim's Progress,' there were more social entertainments and on June 8th, 1900, in the afternoon, *'the children were taken to the top of Benlie for a picnic to celebrate the fall of Pretoria, which they all enjoyed very much.'*

In 1901 we find the children supplied with soup at dinnertime, and more vaccination administered. Education is being seen as a form of social service as well as a system of instruction. That same year Mr MacKay notes : *'the children take a special interest in the free-arm drawing on the walls of the schoolroom which have been specially painted for this purpose.'* In 1904, the teacher suffered *'very sore bereavements'* in his family and two years later he resigned.

Mr Peter Campbell took up duty in March 1906. The names of various assist-

ant teachers are recorded, there is mention of a lecture on alcohol, its nature and use, there are still problems with infectious illness and consequent closure of the school for disinfection.

There are few mentions of social activities, the main record being of school work. In 1909, on the 22nd of February, an important entry reads: *'for the further development of the nature study, practical school gardening is to be introduced forthwith.'*

The school roll was now 116. With assistant teachers coming and going, problems of illness and absenteeism among the pupils, and his own gifted family growing up - one son was to become Medical Officer of Health for Inverness-shire, another lecturer in Classics at Edinburgh University - Mr Campbell stayed only seven years in Abriachan, then moved to a low-ground school.

On 6th October, 1913 Mr James L. Neil took up duty as headmaster. He was the first non-Highland and non-Gaelic-speaking head. He came from Glasgow and had been teaching for a short time on the island of Scalpay, Harris. Finding *'reading and enunciation'* in the school very unsatisfactory he at once started lessons in phonetics.

By early in the following year he was getting homework done in jotters. In summer he had all the children weighed and measured. There is little evidence of the impact of the Great War on the school, though many families must have been bereft of their menfolk. The only report of any 'war effort' by the children is contained in a letter from Mr Morrison, an Inspector, urging the importance of bramble-gathering. Sphagnum moss was also gathered.

In the Inspector's report of 17th March, 1920, we read: *'Singing is of exceptional merit in all respects'*. This is the first indication of this headmaster's particular achievement - the training of the children in choral singing. With a tun-
ing-fork at the ready and a Gaelic-speaking assistant to keep the wording right,
he got the children to create a sound of exceptional purity. The natural, inherited
talent of the children was there. He had the talent to recognise it.

On September 24th of that year the Log Book records: *'Headmaster off duty on
Tuesday, Wednesday, Thursday and Friday of this week attending the Mod in
Oban with a junior choir.'* Luckily he had an assistant who could cope with the
remainder of the pupils in his absence. Thereafter, the choir went on to win many
prizes and trophies in many parts of the Highlands.

In June 1928 they won the Craigmonie Trophy at the Music Festival in Inverness. In September, they were awarded first prize for choral singing in Fort William.
Later that year they gave a concert in the Town Hall in Inverness. The following
year they retained the Craigmonie Trophy and eventually they were to keep it six
times and to secure the highest marks among sixteen school choirs. Their fame
spread all over the Highlands and is still remembered.

During these years the headmaster had to cope with the usual trials - the school
closed several times owing to outbreaks of chickenpox, the water supply failing,

the chimney smoking, sheep breaking into the garden and destroying the crops - yet he managed, by dint of some blustering, to get many things done. A partition in the big classroom gave him an extra classroom, water closets replaced the old dry system, a playground shelter was built and the telephone installed. By this time he had been elected a member of the Educational Institute of Scotland, and had from time to time to attend meetings in Edinburgh. All this activity meant, of course, that his nervous system suffered and as a consequence his staff and his pupils often suffered, too. The few surviving former pupils of his remember with pride the glory of the choir. They also remember inevitably some harsh words and actions which they would prefer to forget. Mr Neil retired in 1935 and, after the death of his wife, lived out his life as a recluse in a house not far from the school, among his books and his music.

The next headmaster, Mr R.A. Denoon, was a very keen gardener. Two years after his appointment the Inspector's report reads: *'the headmaster here has transformed the garden into something very pleasing and deserves very great credit. With the help of the pupils the following improvements have been carried out: flower plots, herbaceous border, lawn, rockery, crazy-paving, hedges, rustic frame with roses, all carefully planned and neatly executed. The productive side is also included and the education aspect kept in view.'* Subsequently the school won a Challenge Cup for gardening. The headmaster arranged lectures on beekeeping for the boys. He kept goats and chickens and set a great example to others trying to help the war effort. By now the school roll had fallen to 54, three-quarters of whom were boarded out children, some of less than average ability.

Mr Denoon (right) and his older pupils, late 1930s

On September 15th, 1944, Mr Denoon records in the Log Book: *'I ceased teaching in Abriachan today and have been appointed to Fort Augustus.'*
In 1945, when the next teacher, Mr MacFarlane, was appointed, a kitchen was built for the service of school meals. Over the following years, in spite of the decrease in the number of pupils, plans went ahead to erect a new building at the top of the playground, for the teaching of practical subjects - wood and metal-working for the boys and cookery for the girls. The idea was to make the school a 'Junior Secondary' so that pupils could finish their education in their home environment. But the decline in numbers continued.

By 1950 the school was reduced to one-teacher level, with its first headmistress, Miss Fraser, in charge. She had been a pupil in the school, a pupil-teacher, an assistant teacher, then head. Her sister, too, had been a pupil, had taught cookery and had cooked for the school. The conversion of the school to a Junior Secondary was abandoned, the equipment removed. The school roll fell to 15, then to 12, to 8, to 4, to 2. On April 2nd, 1958 the Log Book records: *'The school closed today. 8/6d was collected from the sale of articles made by the pupils. Janette Maclean and Hilda Stewart, the only pupils on the roll will attend Tomnacross Junior Secondary School and Glenconvinth Primary School respectively at the commencement of the summer term.'*

above: Mr MacFarlane, headmaster, and Miss Elizabeth Fraser, assistant, late 1940s

The closure of a school is a grievous loss to any community, but clearly, at the time, this was inevitable. Some years were to pass before families with school-age children came to live in the area. They were to be taken by minibus to the school at Dochgarroch, where all the equipment and facilities necessary for modern education were already installed. Miss Fraser, with her sister, moved to another school, before retirement.

In her short story 'The Road of No Return,' the well-known Scottish writer, Jessie Kesson, who spent some of her youth in Abriachan, attending the school for a time, tells of the sense of desolation of those years:

'It had never been a land that sang with colour, except in late autumn. Hard to tell then whether it was the heather, or the red rocks that so assailed the skies and made the loudest impact. At all other times it was a grey land, mottled with silver. Small burns leaping over the dun stones, and rushing down through the birch trees. Yet it had always 'smouldered' behind its greyness. The smoke of its hidden fires would catch at your throat, and envelop you forever. Even at your desk at school, ignorant of where 'the trade winds' blew. Or why they blew at all. You would hide your head between your arms, and your ignorance would find its comfort in the warm, peaty smell of your jersey's sleeves. There was no peat-reek now. The houses scattered on the slope stood with heart-remembered names. Achullen. Balbec. Tullurach. Balmore. But you had now become aware that they were empty. Staring sightless down over Loch Ness. Blind to the tourists' caravans, and the scientific ships, searching for a monster that they had never seen in all their window-wide and watchful years.'

The reminiscences of James Macdonald, Achbuie: born in 1891, Mr Macdonald was encouraged by his son, Ian, to write down his memories of his childhood in Abriachan.

'31st October, 1966.

This day I have completed my seventy-fifth year and it occurs to me if I am to leave you a record of our forebears according to my knowledge it is time I made a start.

My maternal grandfather was a native of Glenurquhart, in early life a saw miller to trade. He came to Abriachan and carried on the trade of meal miller at Balbeg. From all accounts I have heard of him he was a hail-fellow-well-met type of man, jovial of nature and popular with everybody. He took suddenly ill when returning from Loch Laide where he had gone to open the mill dam, toddled home in great pain and died three months later on 11th April 1861 aged about 55 years. It would appear he had been struck with what we call today coronary thrombosis. My mother once told me as a child she overheard her father say to his wife's brother (after returning from Inverness where no doubt they had a dram) that 'although I would die tomorrow I could leave £20 to each of my six daughters.' So he was comparatively well-off financially considering the times.

My grandmother was I think a native of Abriachan and was born in or about 1823. She married in 1846 and was her husband's second wife. She was of medium height and slight of build, intelligent, sagacious and of a commanding and dictatorial manner and was left a widow with six daughters and one son (aged between 1-14 years) to bring up which she did with credit. She was confined to bed for the last three years of her life, tenderly nursed by her daughter Kate and died in September 1918 in the 96th year of her age. They are buried in Kilmore churchyard, Glenurquhart.

My uncle James was the youngest of the family. He was of medium build, thick set with a reddish beard. He was a stone mason to trade and was reckoned a very good tradesman. The contractor of the GPO building on Queensgate was from Achbuie - Tom Macdonald - and my uncle was the foreman mason. Later on he commenced contracting on his own account but was unfortunate in building a school in Harris and failed over it. In 1900 he was engaged by engineer Murdoch Macdonald - later Sir Murdoch - as a masonry overseer on the Aswan Dam where he arrived in May but the following May he contracted typhoid or typhus fever and died within a few days of the disease. In the summer of 1898 he and my brother William built our byre and stable and I remember him quite well when engaged on that job.

122

I was born at Achbuie on Hallowe'en night, 31st October, 1891. My first recollection of life is being among a crowd of elderly people dressed in black. Next I found myself dressed in a frock rolling on the floor of a house I afterwards recognised as that of my grandmother at Taluarach and the old lady coming at me with a besom in her hand and in her shrill voice saying 'oh, you bad boy, if you'll no behave yourself I'll give you a whipping.' Not a very happy recollection of memory's treasure but a salutary lesson to grown-ups as to how they should treat and speak to children ever so young. The occasion I believe was the wedding of my aunt Betsy to John Davidson and this happened either in 1894 or 1895 when I was approaching 3 or 4 years old.

My next clear recollection is of seeing the remains of an old man, a neighbour who died in 1896. 1897 was the year of the Queen's Diamond Jubilee which I remember very well and in that year I went to school. In 1898 I was interested in seeing the new byre and stable being built by my uncle and brother and at that time my Aunt Maggie died. Next year my sister Jessie was called away which was a great grief to us as a household and left a deep impression on my memory.

1900 was the year of the great Church controversy which caused so much bitterness in the Highlands and throughout Scotland. I remember how folk used to argue the pros and cons of the case. Although I could not understand what they fought each other for, I remember how jubilant the minority was on the Lords' decision in 1904. The older people in Abriachan refused to go into the Union but most of the younger generation did and they were about equally divided. I remember my father saying if the Free Church was good enough for his father it was good enough for him. Church going was very popular in those years but whatever the rights and wrongs of the case, church going has been on the decline ever since especially since the 1914 war.

One other memory of early childhood remains with me. In Mr Gladstone's last Liberal Administration - I think in 1896 - there was a picture of him in the centre and all his Cabinet in smaller figures all around. This picture hung in our 'room' and I remember going in one day to find the eyes of the old man fixed on me. I moved all round the room keeping my eyes fixed on the picture but still the eyes followed me no matter where I stood and I concluded this was God. Like Hagar in the wilderness, I could feel 'Thou God seest me.'

above: Balchraggan, Balbeg, Balmore and up to Achbuie c 1900

My School and Schoolmasters.

Dr Mackay, Craigmonie, records in Urquhart and Glenmoriston that the first schoolmaster in Abriachan was Mr McLauchlan who was transferred from Culduthel School against his will. At that time Abriachan was notorious for smuggling and drinking and McLauchlan had a difficult task in trying to bring order out of chaos on the princely salary of £10 per annum. This was about the close of the eighteenth century and he remained there for the rest of his life and was buried in Kirkhill. Dr McLauchlan, one of the Disruption leaders in 1843, was a grandson of the first schoolmaster in Abriachan. Several others followed and one, Maclean, removed to Balloch where he died at a good old age. He was succeeded by Donald Mackay who was my first schoolmaster.

Mackay was a native of Strathconon from where his parents were evicted during the Clearances of 1846. I don't know what training he got for the teaching profession but it must have been very elementary, I fear. His first post was teaching in the 'Ragged' School Inverness - Dr Guthrie's idea of education for the poor. From there he went to Inver and in the early eighties he removed to Abriachan where he remained until his retirement in April 1906. He had one son, Finlay, who was a medical student in Glasgow and two daughters, Jessie and Jeannie. Two other children died in infancy within a week of each other of scarlet fever or diphtheria and it is recorded that his hair turned white in one night as a result. Finlay and his mother died in 1904. Jessie taught in Abriachan and Jeannie married a Mr Stewart and now lives in Newtonmore. After his retirement Donald Mackay went to Dublin with his daughter Mrs Stewart and died there in 1914 aged 74 years and is buried in Fodderty. As a teacher I think his strong point was teaching Bible history from the Creation to the time of Samuel and the Kings but never the New Testament. He was also strong on the Shorter Catechism which we could repeat from beginning to end like the Alphabet. But for the more mundane affairs I am afraid our education was very much neglected. I can still see the old man with his white hair shaded from each side meeting in the centre - his gaunt face, half tile hat, swallow tail coat and spats. In the back pocket of his coat he carried a large red handkerchief with white spots and a four fingered tawse whose tips were wearing done through constant use. It was a constant anxiety for the pupils when they saw his hand going to the pocket whether it was the red hanky or leather strap that appeared but owing to the dilatory method of teaching the boys became bored and it was difficult to maintain discipline in spite of the strap. His principal subjects were grammar and arithmetic, neither of which he taught with any degree of success, but he was a very interesting raconteur and did a turn at lay preaching.

Donald Mackay was succeeded by Peter Campbell, a native of Minard, who was headmaster at Strachur and what a contrast - a real drill sergeant who kept everything going with clockwork precision. There was never a dull moment and the strap was practically unknown. His sharp eye and powerful voice kept discipline and he put his whole heart and strength into the work making up for the older pupils 'the years that the locusts had eaten.' All the boys of my age did not like the change and left school by the summer but I stayed on although I sorely missed the boys. Campbell took an interest in me and was anxious that I should go to Inverness Academy but that did not materialise and instead he arranged for me going into the Railway service which to me a few years later seemed providential, as it saved me from all the horrors and miseries of the First World War.

Mr Campbell had four sons, all brilliant students. Donald Ian was lecturer in Latin at Edinburgh University and was fatally injured by an IRA bomb at King's Cross Station (1939). Alistair is General Manager of the Sun Life of Canada Assurance Co, Montreal, Ruari, chief medical officer for Highland Hospitals and Patrick, chief cashier for Commercial and National Bank, Edinburgh. The three older boys were dux of the Academy and the two older ones were Cambridge dons.

I looked upon Mr Campbell as a very good friend and I revere his memory. He was very strong on recitation for memory training and I still remember many pieces of poetry we had to learn and found much pleasure in it. For himself I think he was too prosaic and practical to find in poetry anything higher than memory training. I often wonder why he left Strachur to come to such an outlandish place as Abriachan and I enquired of him his reason so he told me he wished his family to be educated at Inverness Royal Academy and the School Board had promised him that if he would accept Abriachan they would keep him in mind for a more convenient school later on, which they did when they offered him Balloch in 1913. Mr Campbell was predeceased by his wife and he died about 17 years ago at the age of 87 years and is buried on the west side of Tomnahurich cemetery. Two of his dictums: 'Sit down you dolts, and learn it,' - 'Be like the Maister and lose your hair, you cannot have hair and brains too.' He was very bald and we nicknamed him 'Baldy', a name that followed him to Balloch.

Another schoolmaster, MacGillivray, taught in a thatched biggin slightly west of the present school and his widow who lived to a very old age was still alive when I left home. They had two sons and a daughter. The elder son William was mentally deficient and Angus who was Chief of the Clan was Professor of Ophthalmology in St Andrew's University. The daughter made a runaway marriage with a man Maclean - a teacher who was brought up at Rhivoulich above Loch Laide - much to her mother's disappointment but he was a very clever man and finished up as Rector of Hillhead High School, Glasgow. The present school was built after the passing of the Education Act of 1872 establishing School Boards. When I left it on the 4th of May 1909 there were about 110 pupils, many of them boarded out children and gradually the numbers decreased until only two were left and the school was closed. Maclean had two sons and they were both killed in the first world war.

On receiving an appointment from the Highland Railway at Forres Station, I left home on 13th May 1909 and arriving at Forres Station, presented myself meekly to the Stationmaster John Crowe as the new boy. He looked me up and down and in a very supercilious manner after asking for my name told me to stand aside while I talk to this gentleman (the gentleman I afterwards found was ex-Provost Lawrence.)

Of the social life at Abriachan there was very little in my day but before that they used to have concerts in the school and dances in the Mill. New Year's Day was the great day of the year. We were up early in the morning and had breakfast in lamplight and speldins and unlimited supplies of bread, scones, cake and biscuits, butter, jam, oranges, etc. All the family as far as possible came home for the occasion and all together it was a happy time. Every house was well provided with whisky to welcome visitors and this continued well into the month. At that time the common thing was gallon jars costing 15/- a gallon. The next great day was the annual visit to Inverness for a pair of boots. Stepping on the steamer - clang of bells, thump of paddles, swish of water and movement of the boat - was a great experience for a child.

above: the crew of the paddle steamer, the Gondolier

127

Later it was made obligatory for proprietors to pay compensation to crofters for improvements made by them on their crofts when giving them up; in this connection through the good offices of the Scottish Land Court we received £590 compensation from a recalcitrant landlord who had no intention of paying it if he could avoid it.

My father was of a retrospective nature, not very communicative to his family but inwardly kindly. He was temperate in habits, abstemious in eating and drinking and a non-smoker. As far as I know his peregrinations did not extend beyond Glenurquhart to Forres and Dingwall or Muir of Ord to Carrbridge. He lived for his croft and his church in which he was latterly an elder and looked at things such as holidays, concerts and sport as sheer vanity. He conducted family worship morning and evening without fail and I believe thought this world the centre of creation.

My mother was much more active, more intelligent with a keener appreciation of things. She worked very hard all her life in bringing up a large family on very little except what the croft produced but this was sufficient for their needs. My parents both enjoyed good health until the last few years of their lives and lived contented with their lot. One morning I dreamed that I stood outside the door at my mother's funeral and the dream was so vivid that I spoke about it when I awoke. Later that day my brother came from Abriachan to tell me that Mother had taken a stroke early that morning and three days later on February 17th 1930 she passed away and the funeral was exactly as I saw it in my dream.

There is a nostalgic pleasure in looking back on childhood years spent among a poor but contented peasantry and the solitude of the everlasting hills. Since I left home, conditions are much better for those working on the land but now the 35 crofts or so in Abriachan and Caiplich are all except half a dozen derelict.

Well, that is my story. Eighty years ago my father planted several trees in front of the house. Two still survive, an oak and a rowan tree and it fell to me to turn the key in the door of the old house for the last time with a heavy heart. I am now the only surviving member of the family and, so far as I know, the last of my school classmates.'

.

22

THE BARD

As in most places in the Highlands, Abriachan had what was known as a 'township bard.' He, or she, was someone known to have a gift for composing verse to whom the people looked for a poem to commemorate some happy event such as a wedding or a 'réiteach,' a formal betrothal, when a young man would go to the home of his intended bride to ask for her hand in marriage.

Poems were written in praise of someone who had acted generously on behalf of the community, or to pour scorn on an unsympathetic character. Satire was quite a favourite medium and much appreciated by the lively minded people. In some places, where a wealth of versifying talent existed, there could be rivalry, pleasant or unpleasant, between bards, known as 'flytings.' Humour in verse often relieved tension in any critical situations and had therapeutic value for everyone concerned.

In the late 1800s Mary Macpherson, - known as Màiri Mhòr on account of her stature - a Skye woman, composed powerful verse which did much to put heart into the Highland people during the difficult times of the Clearances. Her poems were recited at ceilidhs and meetings at many places. A passionate advocate of land reform, with a heartfelt conviction that the land belonged to the people, she made a major contribution to the victory of popular candidates in local elections all over the Highlands. She could not write Gaelic, but she could recite eight or nine thousand lines of her own verse, from memory, for a scholar to transcribe.

In older times there had been a class of professional bards, some travelling the country dependant on hospitality and demanding fixed rates for the kind of poetic utterance required. Many formed part of the chief's following, along with his steward, his harper, his piper, his flag-bearer, his fordman, his jester, his cup

bearer, his keeper of the sporran and others. The bard's job, which was hereditary, was to compose praise poems in the chief's honour or to incite the clansmen
to battle.

The training of these bards was rigorous. As students they would be required to
lie daylong in a darkened room, doors and windows closed, their plaids wrapped
round their heads, eyes shut and a large stone on the belly, memorising poems or
tales and also the rules of composition. The highest degree of skill meant the
ability to repeat from memory 350 poems or tales, many of great length.

In the twelfth century the stories of Fionn and his band of warriors were turned
into ballads and sung to music very similar to the plain-song of the early church.
Some of these heroic ballads, perhaps accompanied on the clarsach, were still
sung until the middle years of the twentieth century.

Our bard was not a professional who had made a study of his craft. He had a
croft to work and a family to raise. He was Thomas Macdonald, born in 1822,
and became known as 'Tòmas an Tòdhair,' the Abriachan bard. His grandfather,
John Macdonald, had married Helen Maclauchlan, the daughter of the schoolmaster, who was himself a talented poet. Thomas' gift may thus have been inherited. On his father's side were also many talented people.

In the 'Transactions of the Gaelic Society of Inverness', vol. XXIII, we read:
*'Thomas composed a number of songs and poems, but, like many a Highland
bard, he confined the most of them to local subjects. Those that have any general
interest, however, are really of a comparatively high order.*

*Thomas Macdonald was descended from a family of Macdonalds who, it is
said, migrated at one time from Glen Urquhart and settled in Abriachan. From
the same Macdonalds is believed to have sprung the famous 'Bishop John'
Macdonald of Alvie. There was brain among them all, beyond the average Highlander, and Thomas was by no means the least talented. One of the most prominent features of his compositions is their sarcastic wit, an instrument which he
could use at times with very considerable power.'*

This account of his life and work was written by Alexander Macdonald, himself
a writer, who also said of him that he was a *'master of Gaelic expression',* with
'great fluency of language.'

A poem of his 'In Praise of Glen Urquhart' shows his descriptive skill in that
close observation and feeling for natural beauty which has always been a charac-
teristic of Celtic people. Some verses translated by Mr Norman MacMillan give
a feel of the work:

Oran do Ghleann Urchadain

Tha Gleann Urchadain cho àluinn,
Fo-sgàil nam beann ciar,
Le fìor oibre Nàduir
A' fàs ann an rian;
Gach raon agus àite
Is àilleanta sgiamh
Le neòneanan sàr-gheal
Gu àirde nan sliabh.

Tha Meall-fuar-mhonaidh shuas,
Fo shuaicheantas làn,
Le 'bhàrr mulaich an uachdar
Thair' stuadhaibh nan càrn;
'S gach taobh dheth air iathadh,
O iochdar gu bhàrr,
Le fuaranaibh ciatach
'An iochdar gach sgàirn.

Tha Eanruig 'us Coilltidh
'Cur loinn air a' ghleann,
A' tuirlinn tromh 'n oighreachd
Le gleadhraich na 'n deann;
S tha fonn-chrith le gaoir
Aig gach caochan 'us allt',
Gu mearganta 'taomadh
O aonach nan gleann.

Tha Creag-Neigh 's Creag-Mhònaidh
Air an còmhdach le coill,
'Cur dian air a' chòmhnard
O dhoinneann nan sion;
Tha iasg 'an Loch-Mhioclaidh
Agus eunach 's a' bhéinn
'S tha Rùsgich 'us Diòmhach
Na 'm frith aig na féidh.

In Praise of Glenurquhart

Glenurquhart in its elegance,
In shade of dusky bens
With that special reverence
Stretching through the glen
Each and every field and place
Lie sacred, silent, still;
With snow-white daisies on display
To grace each glen and hill.

The mass and mounds that line the sky
With majesty prevail
Casting shadows from on high
On lower crag and cairn
And etching slowly from each peak
The streams still slowly crawl
From springs the water fills each creek
And silver water falls

There's 'Eanruig' and there's 'Coilltidh'
To complement the glen
Overlooking the estate
As if minded to defend;
And each brook and river runs
With music in its spill;
Brisk and wanton, once begun
Its journey will fulfil.

There's 'Creag Neigh' and 'Creag Mhonaidh'
Well covered by the firs;
Which offer shelter far below
When storming winter stirs.
Loch Mhioclaidh has its share of fish
The marshy moor lies near.
There's 'Ruisgich' and there's 'Diomhach'
Providing for the deer.

His poem in praise of Baillie Stuart, a man well loved and respected, contains a wealth of expression. This also is apparent in the translation by Mr Fred Macaulay of the first four of the thirteen verses.

Oran air Mr W.G. Stiubhart.

(Air fonn 'A' nochd gur faoin mo chadal domh.')

Le fiòr-ghean gràidh, céud soraidh slàn
Do 'n fhleasgach àluinn, òg;
'S na 'n d' fhuair mi iùl gu d' àrdachadh,
Cha 'n fhàgainn thu 's a' cheò;
Is ceann-iuil air thus nan sàr thu,
'N uair thàrladh tu na 'n còir,
Le d' òraidean ga 'n gléusadh dhaibh,
Gu soilleir, réidh-ghlan, fòil.

'S gur lionor buaidh tha sinte riut,
Nach tàr mi ìnnseadh 'n dràsd
Is Gàidheal foinnidh, finealt thu,
Bho chrùn do chinn gu d' shàil;
'S tha macantachd a 's mìleantachd
Co-shìnte ri do ghnàths;
'S tu smachdail, beachdail, inntinneach,
Gun mhi-run gun chion-fàth.

Thug Nàdur gibht mar dìleab dhuit,
Le inntinn fhiòr-ghlan, réidh,
'Toirt eachdraidh bheachdail, chìnntich dhuin
Air iomadh lìnn o chéin;
Le éudmhorachd ga mìneachadh,
Gun dichuimhn o do bhéul,
'S iad uile làn de dhiòmhaireachd,
'S an fhirinn annt' mar stéidh.

Tha tùr 'us mùirn na d' ghiùlan,
Gu fearail, sùnndach, fòil;
As gealtaireachd cha d' ionnsaich thu,
'S cha d' thug thu rum do phròis;
Air nail', cha tugainn dùlan duit
An ùine bhios mi beò,
'S mo dhùrachd cheart cho dlùth riut
'S a tha 'n driùchd air bharr an fheòir.

' With true warmth of feeling I wish the handsome young man a hundred farewells. And if I had been given the talent to exalt you I would not leave you in obscurity.

You were the star among them when you joined their company, with your polished observations, delivered with stately clarity.

Time will not allow me to number your many qualities; you are a Gael of fine mettle from top to toe, your nature is a balanced blend of gentleness and heroic valour, authoritative, decisive, inspiring, never harbouring ill-will, without good reason.

Nature gave you the gift of a crystal-clear balanced mind, giving us studied confident accounts of previous ages, relating them diligently and accurately, and all of them full of wonder and based faithfully on truth.

There is understanding and affection in your attitude, manly, joyful, stately, and you have never known fear nor given undue place to pride. Truly I would never challenge you as long as I live as I feel as close to you as dew on grass.'

That this poem was meant to be sung is evident from the fact that the title of the tune is given. Music was never far from poetry. A note in the 'Highlander' newspaper of 1875 says that he composed a song on smuggling, an activity which was still engaged in at that time in the neighbourhood. Satire was a favourite mode of his, as it had been for his predecessor 'Mr Lachlan.' Sadly, towards the end of his life, when religious precepts were condemning the composing of secular forms of verse, he asked that most of his work should be destroyed. Mercifully a few of his compositions did escape destruction and have been recorded with care.

The other art-form closely linked to that of bardic verse was storytelling. Some of the storytellers were no doubt descendants of the old itinerant minstrels, who, along with the bards, entertained the chiefs of the distant past. They enjoyed the well-earned favours of the time - food and shelter and some applause - and their tales were remembered and repeated many times. They also visited more humble homes and were a source of inspiration for the young as they recounted the heroic deeds of their forebears.

Still today among the few remaining native people of the Abriachan area - a Macdonald here, a Fraser there, maybe a Chisholm or a Maclean - the art and practice of the storyteller lingers. Some incident of daily life acquires a glint of magic when recounted slowly, deliberately, with flashes of wit, many meanderings down byways, with subtle references to former happenings. The teller, feasting on the wonder in his listener's eyes, carries his tale on till at last it must mount to the surprise of the climax. The enjoyment is such that, inevitably, there are calls for more. Storytelling was the mainstay of the ceilidh. It is recognised, today, as an art-form and is being revived.

A descendant of the Bard, now in his 90s, still lives near the family home and retains a love of poetry and song. He has composed some short pieces, which he sings, in the traditional manner, along with many of the older songs, stored in his memory. He also enjoys the telling of tales, recording happenings of yesterday or 70 years ago. They are all part of the pattern of life, all worth a tear or a smile. It is to him, to Hugh, that we turn for a picture of the past, of the events, the places, the people he has known. His store of genealogy is vast. Each field, each hillock, each crag has a name for him, a name not recorded on any map.

'Well, I suppose I'm the oldest one that belongs, now. I'm 92. Yes, 92. I've lived always here in this house or the one before it. My mother's father came from Tore, as we call it, the house just up the hill there. My father's people were from Corro, Corriefoyness, that is. Some of them were tailors. There's a field there they still call 'parc an taillear,' the tailor's field. My father was born in Inverness. He was still called 'Jimmy Tailor.'

His aunt had the place here and then he got it. Before he was married he worked on the boats. He was a steward. He sailed all over the world. Later, when he was home, he worked at fencing. He was a road man for a time. We hadn't a croft. Just the house site and a garden. A good garden. My father kept a good garden. You can still see it. The rhubarb is there and the rasps and the blackcurrants. And there's the apple tree and the damsons. He had great carrots and onions and turnips. And we'd grow tatties, just here and there, wherever there was a bit ground. And we had hens and ducks. And bees. Just in old straw skeps. So we had plenty honey.

There were seven of us children - four girls and three boys - in the house, the old house. It was small but it was quite warm. The roof was thatched with heather. There was a special place where the heather grew with long stalks. Special heather for thatch. We had to renew it maybe every four or five years. And the old thatch made grand manure. Later we sometimes used bracken for thatch.

My mother cooked on the open fire, with the pot hanging on a crook. The kitchen floor was cemented. In the other room the floor was earth and clay. There was a box bed in the kitchen. We lived in the old way. My parents spoke Gaelic, of course. My mother could read and write it too. And she could make up wee poems. She had had good schooling. She thought the world of the master, Mr Mackay. She had good English, too. And my father had good English. The children had to speak English in school. But, of course, we had Gaelic as well, though our parents wanted us to use English, as we'd need it for work later on.

My father would often read the Bible to us, in the evening. And he was a great singer. He had many Gaelic songs, and others he had learnt on his travels. Yes, I learnt many songs from him.

135

In the school we had a good choir - a Gaelic choir. The master, he fairly kept us in order, him and his tuning fork! But the choir did well. Took prizes at the Mod.

My granny made kilts for us, good kilts. I wore one to school when I was wee. Many a time I ripped it, climbing fences, and fixed it with a safety pin!

One of the teachers lived in the house there, next door - Miss Maclennan. She would give us sweeties to keep us quiet and take us outside for lessons in the summertime. We would try to hide the strap when we were with her! On Sundays she would have us to her house to sing hymns. She was good to us.

We'd go up to the school on Sundays, too, to the 'sermon' as we called it, a service taken by a minister from Inverness. I remember the big men squeezing into the desks we used as pews. At school we played shinty and football, yes and rounders, too. Sometimes, in the winter, in bad storms, the school would be closed, for the sake of the children coming from far. Then we'd have a great time sledging, sometimes just on small sheets of corrugated iron. It must have been dangerous! At Hallowe'en we'd have fun playing tricks on the neighbours - flinging sods down the chimney, things like that. Once we let loose a cart and were going to push it down the brae but the man it belonged to got the better of us - he was hiding in it, and jumped out. Did we get a hollering!

above: John Macdonald, son of the Bard and his wife Margaret, née Fraser, Gartallie, grand-parents of Hugh and Jock Macdonald

And, of course we all had our jobs - fetching water from the well and bringing in peats and gathering sticks. A job I didn't like was gathering brambles for my mother to make jelly. And I didn't like going to the peats much. The midges were terrible!

I left school at 14, was apprenticed to a joiner in Inverness. Jock, my older brother, and myself we went into town every day on our bikes. Left them in a shed at the foot of the hill and took the short cut up.

After a while I switched to work with a mason. Jock and I worked together for many years. At places all over. For a while we had lodgings in the town. But I didn't like that much. I liked to be here, at home.

We had good times. There was a lot of folk here when I was young. Folk like ourselves in every house. And some boarded orphans from the town too. In the summertime we'd go dancing at the bridge up yonder, at the crossroads, in the long evenings. And if it was real warm we'd go swimming in the loch. Sometimes it was to Loch Ness, for a swim at the jetty.

Jock and I would often go to fish the wee hill lochs. Sometimes, if we were well away, we'd manage to get a roe for the pot. And we'd be ferreting for rabbits and having a go at the hares. Butcher meat was too dear for us. We'd make do, though. My mother would put nettles in the broth and make jellies and medicines from the wild berries - brambles and sloes. We'd make a kind of tea with dried leaves of willow herb and other plants. And sometimes we'd smoke dried coltsfoot, when tobacco was dear. As long as we had meal for the brose and oatcakes we were all right!

John (Jock) Macdonald, brother of Hugh, photographed making a hazel walking stick, c 1970. Jock was one of the last native Gaelic speakers in the area. 137

We had a neighbour, Seonaid, who had a wee shop, just in the lobby of her house, where we could get sugar and other things. You can see the remains of her house, just down there, where the gooseberry bushes are. And she had a good garden, yes.

About this time it was decided to build a hall. There were joiners and other tradesmen among us, as well as masons. We would work on the building in the evenings and any other spare time. Then, of course we had dances and ceilidhs. Lots of them. And Johnny Finlay, at Leault, he played the fiddle for the dancing. He was a grand fiddler. He'd play all night.

Meantime we had decided to rebuild the old house. The family was all grown up and earning. My mother had done a grand job bringing us all up. We went to stay at Balbeg while the job was done. We started during the trade holidays in July and by October we were finished. It was hard going. We carted the stones from up the hill, with the horse and cart, hewing and shaping them. We got good timber and slate. Jock did all the joiner work, too. See those great ceilings and partitions.

It was much later on when we built on the kitchen and the bathroom that's there now. And by then we had piped water from the well and the electric. And the garage!

When the war started I was called up. To the Royal Engineers. I was sent away to England to train - building bridges and light railways. They called me 'Paddy' Macdonald because of my Highland speech! I was demobbed down

above: the corn mill

Hugh Macdonald, his sister Daisy and their nephew James at Balchraggan, c 1950

there and got home. Then it was back to work. We worked on many buildings in Inverness, myself and Jock. And in places in the country, farms and distilleries and shooting lodges and so on. Sometimes we slept in tents. And the midges! Most often we had lodgings.

Now most of my family have died. I have just the one sister living and she's very good to me. My nieces and nephews come often to see me. And I have good neighbours. I'm on my own, but I have my wee dog, yes, and my cats. And out there the hens, the ducks, the geese. And the bees. So I have plenty company.'

Hugh Macdonald
Balchraggan, 1999

23

THE POST

Ever since the invention of writing, and particularly since the practice of it became more universal, with the spread of educational facilities, the sending of written messages by what came to be known as 'letters' assumed more and more importance. In the Highland area, where communication by word of mouth, the oral style, was, and still is, the most usual way of transmitting items of news, the sending of letters was practised by comparatively few.

By the seventeenth century, with fear of rebellion in the north always present, the centres of power in the south sought to improve communications. In 1669 a foot-post was established between Edinburgh and Inverness, to operate 'wind and weather permitting.'.

By 1695 a Post Office was opened in the Highland capital. Almost a century later, in 1786, the first mail coach came up the Great North Road to Edinburgh, but the hill country was still too wild for a direct delivery to Inverness. Mail was brought by carriers 'riding horse.' Beyond Inverness roads and bridges were non-existent. 'Runners' were employed.

It was at this time that Lachlan Maclauchlan, very much a 'man of letters' was schoolmaster in Abriachan, and, as such, would have been expected to act as 'receiver' of mail for the community. Letters would have been few as many of the people were still illiterate, but, should a written communication arrive, 'Mr Lachlan' would read it to the recipient and write any response needed. Even in comparatively modern times some communications, mostly of an official kind, were taken to the Postmaster for elucidation and the drafting of a reply.

In the early 1800s a 'runner' was carrying mail three times a week between

Inverness and Fort Augustus. Whether he travelled by Loch Ness-side or by the more direct route through Caiplich, is not recorded. One man, known as 'Posta Ruadh' (red-haired postman) covered the whole district between Inverness and the Fort, sleeping the night at Drumnadrochit, 13 miles on the way.

Another postman, Stoddart to name, and known as 'Posta Ban' (fair-haired postman) travelled two or three times a week between Drumnadrochit and Fort Augustus and composed a song which tells us something of his life, his feelings, and also describes the route he took. It translates from the Gaelic thus:

> *Chorus*
>
> *My feelings are sorrowful*
> *Since the sack went on my back*
> *My good humour and mirth are gone*
>
> *When others are sleeping soundly*
> *On their pillows and warm;*
> *Plodding hard on foot*
> *I am then wet and cold.*
>
> *A road, long, winding and crooked*
> *It is awful, by the shore,*
> *At the stroke of twelve o'clock*
> *Setting out to Port Clair.*

This is from the volume: 'Song and Story from Loch Ness Side' by Alexander Macdonald.

As the nineteenth century moved on the volume of mail increased considerably. People from the area had emigrated, to towns or overseas in search of a better life. Some found it, after a struggle, some did not. Most wanted to keep in touch with the homeland and to write letters was the only way. In some cases professional letter-writers were employed, as well as the local schoolmaster. More and more business correspondence, as well as newsprint was circulating through the post.

About 1840 a mail-cart was tried for the first time on the route to Fort Augustus, then a daily horse-post, till, in 1876, a steamboat came every day up the loch. By 1882, ten years after the Education Act which established good schools and schooling all over the Highlands and which saw the building of the great new school in Abriachan, we find the people confident in their ability to express their needs and wishes.

In the Post Office Archives in London there is this interesting entry headed:

'The Postmaster General.

Under Mr Cunninghame's recommendation I submit that a Post Office be established at Abriachan, on Lochness, in accordance with the wishes of the residents, as expressed in the accompanying Memorial forwarded by Mr McDonald Cameron, M.P.

The Salary of the Subpostmaster should be £5 per year and for this I request authority.

(dated) 28 July 1882

Approved. Please inform Mr Cameron.

29 July 1882

Abriachan Sub Post Office established.

Mr McD Cameron M.P.'

So, in November 1882, Mr John Mackenzie of Balchraggan was appointed sub postmaster. Four years later he was granted an allowance for meeting the steamer which carried the mails from Inverness. At about this time a special allowance was also granted for the delivery of mail to the very distant places of Ladycairn and Corriefoyness. Then, in 1903, the allowance for meeting the steamer was withdrawn. Auxiliary (relief) postmen were entitled to a Boot Allowance of 15/- per annum, 12 days holidays and two-thirds of pay when sick.

John Mackenzie retired in 1909 at the age of 60, after suffering a stroke. He continued to live at Balchraggan, with his wife and family, and is still remembered by the oldest member of the community today, as 'the shoemaker.' This was his trade, which he continued to ply, in a small shed, down by the pier, as he waited for the steamer. Sometimes, in stormy weather, it was a lengthy wait. His day was long and arduous. Having collected the mail, carried it up a good mile to his house on the hill, sorted it on his kitchen table, he then had to deliver it, on foot, to the houses scattered over the hillside. He was often on his feet till midnight, battered by gale, rain, snow, whatever the weather might throw at him. His small house is now a rickle of stones, with the little tumble-down wall that enclosed his garden ground. Blackthorn and bird cherry adorn the ruin, its erstwhile occupant and his family have passed into legend.

The next sub postmaster was Mr Donald Fraser, appointed on 1st November, 1909. He had three assistants - Elizabeth Mackenzie, Christina Fraser and Katie Fraser. Ewan Mackenzie Fraser is recorded as a 'rural deliverer', paid 15/- for taking letters to Ladycairn. Whether this was an annual or occasional payment is not stated. After Donald Fraser's death on 14th November 1918, his niece, Mrs Christina Fraser, was appointed sub-post mistress on 18th January, 1919. Her

salary was £16.16.0, she worked six hours a day and had an allowance for paying Old Age Pensions. Conditions were improving. In 1920, on 23rd June, Kenneth Fraser was appointed postman to carry mail as far as Ladycairn for a wage of £1.14/-

In the 1930s the road along the north side of Loch Ness was widened and improved with the result that the volume of traffic along it increased greatly, while traffic on the loch itself grew less. The mails were then carried by bus from Inverness, the postman going down on his special issue bicycle to collect them and bring them to the Post Office for sorting. By this time the positions of post-master and postman were entirely separate.

Soon after 1958, the Post Office, after changing location several times, was to be established on a more permanent basis in the schoolhouse. The school had closed and the house was let to a teacher working in Inverness, whose wife was to run the post office. This she did, from a small 'office' in the entrance porch.

By 1950 William Fraser had been appointed postman. His family had been in the area for generations. He was allowed a pedal cycle by the authorities, but he ran a motor bike at his own expense in order to save time and energy for the working of his croft. This he did to perfection, growing the traditional crops and rearing cattle of first-rate quality. His older sister kept house for him and he also had a 'boarded-out' boy living and working with him.

above: the paddle steamer, the Gondolier, which carried the mails until the 1930s

ABRIACHAN TRIBUTE TO POSTMAN

"You have the distinction of being the last man to carry the mails to the people of Abriachan," said Mr G. D. Thomson, of the Head Post Office, Inverness, when he attended the presentation, in Abriachan Schoolhouse, on Saturday last, marking the retirement of Mr William Fraser, who has been postman in the district for close on twenty years. The delivery of mails is to be motorised. Warm and sincere tributes were paid to Mr Fraser both by Mr Thomson and by residents in the area. The way he never failed to win through to the outlying crofts even in the worst weather and his unfailing helpfulness gained him the respect and affection of everyone.

Mr John Macdonald, Balchraggan, who presided, read messages of goodwill from friends as far away as Fife, Edinburgh and south of the Border, and Mrs Clayton, Corryfoyness, handed to Mr Fraser a gold watch, inscribed by his friends, and a sum of money. During the ceilidh which followed, the company greatly enjoyed the Gaelic singing of Mr John Macdonald, Glenurquhart, and the fiddle-playing of Mr William Grant, Abriachan, as well as the fare provided by the ladies of the district.

The value of his work lay not only in the fact that he delivered letters, parcels, newspapers, telegrams, good news and bad, but that he brought a welcome presence into some places that might be lonely enough in their isolated situations. Born and bred to the local ways, he could understand everyone's hopes, fears, needs. A look, a handshake was the discreet form of sympathy offered in the face of news that was clearly bad, to be followed, perhaps, by an offer of help at the harvest, the clipping, the peats. Good news was celebrated discreetly, too, for one must never tempt providence.

The postman carried this vital link between the people and the outside world, between the people and their kindred in far-off places. News, carried in the traditional way, by word of mouth, news of an accident, illness, sudden death would send helpers hurrying to the affected home, with horse or tractor, medicine, food, whatever was needed. The amount of good or interesting news he brought greatly outweighed the bad. He had heard perhaps on the grapevine, that the snowplough was due to clear the road in the morning, to let the grocer's van through. Hamish at Ballone had his harvest in and would be up in the evening to give Jess a hand with hers. Meg had a broody hen if one were needed to hatch eggs, Jock had a swarm of bees to spare. Good verbal messages with not a hint of malice or scandal.

Beel's retirement was marked with a ceilidh in the schoolhouse and the presentation of a gold watch by a Post Office official from Inverness. It was an old-fashioned ceilidh, with Gaelic songs, story-telling and a good dram along with the tea and cakes. There were many quiet expressions of appreciation of his work. After retiring he survived two serious accidents with his tractor and lived on to fight for his grazing and peat-cutting rights to which the incursion of tree-planting posed a threat. Illness finally caught up with him.

At this time there were to be changes in the structure of the postal delivery. The mail was to arrive ready sorted in a Post Office van driven by a postman from the town. The first man to undertake this form of delivery was Kenneth Chisholm. Luckily he was a countryman by birth, who still worked a croft near town, so was acquainted with the ways of a crofting community and he soon came to know his round.

After Kenneth's retirement John Kay took on the job. He was a countryman too, and a keen gardener, always ready to talk gardens, plants, trees. He was also interested in history and brought several interesting things to add to the collection in the local museum. He knew the area well, having acted in a temporary capacity over the years.

His appointment to Abriachan was not on a permanent basis. His successor was to be William Urquhart, another man from a country background, who soon fitted into his part. His unfailing cheerfulness and his many acts of kindness endeared him to the community. With his friendly and understanding, yet discreet, approach, he was able to help in many times of trouble, particularly among the elderly living alone. Even after his retirement, in June, 2000, after 50 years of service with the Royal Mail, he and his wife Isobel continue to participate in many local activities and Willie brightens many a ceilidh with his gifts as a raconteur.

'the mail must get through...'
Willie Urquhart delivers mail to Helen Fraser, Woodend, Caiplich

145

There is talk, today, of small offices being closed. The Abriachan office had survived largely on account of its relative inaccessibility, particularly in winter, steep hills intervening between it and the next nearest office. With many incoming families now owning Land Rovers and four-wheel drive vehicles, this problem is not so acute, but nevertheless it is important to maintain some focal point and an identity. This small office is fortunate indeed to have preserved its named date stamp - ABRIACHAN - not to have been swallowed up, as so many have, in the overall designation - INVERNESS.

As for inaccessibility, there have been winters, in fairly recent times, when even the Post Office Land Rover could not plough through the drifts on the hill, the 'post' leaving his vehicle, carrying his mailbags like a 'runner' of old, and volunteers helping to distribute the contents to various districts, outliers being asked, by telephone, to collect their letters at the Post Office. The volume and pattern of postal business has, of course, changed over the years, as has the pattern of country living. With many people now commuting daily to Inverness, some find it more convenient to buy stamps at the supermarket where they do their lunchtime shopping. But as the Post Office accepts payment for telephone, electricity and other bills and as there is seldom a queue at a small office, they find it convenient to discharge this sort of business locally. Bank accounts and direct debits are devices not yet widely used by members of the older generation. They still like to see the colour of their money! At Christmas time there is much activity in the parcels department, when the lack of a queue is a blessing!

As we enter the modern age, with its power of telecommunication, some commercial enterprises are emerging in the area and are making use of postal services for the despatch of 'real' as opposed to 'virtual' products. The local office has moved with the times too. Though the counter is still a table in the porch with scales so old that a similar model is to be seen in Inverness museum, computerisation is imminent. It is hoped that small outposts of the postal service, such as the one in Abriachan which has passed its centenary, may be allowed to maintain their place in the vast scheme of communication.

24

RELIGION

As we have seen, Christianity came in its earliest stages to the vicinity of Abriachan with the passage of Columba on his way to Inverness and the settlement of the monks at Kilianan on the shore of Loch Ness. In the oak groves just up the hill from the settlement there must have been ceremonies conducted by the Druids.

What notions of good and evil, what visions of eternity were in the hearts and minds of the first settlers, those in the bleak uplands, we can only surmise. Those things that fostered life - the elements of earth, air, fire and water - must clearly have been the object of respect, amounting to veneration. Family groups living in close proximity must have evolved a certain moral code in the furtherance of life itself. The burial rites, particularly of a person who had risen to a leading position in a community, would seem to indicate belief in a future life, since goods to facilitate the journey ahead were laid in the grave. Storm, thunder, rainbow, these phenomena must have spoken of unseen powers.

By way of myth and legend we can learn that, in later ages, in the time of the Celts, the spiritual foundation of their attitude to life lay in a feeling of harmony between the land and all forms of life existing on it.

'I am a wave of the sea,' said Amergin, an Irish poet of this time. And: *'I am a hawk on a cliff, I am a tear of the sun, I am fair among flowers.'* There was a sun-god - Lugh; a sea-god - Mamannan, and many other gods and goddesses. Time was calculated in phases of the moon. The fact that many of the early proponents of Christianity shared this respect for, and love of, natural things must have eased the transition from pagan cults. St Columba, in particular, and, later, St Francis of Assisi entered happily into this form of 'brotherhood.'

Forms of worship in the early Celtic church had a simplicity which must have made a direct appeal to the people of the time. Later forms, emanating from Rome, may have become more complicated but converts combined their innate veneration of the phenomena of nature with due regard for a single supreme deity of whom these phenomena were manifestations. The fact of the blood-sacrifice of this God's earthly son, and the fact that he was hung on a tree, must have made a forceful impact on these early peoples. It is thought that the Druids may have prophesied the coming of Christ.

With the growing strength of influence from the south, the arrival of feudalism in political affairs, Roman Catholicism became, by the Middle Ages, the estab-lished form of Christianity in the Highlands. The many small, ruined chapels bear witness to the demise of the early Celtic forms of worship. The big Abbeys, now also, many of them, in ruins, show the growth of affluence in Church affairs, which was itself partly the cause of further downfall. In the late sixteenth century, with the reform of the Church, the new form of worship, labelled Protestantism, found its way into the Highlands. In many remote areas its intrusion was resisted. The priest was an important member of the community. As well as seeing to the spiritual needs of his congregation he also helped them in everyday matters, hav-ing access to the chief and also to higher church authorities who owned land and wielded secular power.

There is no evidence of Abriachan Frasers, not even those who took the 'boll o' meal' in order to qualify as clan members, having adhered to the old faith. Many staunch Jacobites had become Episcopalians, others preferred the Presbyterian order. 'Easter and Wester Abriachan', that is the lands to the east and west of the dividing gully, had for long been Church lands, under the jurisdiction, and in the gift, of the bishopric of Moray. Until very recent times a levy was paid to the church authorities by every tenant. The people became strictly Presbyterian, at-tending services at a preaching site at Kilianan, then, from the late eighteenth century, in the schoolroom, where the master also held catechism classes for adults as well as children. At Communion times, which came round quarterly, great efforts would be made to reach a church, which might be many miles away. Food was carried, the women's skirt pockets filled with oatcakes and cheese, and com-municants would stay overnight with relatives or friends before the long journey home.

When, after the Disruption in the Church of Scotland in 1843, the Abriachan schoolmaster, Donald Tolmie, seceded to the Free Church, he had to resign, in spite of petitions by the people. He had been a popular teacher and member of the community, helping in many situations, such as rent increases, disputes over boundaries and so on. Many people, perhaps following his lead, went over to the Free Church.

One of the nearest places of worship at this time was several miles away on the other side of Loch Ness. Attendance at the service took up the whole day. People still today can recall the crossing in the small ferry boat at Bona, the men rowing and the company singing psalms, the sound carrying across the water on calm summer days. The young people were so hungry by evening that they feasted on whatever wild fruits were in season, sometimes on turnips from the edge of a friendly field. Services were also held in barns, mills, or other buildings for those who could not travel far. In some parts an outlying field was used, the preacher having a moveable wooden shelter to protect him from the weather. One open-air preaching site is on the heights between Abriachan and Kiltarlity. To many remote places the gospel was carried by the 'Men,' elders of the Church who went from house to house leading prayers and Bible readings.

At about the time of the Disruption, the mid to late nineteenth century, an evangelical movement was appearing in the Highlands and was gradually to become a force affecting many people's lives. Some ministers of religion were preaching acceptance of the many hardships involved in the 'Clearances,' the forced evictions of people from their homes, saying that they were punishment for sin. Music and dance, the composing of songs and poems, the artistic expression of a whole people in their traditional way of living, were condemned as ungodly. Writings and musical instruments were burnt.

Services continued to be held in the schoolroom, as they had been in the days of 'Mr Lachlan' in the late eighteenth century. 'Going to the Sermon' became the practice of most people every Sunday. A Church of Scotland minister would come one Sunday, a Free Church minister the next, members of the congregation having to squeeze themselves into the new-fangled desks. The sermon, delivered in Gaelic and based on the Scriptures, was the most important part of the service. The fine preaching was much appreciated. Still today it is spoken of as an inspiration for the leading of a good life and for the retention of Gaelic, the 'language of Eden.' The psalms were sung in the traditional fashion, a precentor intoning the first line. The Bible continued to be a bedrock, many families having a daily reading by the head of the house. Books of sermons, notably Spurgeon's, were to be found in most houses and the 'Pilgrim's Progress' was widely read, sometimes a portrait of Bunyan adorning the kitchen wall.

There was, until quite recently, by all Church members, a strict adherence to the observance of the Sabbath. Peats were brought in, water-pails filled, potatoes scrubbed, boots cleaned, on Saturday evening, so that Sunday could be given to God. One elderly man of Abriachan still remembers being chided, as a boy, for whistling on a Sunday. Today a service is held, once a month during the summer in the hall. Music is provided on a small harmonium or a keyboard. As many people now have cars, attendance at the church at Bona, some five miles distant, is easy. Lay preachers also help to organise prayer meetings, as did the 'Men' of old. The fervour of former times may be lacking, but the ethos is still there.

In 1973, a cousin of Tom Fraser, Balchraggan, also called Tom Fraser, or Tom Gow, was interviewed by Dr Marinell Ash. Here is how he described the funerals remembered from his youth:

'Ah, yes, a Highland funeral. The service was always at the house and after the service was finished there was whisky and biscuits and cheese passed round. And then the remains went off walking. They always walked with the remains for three or four miles quite often. Somebody went in front and if they met anybody coming to the funeral they got a glass of whisky. At the churchyard there was the service, again just before the coffin was lowered in the grave and as the people left the gate - the churchyard - they got another dram because it was very, very hard work - a funeral in them days. Everybody said that a funeral was a day's work.'

'There were a lot of weddings in those days...usually the wedding took place at the house where the daughter was that was getting married, and sometimes in the summer the wedding was outside, the reception would be in the house and then after the reception in the evening there was a dance in the barn, with lanterns the only light till five, six in the morning..weddings would go on for four or five days, the guests would dance and drink.'

above: the wedding of Margaret Fraser and John Forbes at Achbuie, 1903

25

NAMES - PLACES AND PEOPLE

The Celt, with his strong feeling of affinity with the natural world, was in tensely sensitive to the beauty and mystery of his surroundings. This finds expression in the amazing fertility of the Gaelic language, in its naming of every natural feature - every hill, rock, burn, particular area of ground, be it wet, dry, stony, flat. There are, for instance, over a dozen different words for high ground, the type of country the Gael knew best. 'Beinn' is a high hill, 'meall' a rounded hill, 'cnoc' a small hill, 'ard' a pointed hill, 'druim' a ridge, 'leitir' a slope, 'aonach' rocky, steep ground. Brae, tor, tom also indicate height. Some hills were named for their resemblance to people or for events that took place on or near them. Thus, the hill of the 'bald man' or the 'hill of history.'

Fields, too, were so named. The 'field of the sword' is a place where an eighteenth century weapon was found. Could it, one wonders, indicate a skirmish with a Redcoat making west? The prefix 'bal' indicates a settlement. In Abriachan 'Balmore' is the large settlement, 'Balbeg' the small one, 'Balchraggan' is the settlement on rocky ground. 'Achadh,' abbreviated to 'ach' meaning field, is a common prefix. Over the years most names have been anglicised. On the high ground across the old road to Glenurquhart, in a place once a shieling area, there is the farm of Achpopuli. This means the field of the tent: 'Achadh Poible', field of the tent. It is said that at one time the people from the glen would hold a fair there, setting up small booths and selling or exchanging goods - perhaps manufactured things, horn spoons, wooden plates and so on. It would have been an occasion for a welcome exchange of news and gossip and no doubt some eating and drinking, and surely a song and a dance.

The ground at the back of the schoolhouse was known as the place of stones.

These stones have now been identified as clearance heaps, stones piled up to make way for the cultivation of small crops of grain in prehistoric times. A hut circle lies just outside the wall of the old playground.

Walking up from the village hall and bearing right where the road branches, just past the former schoolmaster's house at Leault (this means a half-burn - Gaelic leth allt - that is, a burn with one bank higher than the other) and walking up into Caiplich, on the right is Cnoc na h-Eachdraidhe, the hill of history. This name probably refers to the prehistoric settlement there, or possibly, to a skirmish that may well have taken place there in later times. On the left are two places, Tomachoin west and Tomachoin east, each bearing the name 'hillock of the hounds.' Hounds played a very important part in the old hunting days. They were said, in the legends, to have the power of speech. Certainly, like the sheep-dogs of today, they probably had an uncanny understanding of their master's words. Up the hill, to the right, An Leacainn denotes a hill slope, and beyond Creag na h-eigheachd is the rock of shouting. Meall na h-earba, the hill of the roe-deer is close by. Could the shouting have been to the hounds? Carn a' bhodaich, the old man's cairn, is also in the vicinity. Did he die on the hill, perhaps out hunting, and was buried there?

Further along, and a short distance from the road lies Ballone, once a small settlement, on marshy ground, now one substantial croft, and nearby is Balnagriasechin, the place of the shoemakers. At one time seven shoemakers lived and worked here. Returning to the road we find Carn na Baintearn, a place named for a cairn at the roadside, said to mark the spot where a 'lady's' coffin was rested on the way to burial in Inverness. A Grant lady?

Back at the hall, and going down the road and turning left at the bridge, through Balmore, we climb to Achbuie, the yellow field, so named for the profusion of whin which lights up the area in early summer. Here are two crofts, with modernised houses and below them, at Achcullin - Gaelic cuileann - the field of the holly, more croft ground, the buildings ruined. Moving east, along a track now largely overgrown, but which the people used to take as a shortcut to Inverness, the women travelling barefoot and carrying baskets of eggs or hazelnuts, we come to the Bealach A' chadha, the steep pass, and to the Slochd an Famhair, the pit of the giant, a secret place, well suited to the brewing of an illicit dram. A little further on is the Creag nan Gobhar, the goat rock. Until quite recent times feral goats lived among the crags here. Dominating all this once busy area is the Cnoc an Duine, the hill of the man. You can see him there, lying peacefully on his back, as he has done through many millennia.

Returning through Balmore to the road-end and looking across to the Leitir, the slope, which was common grazing and which bore a transversal track up to the moss where peat was cut, and which has been afforested, the shape of Meall a'

bhàthaich, the hill of the byre or cattle shelter can be clearly seen. It may have been the place where, in a hollow, the cattle were gathered on their way to follow the drove to market. Flowing from the Leitir is the burn called Allt nan Clachan Breaca, the burn of the speckled stones. When the water gleams in sunlight one wonders - gold? Perhaps not, but there is said to be silver in many hill burns. Taking the road to the right through Balchraggan we find the way to the bard's house, up the hill to the right. Its name, Tigh an Tòdhair, is thought to mean either the house on the bleaching green (tòdhair - bleach) perhaps from the time when flax was grown, or the house on the midden, meaning a good heap of valuable dung. To the west lies Cnoc Bheinnellidh, the hill of the deer-trap, so called in the days when deer were driven into a hollow for slaughter. Further along is the settlement of Coire Foithaneas, anglicised to Corriefoyness, the hollow by the waterfall, where, until the mid nineteenth century, there was room for five families, and where one field is still known as the Parc an Taillear, the field of the tailor.

These are only a few of the names of the more prominent features of the area, names which have been mostly anglicised and which have found their way onto maps at various times. To the people whose families have lived and worked in the area for generations each burn, each field, each rock has memories and associations peculiar to them. Burns and rocks formed the natural boundaries between lands before wire fences were invented. Paths were worn through the heather to

make easier access to neighbours' houses. The names of features such as these will never find their way on to official maps.

Along the road to Corriefoyness and down to the left there is a place known to very few, the place of the apple tree. Sure enough, after a walk among boulders, through bracken and scrub, you come on it, an apple tree that blossoms every spring and beside it a small green shelf of ground. Here, it is said, a recluse lived contentedly enough for many years, feasting on apples, with hazelnuts and berries in autumn, snaring a rabbit for the pot, making broth of all the wild plants, with no authorities to question his rights or his welfare. Did he plant the apple tree, did it grow from a bird-dropped seed?

Back to the road and up to the hill ground on the right we come to the place of the 'little houses.' This was shieling ground and the shelters built to house the people tending the cattle in summer would very likely have been built on the sites of prehistoric dwellings which are here. Above Corriefoyness, up the hill to the west, is a cairn. This is marked on the map, but it is not generally known that it marks the spot where a woman, returning to Abriachan from the woollen mill in Glenurquhart with her cloth, hearing a cry, whether of anger or distress she was not sure, alerted the people in the nearest house at Corriefoyness. Going up the hill they found a man, a keeper on the estate, who had collapsed from a heart attack and was dying. Down the old 'funeral road', where the coffins were carried shoulder-high to a conveyance on the roadside, a place known as Balochan would seem to indicate a settlement near a small loch. There is no sign of former habitation and the water has drained away, but the name makes it yet another secret place. Also very secret and unmarked are the places where the distillers plied their trade. A famous one, which can still be clearly seen, was in the rocks above the inn by Loch Ness. One on the far shore of Loch Laide and one below

above: Tom Fraser, Balchraggan, with helpers at the tattie-howking, Abriachan, 1943

Balchraggan can just be made out, the roofs of thatch long since fallen away, but small stone walls standing. So the stories remain and the vanished people live on in the mind and heart.

People, the people of recent times, had designations all their own too. They were given names not found in any baptismal records by those who knew and understood them. Sometimes it was by the names of their place that they were known, sometimes by their occupation. Thus one William Fraser was Willy Balnagriasechin, another Bill-the-Post. A designation could be carried on through the generations. James Macdonald was Jimmy Taylor, so-called from his grandfather's occupation. Another Macdonald was known as the 'breabadair,' the weaver. He had never used a loom, but his grandfather had had the skill. One man, not long dead, was known as the 'Boxer', not on account of any pugilistic ability but because he was a gifted player of the 'box', the accordion. The 'swapper' was the man who practised the old art of barter, not necessarily always to his own advantage. The 'cromadh' had a crick in the neck which gave him a bent or twisted look. The 'balach,' the boy, was he a character who refused to grow up? He was certainly a lively and good-natured man. One who went out to South Africa looking for a better life, but who returned at the outbreak of the Boer War, was known, till he died, as 'Kruger.'

In a humorous poem written by the bard, describing a wedding in the part of Caiplich known as Street we find a collection of nicknames. The third verse reads:

'When we arrived at what we call the 'Street'
Fine banners were spread and mounted aloft,
'Earl Sutherland' 'Lord Seafield' 'Doctor William' 'White Rock'
'Thomas from Corrick' 'Humpbacked Roderick' and 'the King.'

Anyone who perhaps thought too highly of himself was mercilessly satirised in his title. It was all accepted quite happily. John Mackenzie, the first postmaster in Abriachan, was always known as the 'shoemaker.' And there was the 'Trapper'

above: Finlay Maclean, Achpopuli; John Mackenzie, Lochend; Willie Grant, the fiddler, and John Logan, Achbuie, the ' Boxer,' at the clipping in 1965

155

who kept the rabbit population under control. The 'drover' - 'drobhair' - was the man who relished the days when the cattle were driven to market in Inverness. The Abriachan beasts were sometimes hard to handle. A large horned creature from these high grounds once stumbled into a dairy, causing as much confusion as the famous bull in a china shop! These names, bestowed with affection and understanding, and with wit, gave people a special sense of identity and of a close link with the community of which they were a part.

Eona MacNicol's grandfather lived at Druim - the ridge on the shoulder of the hill leading to Caiplich. Here is how she describes him:

'But grandpa must follow the course of the Tallurach burn, far up till it winds free of bushes and comes out thin, clear on the open moor. It is a bare landscape, quintessential, austere. There is a hill face, veiling itself at times with mist, like some holy mountain. There is a small reed-fringed lochan where waterfowl cry. And there is the moor, with a cold sweet air blowing over its bog myrtle and heather. Hill, lochan and moor. The three. And that is all. There grandpa's solitary croft lies. His forefathers wrested it from the moor. They scratched out little squares and lifted off the heather and went through the soil beneath, sifting out by hand every individual stone. Thin oats for food and thin barley for drink grew as best they could against the wind. There were potatoes and turnips and a little grassland forever being encroached upon by heather and bulrushes.

Above the croft the cottage stands, twin rowan trees growing by the gable and one wild rose bush. A path of flat stones lead through the swampy land down to the well. The well has three stones for walls, a fourth stone for its roof, with fern sprouting between them. And in it lives a fish, a tiny priestess keeping the water clear. This is his world, his universe: he has no identity apart from it.'

Eona's grandfather, Donald Fraser, at Druim, c1900

26

THE SUMMER WALKERS

Welcome visitors to the area were the 'summer walkers', not those who come today, from all over the world, kitted out for spending a holiday walking the hills, but what were known as vagrants, wanderers. Sometimes a single man would appear, perhaps on his way from a spell of work in the east to his home in the west, taking the familiar track through the hills. One man who did this every year became a familiar figure and was always warmly received. He would get a sleep at the fire, a bowl of morning brose and oatcakes to see him on his journey, with 'see you next year' and a parting wave.

Most often they came in company. Their coming was looked for, and they were welcomed. In the old tradition, a stranger, be he friend or enemy, was never refused food or shelter. There were those who took advantage of this custom, and left their hosts impoverished. The wanderers were independent in their ways, making their shelters of willow-wands and tarpaulin and cooking over a wayside fire. Their coming would be noted from afar - a little procession of men and women, young and old, some walking, some riding in a ramshackle cart drawn by a lean horse, dogs racing ahead or staying to heel.

Many of the company were descendants of clansmen who had been 'out in the '45,' had taken to the heather and never returned to stay in settled conditions. They still had pride in their ancestry and were happy with their style of life. Some were skilled craftsmen, perhaps erstwhile smiths, highly regarded members of a community, who had adapted their skills to the making of tin-ware. The goods they produced were of a solid standard and would last for years. Some worked in silver, others made horn spoons.

Their knowledge of the uses of plants as food and medicine made them adept at living off the land. A stew of rabbit flavoured with thyme and a dash of wild garlic made a memorable meal. Summer berries, autumn nuts, gull's eggs, fish from the burn, the odd game animal or bird, caught with skill and cunning, wild honey, herbs of all kinds, meant that they could live as well as the hunter-gatherers of old.

Many of these travellers had vast stores of traditional tales tucked away in their minds, handed down through the generations, ready for the telling, along with a tune scraped from an old fiddle. They were also, like the wandering bards of past ages, bearers of news from other parts. In the days before the advent of radio and when newspapers were scarce and many could not read, this made them doubly welcome. Avid listeners would greet them when they stopped to unload their wares, put up their little shelters and light their fires - as they settled for a stay of a week, or longer, on a patch of wayside grass. If an extra hand were needed to get in a crop of oats while the weather held, if turnips needed singling, if the tatties were ready for lifting or the peats for carting home, a 'walker' could always be called on to help. His reward might not be money, for that was scarce. But barter came more easily and meant the reality of a goodly portion of butter, milk, eggs, rabbit skins to make winter clothing. So everyone was satisfied.

'the wanderers were independent in their ways......' - summer walkers in the 1930s

Other summer visitors were the 'packmen,' who arrived singly, walking miles along the old tracks and drove roads, carrying their wares on their backs. For people with scant means of access to markets, their coming was welcomed, particularly by the women, who caught a glimpse of luxury at the sight of ribbons and lace among the mundane buttons and threads as the pack was opened on the doorstep. The packmen dealt in barter, too, though money was welcome if it could be spared. And they carried news, which was as welcome as their wares, news from the town where they bought their stock, news of the wider world, of political intrigue, news of distant friends or relatives at whose houses they had called. Occasionally, a strange character would arrive, someone clearly schooled in the ways of the world, who had been to many parts but who preferred his own company and that of the hills and forests. Encountered at the right moment he would delight a listener or two with his tales and would share his experiences and his knowledge of the contents of books of many kinds. He must have inspired many young men, over the years, to go exploring.

Still to be seen among a tangle of bushes and grasses along the road to Balchraggan are the remains of a small house, where a 'walker' family would live, in the bad weather, between wanderings. Planning regulations did not apply in the nineteenth or early twentieth centuries! A beautiful gean tree at the spot is still known as 'Henny's tree.' 'Henny' evidently kept poultry on quite a scale; he and his family spent winters there, their wants seen to by kindly neighbours.

Members of the old wandering families still come about in the summer months, in old cars or trucks, bringing bought goods, small textiles, knitting wool and so on. Most of them are settled now, in the towns, and no longer have that look of sparse, but healthy living. Some still hanker for the freedom of the road and tour the country, dealing in scrap metal and spare parts. The old stories are dying as radio, television and the Internet dominate most lives. Some have been faithfully recorded and published in book form. So they can still carry you into that world of legend, where there is room for heroes, where gods speak, where the little people go dancing under the hill and all things are possible.

27

OTHER WORLDS

For the Celts, all natural features were endowed with sanctity. It could not be otherwise, for human life depended on a harmonious relationship with all other forms of life - animal life, plant life - and with the elements of earth, air, fire, water. And there were many mysteries - wonders to be observed, wonders that could not be explained. Room was left for the magic of uncertainty. There was the sky above and a depth of earth beneath. That was sure. But pure water springing from the ground, trees that grew from minute seeds into colossal living structures, deeply rooted in the earth and reaching high into the sky, these were things that caused wonder in the mind and heart.

Water being the basic element essential to the continuance of life, springs were venerated for their health-giving properties. Water could cleanse inwardly and outwardly. They were fit places for the habitation of a goddess. And the trees that grew nearby had a touch of magic about them, too. It was a grove of nine hazels which imparted knowledge to the salmon.

The early Christian missionaries had wisely refrained from condemning many of the beliefs they found, discreetly adapting them, and thus converting the goddess of the spring to an equally attractive Christian saint. The spring at Kilianan is known as Columba's Font. Not far away is St Ninian's well and there are many others. The descendants of these Celtic peoples have, until quite recently, retained a belief in 'supernatural' powers, powers which could live happily with a Christianised version of human life and death and immortality. Who were the fairy-folk who danced on the green, flitted about the sky and cast love-spells on human men and women? Were they, perhaps, angels? The water-horse, also known as the kelpie, was never Christianised. He's a relic of the belief in transformation, when one animal or human could take on the form of another, perhaps with evil intent. Ride on this fine horse's back and he will become a water-creature and convey you to the underworld, in the depths. One Abriachan woman, not long dead, would not pass Loch Laide at dusk. Fear lingers.

'Morag would go down to the pool to meet the kelpie and very often when they got tired of talking they had a game of skiffers, for the kelpie always had a supply of pearls on him. Morag sometimes thought to herself that there must be a small fortune in pearls in the pool as a result of their games but since she was not interested in money the idea never bothered her. To please the kelpie, however, she did at last accept the pearl necklace he had made for her.

'It suits you fine' he told her with a glint of triumph in his strange old eyes when she put it on for the first time. 'You look real bonny with them on, mistress.'

The kelpie was speaking no more than the truth when he said this, for flax-white hair is fine with pearls and so are rowan-red cheeks and blue eyes with a sparkle of good nature in them. Morag had all these and a good black dress to wear with them as well, and though she laughed at the kelpie for a flatterer she could still see in her mirror the bonny picture she made when she wore them.'

from Mollie Hunter: 'The Kelpie's Pearls', set in Abriachan.

In what is now a small ruin on the moor just up from the schoolhouse there lived, in the early years of the nineteenth century, a woman who was said to have some truck with the fairy-folk. Eccentric she undoubtedly was, living her own way in her one-room dwelling. Neighbours would look to her in times of illness, when she would nurse a sick child with unending patience. But.....a witch? Her brother, who lived not far away, angered at the rumours, one day shot a hare, then took malicious neighbours up to see his sister alive, thus proving she was no witch, for witches often took the form of hares.

Belief in the power of the 'evil eye' was another source of fear which haunted people's lives. A curse could be put on a person or on a valued beast, so that they would wilt and die. Recourse had to be found to those who could work counter-action. A woman in Caiplich, not long dead, remembered a man who had to walk, in silence, the fifty miles to Speyside to consult the only person who could rid him of an evil spell. She also remembered a cockerel being buried alive under the doorstep of a house where lived a cherished epileptic daughter.

When an elderly man who lived alone was found lying dead in the barn at his home, a woman who had long known him said that when she last saw him making his way up to his place on the hill, a few days before his death, she had had the strongest feeling that he was not walking alone. There was no sun that day, yet he cast a shadow. An angel of death? There is no doubt that people living quiet lives, perhaps alone after the deaths of relatives, in close touch with the still forces of nature, do have faculties of perception which the urban dweller has lost. This same woman would not burn the branches of a dead rowan tree on the fire in her house, though it was winter and she was short of fuel. The rowan is the protector of the household. There is one near every door.

At Moine Dubh, near the foot of the road to Achpopuli lived, sixty years ago, Margaret Noble, who had the 'second sight.' She must have often wished she had been spared this faculty, for it was most often sad things she saw, premonitions of death in the form of funeral processions passing before her eyes.

The powers of perception and imagination in the people of older times led to that vast store of poetry, story and song which enriched the lives of the generations. Glimpses of worlds within worlds must have been a source of magic which would have given a richness to life, however hard the circumstances of poverty or war. And there was always humour about, too.

Down on the shore of the 'big loch,' Loch Ness, is a huge boulder - Clach Mhor. It is said that a witch in Abriachan fell out with her counterpart on the opposite shore, at Dores. The two hurled boulders at each other across the loch. Once, the witch of Dores missed her mark, the boulder fell short, where it still lies, on the shore. And the 'monster' in that big loch, down there - what of him? There is no doubt that creatures of many kinds have been seen swimming in those waters - otters, deer, even a seal - by the people living near the shore. If there has been one more elusive creature, who prefers the depths to the surface and who still evades us most of the time - so be it.

The powers of science and technology have not been able to prove its existence yet. They are still probing their way into greater mysteries. The links with our forebears and their vivid ways of interpreting the universe grow stronger as we progress.

above: Margaret Noble in front of her thatched house at Moine Dubh (black peat)

28

INVERNESS FIELD CLUB AND ABRIACHAN

In early November 1875 Professor Young of Glasgow University delivered three lectures on the geography and geology of Scotland in the Music Hall, Inverness. Mary Ettles, a lady of Inverness, who died about 1870, had bequeathed money to provide for lectures such as these. They were very well attended and, as a follow-up, the Professor organised an excursion to Abriachan, for Saturday, November 6th, to study the formation of the Ness Valley and the geological features of the area. An account of the excursion was published by the 'Inverness Courier.' Unfortunately the weather broke during the night previous to the planned outing, so that on the Saturday morning there was *'persistent rainfall and a shroud of mist enveloping the valley.'* Some Academy boys, eager to go on the outing, had to be disappointed. *'The departure was postponed for an hour while the party waited at Mr Grant's coach office for an improvement in the weather. None came and at half past eleven seven people, including Dr Young, set out in an omnibus from the Post Office, four inside and three perched on the box, to survey the country.'*

At Craig Dunain the party dismounted, and Dr Young gave a lucid account of the geological formation of the area. After luncheon with Dr Aitken, the superintendent of the hospital, they moved on to inspect the quarry at the side of the road leading up to Abriachan *'which yields a fine reddish stone, now frequently used for monuments.'* Small pieces of this rock were broken off with the hammer. Dr Young's discourse was much appreciated and the outing enjoyed, in spite of the adverse weather conditions. Soon thereafter it was decided to establish in Inverness, a Scientific Society, with its *'indispensable adjunct, a Field Club'.* The objects of the Society were *'generally to promote scientific study and investigation and specially to explore the district for the purpose of inquiring into its geology, botany, natural history, archaeology etc.'*

163

At the first meeting in January 1876, Mr William Jolly, a school inspector, took the chair. In his opening remarks he said: '*The tendency of the time is to make us narrow-souled, low-toned money-seekers and place-hunters, instead of the erect, heaven-aspiring, intellectual and emotional men and women that God wishes us to be. The thirst for knowledge and the pursuit of science compensate, yet how little we have done for science in Inverness? We have at last formed an Association for scientific pursuits called 'The Inverness Scientific Society and Field Club.'*

Mr Jolly also quoted Walt Whitman:
> '*All truths exist in all things.*
> *I believe a blade of grass is no less than*
> *The journey work of the stars.*
> *A mouse is miracle enough to stagger sextillions of infidels.*'

By the following year members of the Society had taken over and rearranged the material previously in the hands of the Northern Institute, in order to set up a museum and were urging on the establishment of a School of Art and Science, and a Free Library. On September 21st 1878, a party came out to look at the graveyard at Kilianan. They inspected the sculptured stone and the suggestion was made that it might have been brought from the tomb of one of the Knights Templar. The idea was not corroborated. They did not stop long, as they were on their way to Drumnadrochit. They had time to wonder at an unusual dragonfly!

At a meeting of the Society in Inverness in 1883, Mr Wallace read a letter from James MacKintosh of Polmailly Wood, in Glen Urquhart concerning Creag nan Uamh, the rock of caves, and the giant boulder, Clach nam Fiann.

'*As this place,*' the letter reads, '*will continue to be interesting to the geologist, it will also be interesting to antiquarians on account of the smuggling days of the people of Abriachan, who were considered the best at making whisky in the North Highlands, except, perhaps, the people of Strathglass. But the people of Abriachan were certainly the most cunning smugglers to escape the Inland Revenue officers. They had their bothies for making the malt underground, and sometimes in the face of steep rocks where none but themselves and the goats could get into them. They had the kiln for drying the malt in the silent grove, or on the lonely moor. And they had a portable hand-mill for grinding the malt as well on the top of the hill as in the middle of the wood. They would distil their whisky in broad daylight, without raising any smoke from the fire. They gathered the old stumps of burnt heather and of juniper bushes for making a fire that would raise no smoke.*'

On 5th June 1886 Dr Aitken led a party to Abriachan. They visited the graveyard at Kilianan and saw the sculptured grave stone and the Font Stone. They discussed the possibility, which had been suggested by Mr Fraser-Mackintosh, the noted historian, that the church of Bona originally stood here. Dr Aitken

showed a drawing by Grove, in volume III of the 'Beauties of Scotland' by Forsyth, published in 1808, representing a ruined chapel at Kilianan. No-one, he said, had heard tell of such a building, or ruin.

They inspected the granite quarry and made their way up the gorge to the Schoolhouse. Dr Aitken had collected much information on the history of the area. He had also made a study of the meaning of the name Abriachan, quoting four possible explanations:

1) that it may refer to a Druid Uaigh Briachan, said to have been buried in the area.

2) according to Robertson in his 'Gaelic Topography' 'Abhir-riabhach-an' means 'the confluence of the greyish streams,' that is the confluence of the burn with Loch Ness.

3) the derivation 'aber' meaning 'mouth,' 'riach' (riabhach) 'grey' and 'an' a contraction of 'amhan', a river, so Abriachan means 'the mouth of the grey river.' The native name has been spelt with an 'O', thus 'Obriachan.' This is, apparently, common usage.

4) a letter from the Rev Mr Mackenzie of Kilmorack, a Gaelic scholar, quoted by Dr Aitken, states: *'I think you are safe in regarding 'Aber-riach-an.'* He goes on to say: *'descriptions of physical features so generally rule names that you may look for no other explanation until these fail,'* and *'such a stream as you describe could not fail to strike the eye of the ancient Celt, who was an ardent lover of nature and who was possessed, in his language, of a wealth of descriptive expression truly wonderful.....it seems to me that the true etymology is, and must be, 'Aber-riach-an' - 'confluence of the pretty stream.'*

The Rev Mr Macpherson of Dores had told Dr Aitken of a tradition in his parish, which faces Abriachan across Loch Ness, that a hero of the name of Iachan had been slain there and had given his name to the place. Dr Aitken then went on to describe the 'Robbers' Cave.' A daring cattle-lifter of the nineteenth century, Samuel Cameron, sought shelter there, in the cave of the Red Crag, high in the granite cliffs of Abriachan. Sheriff Mackenzie of Inverness had long wished to catch him, but his stronghold, which dominated the country, was almost inaccessible. One day, however, when out hunting, the sheriff found himself in the neighbourhood of the cave. Then, according to the words of one Maclean, a centenarian, *'with the delight of a vulture hovering over its devoted prey, and with the agility of the tiger advancing to spring upon his prey, the person of the outlawed Highlander, with a visage so overgrown with hair as to resemble the shaggy goats that alone shared with him the mountains, might have been seen rapidly descending the face of the cliff or screening himself behind the stunted pine and birch trees.*

When the sheriff came near, the outlaw sprang forward, seized him by the neck, and pointing his pistol at his breast, shouted: 'unless you will solemnly swear to reverse my sentence and declare me a free man at the Cross of Inverness on Friday first, I will instantly shoot you.' Needless to say, the sheriff complied and subsequently Cameron gave up his thieving ways and lived an exemplary life for the rest of his days, rearing a large family.'

Later Dr Aitken goes on to describe the constituents of the Abriachan granite and the process of its formation and to point out other rocks, including diorite. He had collected much interesting information on the history and traditions of the area and was accorded a very hearty vote of thanks by the members of the Society on their return to Inverness.

On 16th July 1892, a party of Society members set off in two large waggonettes for an excursion to Kiltarlity and Abriachan. At Kiltarlity, the planting of trees by 'natural' process was referred to by Mr James Gossip, the leader. The trees - Scotch fir - planted by a forebear of Lord Lovat, were protected during early growth by coarse trellis-work which acted as a wind-force breaker, but did not prevent free circulation of air. They looked at the big kiln at Clunes, where the working of the limestone had given employment to local people in the Caiplich area. They also stopped at the churchyard at Glenconvinth where there are many sculptured grave-slabs and the remains of a chapel and where many Abriachan people are buried.

In 1919, on 26th July, a party of members left Inverness *'in three brakes'* to visit the graveyard at Kilianan. A cup-marked stone near Loch Laide was also examined with interest. The following year, 1920, on 19th June, a party of 40 members, in two brakes, had an excursion to Lochend. Here one of the early Christian missionaries - St Curadan - lived and worked. In an old burying ground are the remains of what is thought to be a small chapel and on the path over the hill to Caiplich is a stone - Clach Churadain - where it is said the Saint would rest on his way over to preach to the people there.

The members saw the place known as 'Battlefield' above Dochgarroch, where a clan fight had taken place in the late seventeenth century. They then went along the canal bank to see the site of Castle Spioradan, which was destroyed by the making of the towpath and the raising of the water-level, when the canal was built. The ruins were used as a quarry, the stones taken by builders. This castle was in a commanding position at a ford over the river Ness, a ford used in subsequent years by drovers taking their cattle from the Aird and Caiplich to southern markets. Many struggles between Mackintoshes, Macdonalds, Macleans, Urquharts, Grants, Frasers had taken place in the area. The name of the castle - Spioradan - signifies a haunting by the ghosts of the slain. Votes of thanks were warmly accorded to Colonel J.E.B. Baillie of Dochfour, to the Rev Mr Macfarlane and to Mr Mackenzie, the gardener.

On 25th May 1921, we find the Field Club again in Abriachan, when Dean of Guild Fraser led a party of 20 to the area. Their first impression was of the *'gorgeous display of broom and whin.'* This always lights up the landscape in early summer. Accompanied by Mr Donald Macdonald of Reindoul, Abriachan, and the Rev Mr Macfarlane, their first stop was at Kilianan. It was explained that the prefix 'Kil' indicated a cell or small structure made of wattles and thatched with bracken or heather. Though there is no living tradition of a chapel having been built here, as previous speakers had pointed out, yet Kilianan was known as a preaching site.

Mr Fraser spoke of the various derivations of the name Abriachan and of the history of the place, mentioning in particular the good work done by teachers over the years, Lachlan Maclauchlan, Neil Maclean, Donald Tolmie, who was known as "an Talamach." He came from Laggan and had married a young woman from Kiltarlity. Thereafter the party was *'most hospitably entertained'* by Mr and Mrs Macdonald of Reindoul who were cordially thanked for their help. The drive home was by way of Kiltarlity.

In September 1975, to mark the centenary of the founding of the Field Club, which was the result of an outing to the Abriachan area, members came out again to see the places visited by their predecessors on that dreich day in November 1875. They were blessed with better weather. Among them were geologists, botanists, archaeologists, historians, geographers, and many with a simple love of the hill country and its people. None were disappointed.

Some walked or scrambled the precipitous way up the burn from the churchyard at Kilianan. Some inspected the remains of a smuggling bothy on the far shore of Loch Laide. Some wandered through the site of the Bronze/Iron Age settlement on the hill-slope by the Caiplich road. This is a new discovery since the last recorded Field Club visit to the area and was a source of much interest. Much interest was also shown in the collection of artefacts and documents relating to the area, at that time housed in the village hall. On the way down to the main road, some members went to look at the old houses at Achcullin and gathered a basket-full of edible fungi into the bargain. The outing was enjoyed, as had been that of 100 years before. Since that day members of the Field Club have been to Abriachan many times, individually or in small groups, have made photographic records of field structures, old roads, dykes, flowers, wild life, helping to build up a picture for generations to come. It continues to live up to its old motto 'Seek and Reveal.'

Sadly, since its Jubilee year in 1925 the Field Club has not issued volumes of transactions owing to rising costs. It has, however, published several noteworthy books on various historical themes, including, in 1975, its Centenary volume 'The Hub of the Highlands,' which continues to sell today. Between 1990 and 1993 three very attractive illustrated 'year books' were brought out. These contain accounts of lectures, excursions and field studies. At this time a section for junior members was formed and in August a party came out to visit the Croft

Museum in Abriachan. In October of that year a party of senior members also came to the museum. Much interest was shown in the collection of old implements and artefacts and in the documents and photographs relating to the area.

It will be seen that, during its early years, the Field Club found Abriachan an interesting and attractive place to visit, comparatively easy of access, yet sufficiently remote, as the road rises to close on 800 feet, to provide a complete contrast to the flat, cultivated lands and the lifestyle of the Inverness area. It is good that the interest is continuing and that plans are being made for an excursion to the area in the year 2000, in celebration of the Club's 125th year, when the new developments can be studied at first hand.

the steading at Druim

29

INCOMERS

In the years after the Second World War changes were taking place all over the Highlands. Families had lost fathers and sons. Young men and women had seen service in various parts of the world and some were not inclined to return to the hard life of subsistence farming. Some had married and settled in other parts or overseas.

The biggest change in the Abriachan area was brought about by the break-up, in 1945, of the Seafield estate. That part which included most of Glen Urquhart and extended to Abriachan had become known as Balmacaan estate. It was designated a *'Valuable Agricultural and Sporting Estate'* of 49,700 acres, and included the mansion and the Home Farm of Balmacaan in Drumnadrochit and some 200 'Lots' with the *'Grouse Moor of Abriachan'* and *'Trout Fishing in Loch Lait'*, also *'a large part of Loch Ness and nearly all of the Vale of Urquhart extending in all to 49,700 acres.'*

Many of the crofts in Abriachan had grazing rights on the 'grouse moor.' The catalogue of sale states: *'the extensive grouse moors shown as lot 103 will be offered with the adjoining crofts as one block. The crofts which have been selected as those which have sheep grazing rights over the moors, so that the Purchaser of the whole block will also become proprietor of the dominant tenements as far as the sheep grazing is concerned, and the whole of the rights will thus be under his control subject to the current leases.'*

All timber 'standing and fallen' was included in the sale of each lot, with the exception of that sold to the Ministry of Supply, under contract. This included timber in Abriachan, in the School Wood, Rinudin and Caiplich. The contractors had a sawmill at No 1 Caiplich, which became known as Woodend. Much of the felled woodland was subsequently replanted by the Forestry Commission. The sale of the estate was held in the Blairbeg Public Hall in Drumnadrochit on November 6th and 7th, 1945. Several sitting tenants in Abriachan bought their places for nominal sums. One incomer bought several places, some of them tenanted.

INVERNESS-SHIRE

Fifteen miles from Inverness: on the main road from Inverness to Fort William

A Unique Opportunity to acquire a Sporting Estate, Farm or Cottage in one of the loveliest parts of Scotland, in the

Break-up Sale of the Valuable Agricultural and Sporting Estates

known as

Balmacaan Estate

Comprising some 200 Lots, and including

A large part of LOCH NESS and nearly the whole of the Vale of Urquhart

extending in all to

approximately 49,700 Acres

with actual and estimated Rental of **£5,800 per annum**

The Sale includes

BALMACAAN HOUSE, HOME FARM, GROUSE MOOR,
and extensive Salmon Fishing
BALMACAAN DEER FOREST with Lochs
VALUABLE SPORTING MOORS with Lochs
SALMON FISHING in Loch Ness
THE CHALET at DIVACH and the Falls
Many Farms, some bounded with Salmon Rivers
Numerous Crofts, on Loch Ness Side and in the Vale
Houses, Cottages, Lewiston Arms Hotel
Two Important Feus of £110 and £272 per annum,
payable by Forestry Commissioners
Numerous Feus in the Villages of Drumnadrochit,
Lewiston and Milton

To be offered for SALE BY AUCTION, in numerous Lots,
by

Messrs. JACKSON STOPS & STAFF

In conjunction with

Messrs. NICHOLAS

at the

BLAIRBEG PUBLIC HALL, DRUMNADROCHIT

on

Tuesday and Wednesday, November 6th and 7th, 1945

at 12 noon each day

Solicitors: Messrs. STEEDMAN, RAMAGE & CO., 6, Alva Street, EDINBURGH 2,
Messrs. TITMUS, SAINER & WEBB, 61, Carey Street, LONDON, W.C. 2.
Messrs. GEORGE ROSS & NOBLE, 41a, High Street, INVERNESS.

Auctioneers: Messrs. NICHOLAS, 1, Station Road, READING. (Tel. 4441).
Messrs. JACKSON STOPS & STAFF, 15, Bond Street, Leeds 1. (Tel. 31941).
Also at London, Northampton, Cirencester, Yeovil, Chichester, etc.

above: page from the catalogue for the sale of the Balmacaan Estate, 1945

A typical holding offered for sale was that of no 4, Caiplich, one of the 'New Lots' created some seventy years previously. In the catalogue of sale it is described as:

'New Lot no 4 Caiplich and part New Lot no 5 Caiplich, area 40 acres approximately. House with 3 bedrooms, sitting-room, kitchen and pantry. Buildings include Byre for eight, stable for four, Barn. Let on lease 14 years from 1939, break at 1946, to Mr A McMillan, at £8.0.0 per annum in addition to an amount for insurance. Estimated value of shooting £2.0.0. per annum.' (illustrated above left)

The date over the door of the house was 1911. It was an 'improved' dwelling built near the remains of the original small, thatch-roofed house. The steading was well-built and roofed with corrugated iron. The house was of local granite and whinstone, the fine roof timbers supplied by the estate, as also the Ballachulish slates. Water was drawn in pails from a well.

By the mid-1950s several new enterprises were being started up in the area. An ex-Army officer from Cornwall bought a croft with ground on the slopes facing south-south-east down towards Loch Ness. Here he planted strawberries, raspberries and daffodils. They did well for several years and provided a few seasonal jobs. The daffodils still bloom amid the encroaching bracken. The wild sloes are there for the picking.

A mink farm was established at about this time in a fairly remote area - Blackfold. This was something looked on with a certain amount of mistrust, as the creatures were an alien element in croft land, stories of their depredations as escapees in other parts having spread. At least they were a deterrent to low-flying aircraft which were obliged to keep their distance as the noise was fatal, inducing the parent animals to devour their young. Another incomer, ex-R.A.F., who had suffered badly during the war, brought in dairy cattle and other livestock, goats and poultry. But his Friesian cows were not hardy enough to withstand a Highland winter and the dairying had to go.

These enterprises did not prosper, but one which did was the planting of conifers by the Forestry Commission. A man who had bought several places when the estate was sold - also ex-R.A.F. - and whose many ideas for making a living in the heights had not succeeded, now decided to sell some of the land he had acquired to the Forestry Commission for planting, ignoring the fact that much of it formed common grazing for several crofts. He was duly warned but paid no attention. When a start was made to fencing off the moorland prior to planting action had to be taken.

Lawyers were consulted, legal aid was granted and the case was taken to the Court of Session in Edinburgh. After two days hearing of evidence, in February 1959, Lord Cameron declared that Miss N. Fraser of Woodend, No 1 Caiplich, Abriachan, Inverness (in whose name the case had been fought, as representing the five share-holders in the common grazing) was *'granted declarator that she has a right to graze stock on 315 acres of moorland adjoining her holding; to cut, stack and cart peats for her domestic use and to have access to the moorland.'*

This was an important action as Lord Cameron wished it to be regarded as a test case to be quoted in further disputes which might arise. Over the following years, as the crofts involved changed hands and crofting practices altered, much of the area was eventually planted, some small compensation being paid by the Forestry Commission to erstwhile graziers. One area, adjoining the road, was, however, to remain unplanted for good. After a very heavy burning of the heather the foundations of eleven small prehistoric dwellings and some dividing walls were clearly shown up. This was formally identified as a bronze/iron age settlement and is now scheduled as an ancient monument. The Forestry Commission, recognising this, made an 'amenity planting' at the eastern edge of the settlement.

Subsequently, the Forestry Commissioners were to become our biggest incoming absentee landowners. As small amounts of compensation were paid to the new owners of crofts many acres of former grazing ground were planted with serried rows of conifers. Gradually, the contours of the landscape changed. Long vistas were reduced. The old roads to the peat banks disappeared. One landowner refused to give up his grazing, though he had never put stock on the ground. His portion of the hill still glows with heather-bloom in August, a few scattered birches stand aloof, the autumn bracken is a harvest gold. Shelter-belts of conifers are always welcome, but close-planted forest which inhibit the growth of native trees, plants and flowers have a smothering effect on the natural life of the place.

One planting in which the Commission took pride and which has been a real asset is that on the former grazing of the slope facing the Schoolhouse, the Leitir, where the natural regeneration of birch was allowed to remain, along with some hazel and rowan, an edging of larch was made and different kinds of conifers were introduced. This is an 'amenity planting' of great beauty and has been much admired.

Colonel Merry of Belladrum had bought the croft of Lochlait at the sale in 1945, in order to obtain the fishing on Loch Laide. His grandson remembers days on the Loch, and shooting on the adjoining moor.

THE LOCH AND THE HILL

When my grandfather, Eion Merry of Belladrum went off to war with his regiment, the Blues, he was dark-haired, six years married and a father. One of his last messages home was for the leg bones of a hind to be sent down from Benula, the deer forest he rented (Belladrum having none of its own,) to his soldier servant with which to 'bone' his boots. His wife and daughter waited five years before they saw him again. His hair was white by then.

One of the first things he did on his return was to buy Lochlait. This had never been part of Belladrum - it was a Balmacaan (Seafield) croft. But its significance to Eoin was the fishing rights it brought on Loch Laide. He had been a lifelong keen fisherman on the Beauly River, and after all the fighting, he wanted to settle down to cast over the calm trout waters of Loch Laide in his leisure hours. Now, such a trivial reason for a transaction would doubtless raise the hackles of any self-respecting land reformer. But that was the way in the bad old days, and so far as I know, Eion's relations with the family there, the Frasers, were always very good.

Looking back in his fishing book, some good baskets of trout were landed in the postwar years, sometimes as many as 50. Since then the catches have declined. Perhaps the skill of the fishermen has diminished, or the number of bank fishermen has increased beyond sustainability - there is no more depressing sight than the line of static rods sometimes seen along the 'stones.' Or perhaps acid rain is to blame, or the diversion of Allt Lon na Fiodhaige, the main feeder burn into the loch, into the Reelig burn and its only partial restoration into its old course, has harmed the spawning. Whatever, it is a shame, because the Loch Laide trout were the best eaters in the district. Always very pink, reputedly because of a diet of freshwater shrimps, they came in all sizes, up to the legendary ten-pounder caught in the Bishop's Bed (by the lily pads at the western end of the loch) though whether Bishop was the fisherman's name or his style, I never knew.

We shared the boat fishing on Loch Laide with the Frasers of Reelig. Taking the measure of the breeze down at Phoineas, we would gauge what sort of day it might bring on the loch, always allowing for it to blow harder up there. Too strong, and there would be white horses - no good. Too weak for even a ripple - no good. Coming from the east - no good either. A gentle west wind and dull conditions were perfect - though often, we would set out on such a day, only to find we were blasted off the loch later. My pregnant mother and Eion's old tutor, Sir John Mackay Thomson, who had become his closest friend, found them-

selves close to shipwreck once when a gale blew up with Kenny Stewart, the Belladrum keeper at the oars. Kenny, whose son Fraser now farms at Achnaharry and Belladrum Mill, was a great man and a good keeper, but he was not fond of life afloat. He was known to us as 'the Seaman.'

The rods were assembled when we got up there. Jock Stewart, Kenny's successor, had a habit of running the rod ferrule through our hair as children, and then down the side of his nose, giving it just enough natural grease to stop it sticking when it came to taking down the rod. There was always a lot of discussion over the fly box, but in the end, opinion usually favoured a killer combination of blue zulu and bloody butcher on the droppers and a kingfisher on the tail. The hot seat was in the stern, best for trawling when Jock rowed from one part of the loch to another, and we took it in turns to sit there.

Jock was amazingly patient with my brother and me in our early fishing years, as we thrashed the loch inelegantly. I remember his tackety boots braced against the varnished blocks on the floor of the beautiful but heavy clinker-built boat, as he worked the oars gently to keep us broadside on to the wind while we bobbed along the 'stones,' the best part of the loch for catching trout. Somehow he managed to do this while stoking his pipe which was filled with Tam-o-Shanter baccy, and had a sort of metal weather shield, or while helping us untangle a hopeless

ravel of nylon and flies. Naturally taciturn, he amazed us once with a fine rendition of 'John Brown's body lies a-moulderin' in the grave' as we lurched down the hill in his Landrover. It must have been one of those rare occasions, a day when we hadn't hooked some sensitive part of his anatomy on a wild back cast.

On a fine day, we waded around the boathouse at lunchtime, catching sticklebacks in jam jars to take home, in the vain hope that they would live in a fish tank. But raw weather saw a retreat to the lunch hut

Col. Eion Merry of Belladrum and Jean Merry at Loch Laide

where there was a generous stove. Sometimes my grandparents lunched in their car, a two-tone Humber Super Snipe station wagon with bird's eye walnut picnic tables that folded down out of the backs of the front seats. Always, the collie dog from the Postie's croft paid us a visit. And in the spring, we took gulls eggs from the island (probably an imprisonable offence now) to eat for breakfast.

For much of the year, Belladrum moor, as Druim Ba and the neighbouring ground were known, earned its livelihood as part of the Belladrum estate. It provided grazing for the estate's flock of black face sheep, which were overseen by the shepherd, Bob Campbell, from his house at Blairmore, over in Glen Convinth. Besides this, it furnished the surrounding crofts with peats.

But in the late summer months, in keeping with the gaiety of the season, it assumed its more frivolous - and supposedly subsidiary rôle - providing a sporting pastime for my family, the Merrys of Belladrum. Only a small area of ground as grouse moors go - less than 2000 acres - it offered a disproportionate amount of enjoyment for its size. I never remember a blank day. Sometimes it yielded as much as 60 brace of grouse, while at the western end towards Cudrish, there was always a good number of blackgame. So far as I know, it was only ever a dogging moor.

Shooting days began with an early breakfast at Phoineas. Then to the Belladrum kennels, to join up with Jock Stewart, the keeper. Jock was the most charming, mild-mannered of men, and a great hero and friend to my brother James and me. The kennels were full of every kind of trap and poison, quite normal then, and the interior of the dogs' accommodation, with its strong odours and echoing dark corridors had a slightly menacing air about it. The gun room, which was attached to Jock's house, beside housing a large number of sporting guns, also boasted captured weapons from various wars, including a Mauser and a Luger pistol.

We headed for the hill, us children crammed with dogs and the kennel boy into an ancient Landrover. Halfway up, passing Battan forest, momentum began to die and Jock clattered around amongst the low gears in an attempt to keep forward movement, resulting in a series of knee-banging jolts. It always seemed touch and go as to whether the old engine would make it.

Before the ages of 11 or 12, when we were allowed to start carrying a gun on the hill, we were attached to a dog. My regular companion was Ben, a springer spaniel, who towed my short legs across the heather with such relentless energy that even when he had upended me in a bog, he ploughed on regardless, nose hoovering up the scents of an August day. After the first two hundred yards of water-skiing behind Ben, often I cast a wistful glance back over my shoulder at the road, thinking it would be a few long hours before I saw it again.

The guns, my grandfather, Eion Merry, sometimes my grandmother Jean, my

father and guests, fanned out in a line of four or five, and walked in front, keep-
ing in line in case the dogs ran over any birds; the camp followers trudged along
in between the guns. Whilst on the leash, the pointers were the responsibility of
the kennel boy...a short distance from the cars, Jock took the first one and then
loosed it. Away it went, sleek and beautiful, eating the distances, as it quartered
the ground, working the wind. Depending on the way the wind had taken us,
lunch, which we carried in old gas mask bags, was taken lying in the heather.
Often, we stopped by a spring, over near Loch na Cuilce. But, occasionally, if
the ladies hadn't joined us, we would meet them at a prearranged spot with a
wicker basket full of baps filled with thick cut ham, Orkney cheddar in oatcakes,
fruitcake and tins of Tennants (sporting Flora, Heather and the rest of the girls
on the back) poured into horn mugs for the grown-ups. Jock and the kennel boy
took themselves off a little way to eat their pieces, the dogs' gazes following
every morsel from hand to mouth. After lunch, a brief while on ones back on the
springy heather, before setting off on another beat. On some days we could look
across towards Reelig moor and see our Fraser neighbours lined out on a similar
quest. It was on that piece of hill that Donnie Riddell, the piper and fiddler
composed much of his music. He worked as the Reelig keeper, and told me that if
he went out walking across the moor all day, and took no sustenance with him
(solid or liquid!) the compositions just entered his head. At the end of the day,
back at the cars, Jock laid out the bag. And after due appreciation, we set off
down the hill to a rigid ritual of gun cleaning and tea. A few days later, the rich
enticing smell of grouse would permeate the house. Knowing from an early age
the satisfaction of eating what you have killed, we ate the birds on pieces of fried
bread, with beetroot, bread crumbs and bread sauce - though I have a feeling I
disappointed my parents by asking for ketchup.

I was 21 when my mother sold Belladrum. The moor was split off from the rest
of the estate and a year or so later I hopped over the forestry furrows that cov-
ered it with sadness. I am a planter of trees myself, but I couldn't help feeling that
this was a kind of desecration of a beautiful piece of hill, so full of memories.
Had it continued in our ownership, I might have been forced to similar measures
by the realities of life in a fragile Highland economy. I am glad I did not have to
make that decision. The seedlings were of a species then very much in vogue -
south californian lodgepole - and heavily promoted by the Forestry Commis-
sion. Too late, lodgepole, or the seed source it came from - has been found to be
unsuited to our environment, good only for pulp and christmas trees. Looking
back on those times, only thirty years ago or so, I know now that they belonged
to a quite separate era. But we are lucky to have had all that.

Joe Gibbs, Belladrum.

30

WRITERS IN ABRIACHAN

Poetry was the form of expression which always came most naturally to the people of the Highlands, poetry in the form of song. This poetry could express the personal emotions of love, sorrow, anger, jealousy or joy, or the feeling of a whole community about some happening which concerned them all. Humour and satire were often indulged in. These songs were memorised and happily repeated in the oral tradition. In very old times, writing, though it was practised by a few, was frowned upon by the ancient mentors, the Druids, who considered it was bad for the memory. Poems, even of considerable length, must be memorised, along with stories. In this way many songs and stories have been lost, except for those transcribed and translated from the Gaelic by collectors last century.

In Abriachan many songs and stories were undoubtedly composed and have been lost. The first record we have of written material is in the work of Lachlan Maclauchlan, the late eighteenth century schoolmaster. His poetic gift was bequeathed, through his daughter, to the forebear of Thomas Macdonald, the Abriachan bard.

In the late 1800s Alexander Macdonald, who had risen through sheer hard work to become accountant for the Highland Railway, was contributing papers to the Gaelic Society of Inverness, of which he was an early member, and articles on Highland history to many papers and journals. Many of these were collected in a volume 'Story and Song from Loch Ness-side' published in 1914. His special interest was in Gaelic music and song.

He came from nearby Glen Moriston and was known as 'Gleannach' - 'from the Glen.' In the preface to the book he says:

'Few districts in Scotland can vie with Loch Ness-side for song and story. It is a land of poetry and romance ... where bards sang for generations untold and where seanachies never wearied of relating tales of the days of old. The author is a native of this poetic country, whose privilege it was, as a boy, to listen with rapturous attention to those stories and songs.'

He had married into a Macdonald family from Achcullin, in Abriachan, a family which had produced hereditary pipers to the lairds of Grant. His work took him to live in Inverness but his daughter Màiri, who died in December 1979, remembered vividly the happy summer days they spent at Achcullin with her mother's people. She had inherited her father's interest in Highland history and his literary skills, and was to contribute many articles to various journals as well as papers read at meetings of the Gaelic Society of Inverness.

The Gaelic Society published two books by Màiri Macdonald: in 1982 a collection of tales from the history of Inverness and district - 'By the Banks of the Ness' and two years later a novel 'Highland Corronach' which tells the life story of a man very like her father. I quote from the foreword to this story:

'I have tried to write this story in the form of a corronach, the traditional lament of the Celt ... I have named the parts after different variations of the ancient piobaireachd and tried to keep the tempo of the various parts in line with the tempo of these variations. Words alone, without a sense of music behind them means so little to the Highlander ... A Highland lament always ended on a note of hope.'

The music of the pipes was the lifeblood of the Macdonalds of Achcullin. Màiri was proud to claim descent, through her father, from one of the 'Seven Men of Glenmoriston' who sheltered the Prince in a remote cave during the time after Culloden. A former ancestor, Alexander Macdonald, had kept the inn at Aonach, in Glen Moriston, where, each year, he and the Lord of the Isles would exchange shirts in a sign of fidelity. Later the inn was visited by Johnson and Boswell, when the doctor was so impressed by his host's daughter's intellectual capacity that he left with her a book on arithmetic! In her house in Inverness Màiri Macdonald kept many mementoes of her mother's home in Abriachan - a spinning wheel, a shawl and some lovely dishes. From her father's family she had a powder horn given to Macdonald of Aonach by the Prince.

A contemporary of Màiri Macdonald - Eona Fraser - became a writer of great distinction. Her forbears on both sides of the family were from Abriachan, from Druim and from lower Balmore. Her father, from very small beginnings, had built up a business and moved to Inverness, where Eona was born and educated. From a very early age she would be taken by her father to Abriachan, looking at the old places and learning about the old ways. Her book, 'The Hallowe'en Hero,' is a collection of stories set in Abriachan, written very much in the style of the old story-tellers, with touches of magic in the perception of people and places. One, 'A Window Westwards,' tells how her grandfather, in a state of melancholy after being taken from his home in Abriachan to be cared for by the family in Inverness, was only restored to health when a window was opened in the west wall of the house to allow him a glimpse of his beloved country. Eona married a minister, Roy MacNicol, and lived for many years in India. After her return she settled in south Scotland and wrote several books reflecting life there. She had also written two books on the life of Saint Columba and many short stories. She retained her love of Abriachan and would visit frequently.

Another writer whose work came to be very highly praised, a Macdonald by birth, spent only a short time in Abriachan, but a time which was one of the most important in her life and which was to colour much of her subsequent writing. She came, as a young woman, to live on a croft high in the hills, at Achbuie, after suffering illness as a result of her upbringing in an orphanage. Her health improved in the clean air and she married another orphan, John Kesson, who was 'boarded' in a nearby croft house. They lived for many years as farm workers and eventually in London, where Jessie found work of various kinds. Jessie Kesson, as she was to be known, wrote of her experiences in Abriachan. In one early piece 'The Red Rock' written for radio, Abriachan is instantly recognised, the beautiful red granite cliffs the setting for a sad tale. Both Eona and Jessie recognised the sadness that could exist in idyllic surroundings.

Jessie wrote a lot for the B.B.C., many short stories and other pieces. Her first, best-known book, 'The White Bird Passes,' reflects her childhood experiences of life as an orphan. It has been dramatised for television. Her second, 'Glitter of Mica,' is in a sense autobiographical, for it tells of the kind of life she experienced with her husband as a farm worker. 'Another Time, Another Place,' a story about the coming of Italian prisoners of war to work on a farm, has been made into a film. In a book of short stories, 'Where the Apple Ripens,' one, 'Road of No Return,' originally written for broadcasting, tells of her coming back to Abriachan on a visit, of the memories of her youth, of the reality of today.

After her death Jessie's ashes were scattered, as she had requested, at the foot of the Red Rock and a rowan tree was planted at the roadside on the way to Caiplich.

In the 1950s Mollie Hunter, with her husband and small son, came to live for a time in Abriachan. She was enchanted with the place, came to know the people, the stories, the way of life. She would walk about, talking to people, looking at things. The result was a book which has become a classic - 'The Kelpie's Pearls.' This tells the story of an old woman's encounter with a kelpie which lived in a pool in a burn beside her house, her meeting with the boy Torquil and all the following strange happenings. Mollie Hunter subsequently wrote many novels based on historical themes for children and adults. She has been much in demand as a speaker in schools and at literary events, in this country and abroad. Her work is known in many parts of the world.

A young writer who has a strong affinity with Abriachan, perhaps because his mother's people came from 'the glen', as nearby Glen Urquhart is known to the hill people, is Kenneth Steven. He has written several novels, but his first love is poetry. Poems of his have appeared in many publications here and overseas.

A couple of miles up the road from Abriachan, towards Kiltarlity, a former croft house and steading have been enlarged and made into a 'workshop' for aspiring writers. Well-known writers come to act as tutors. One wonders what can be learnt in a week, even with intensive study and practice, but no doubt the ambience is congenial and advice and criticism, and also encouragement, can help. Writing, like any form of art, is basically a lonely business. The setting of this 'workshop' is superb, open to the vastness of moor and distant hills, yet within walking distance of a friendly hostelry. We look forward to more work with a bearing on the locality, where life has always been akin to that in any part of the Highlands.

My own writing owes everything to my experience of living and working in the community that was, and now still is, Abriachan. Short stories and documentaries for broadcasting and several books all came from these hills and from the life that they generated.

above: Katharine Stewart, Hugh Macdonald and Eona MacNicol on the school brae

'*ABRIACHAN*'

Mystical place with your deep loch
Like a fox's eye.
You give up your secrets stubbornly
As an old man in the sea of his bed
Hands broken and head shrewd-sighted.

You keep on luring me back
Like a half-forgotten lover
Offer me nothing to drink
But the ice-fisted cold of the stream
Nor soles for my tired feet
Only the scar of heather
And miles of walking.

Yet in the strange nights
The moon opens her mouth over the white land's bones
And there is dancing and song
Far off where your ghosts remain.

Ken Steven

'*I see the hazel; I see the holly;*
I see the birch growing and in leaf;
I would travel with you through woods and trees
Where we used to gather
The warmth loving primroses and blossoms from the branches...
Beautiful is each branch under the breath of summer...'

fragment of an eighteenth century love poem, written in Abriachan and translated from the Gaelic.

31

HIGHLAND VILLAGE 1970

After the closure of the school in 1958 the premises were cleared of furnishings and equipment and for a time were used as a store by the Education Authority. Then, a few years later the place was made into a field centre for pupils of the High School in Inverness. Bunk beds, made in the woodwork department, were installed. The new classroom which had been built in the playground after the war became a canteen equipped with Calor Gas cookers. The Centre became a base for outdoor activities - hill-walking, canoeing, orienteering. Geographical, biological, botanical and other surveys were made under the guidance of teachers. The art department was actively involved, sketching and painting parties coming out regularly. Groups could stay for a day, a weekend or longer.

In 1968 secondary schools in the crofting counties were notified of a scheme, to be financed by Lord Dulverton, sponsored by the Crofters Commission and supported by the Scottish Civic Trust and the Education Department, for pupils to initiate and carry out projects for 'the improvement in the appearance of a village' in their area, the work to be completed in 1970, which was to be European Conservation year.

Inverness High School submitted a plan which was to consist of four main parts. Firstly - the tidying-up of the old burying-ground at Kilianan. This meant cutting weeds and overgrown bushes, repairing gates and fences, making steps and planting decorative trees, some hedging and bulbs. Secondly - the village hall was cleaned, guttering repaired, walls painted, the surrounds fenced off and planted with trees and bulbs. Thirdly - the biggest undertaking - was the reconditioning of the old croft house at Druim. The garden there was also cleared and replanted. The fourth part of the plan was the setting-up of a Croft Museum, part of it in the refurbished house at Druim, part in the village hall, then unused for a number of years.

A small privately-owned collection of implements and artefacts was made over to the project, and subsequently added to, with many further acquisitions. The hall was also to become an interpretation centre for the area, covering its history and traditions, natural history, geology. Abriachan is not, of course, a village but a scattered crofting area. The scheme was nevertheless approved, the work went on, and in June, 1970, the project was awarded the Civic Trust Plaque.

The following year a second phase of the scheme was initiated by the Crofters Commission, financed by the Highlands and islands Development Board and the Countryside Commission. This led to the development of the project in several ways, including the installation of electric lighting in the house at Druim, the planting of the garden there with heaths and the publication of a small booklet on the area, illustrated with photographs and drawings by the pupils.

Work on the project had involved many departments in the school. The reconditioning of the old house at Druim meant that wood-workers became virtually builders, repairing floors, ceilings, rhones, down pipes, clearing drains and acquiring skills in the use of plaster and paint. Biology people turned their hands to making the garden and to planting trees at the hall. The art department produced hand-lettered information sheets and labels for the artefacts, as well as arranging the collection to advantage.

the collection in the hall as part of the 'Highland Village 1970' project   183

The pupils, most of whom knew only town life, benefited greatly by finding out how country people lived, from identifying forms of natural life - plants, birds, even insects - and from seeing the actual results of their work - a freshly painted wall gleaming in the sunlight, a cleared pathway, some newly planted trees. Many were to come back in later years, some with wives, husbands, families, to see how the work had progressed.

The croft house, appropriately furnished and equipped, and the collection in the hall were to prove attractive to many visitors over the years. School groups from many places also came, making study tours and enjoying a day in the hills.

In September, 1970, after the completion of the first stage of the project, a reunion of former inhabitants of Abriachan was held. A small notice in the 'Inverness Courier' resulted in a great number of responses, some from people living far afield, in West Lothian and Dundee. Transport from Inverness was arranged. Former pupils, relatives of former teachers, people with every sort of connection with the place turned up.

There was much interest and enjoyment for people meeting again in remembered surroundings after many years apart. The house and steading at Druim were inspected and all the artefacts, photographs and documents in the hall. For the men, the old implements were of particular interest, bringing memories of hard labour in the fields. The women found the school group photographs fascinating, as they picked out the faces of old friends.

After a meal of soup, sausage-rolls, cakes and tea, the company settled down to a ceilidh in the big school-room, with music from Donald Riddell, the piper from Clunes, and Willie Grant, the fiddler from Abriachan. Some former members of the Abriachan School Gaelic Choir, together again after many years, sang some of their repertoire. Some sang solo, to much applause. The evening finished with an eightsome reel, many fond farewells and the sound of 'haste ye back.'

32

WILDLIFE

*T*he wildlife of the area - animal, bird, insect, plant - continues to thrive, though many factors threaten. Over recent years changes in agricultural practice, afforestation, the use of chemical agents as fertiliser and pest control, the coming of the tourists (among them egg and plant collectors) have all intruded on the natural wellbeing of many forms of life.

In very early times parts of the area would have been thickly wooded, the woods providing a habitat for bears, boar and wolves, as well as less fierce creatures. The bear disappeared in the distant past, the boar was hunted to extinction some three hundred years ago, the last wolf in Caiplich was killed, it is said, in 1464. The area was known as 'a lady's hunting place.'

There is talk, today, of reintroducing the wolf and the boar to some parts of the Highlands, along with the beaver. These ideas, of course, need very full discussion, and, perhaps, experimentation, before any action is taken. Meanwhile, today, one descendant of the early species is still with us - the red deer. He and his kind have had to adapt, of course, to living on the bare hillside and moor since his natural habitat of woodland disappeared. He is magnificent with his antlered head, his strength, his speed, his whole bearing. He was, indeed still is, a totem animal. Poets have sung of him, painters portrayed him. Duncan Bàn Macintyre, the eighteenth century poet, writing in Gaelic, in his 'Praise of Ben Dorain' describes him thus:

> *'He's the wild-headed deer*
> *Of the white hip and rear*
> *And the high-tined head-gear*
> *Who was noisy in roaring,*
> *He dwells on Ben Dorain*
> *Too much for my telling*
> *The proud stags galore on*
> *Yon moor that are dwelling.'*

185

Duncan Bàn knew the stags well as he worked with them on his beloved hills. For Victorian artists the stag was merely a subject for portraiture.

Occasionally, in a hard season, he comes down to field level, a six-foot fence proving no deterrent to his foraging intrusion. Since the days of the lucrative deer-hunting indulged in by the landlords of the nineteenth century, when the 'deer-forests' were created, red deer numbers have increased so greatly that there has to be drastic culling of the hinds to keep the numbers in check. With the huge numbers roaming the hills the amount of natural feeding is becoming inadequate with the consequent starvation and damage to the environment in the destruction of naturally regenerated trees and other plants.

Their cousins, the roe deer, are here in considerable numbers, too. They are a delight to watch as they scamper up the hillside at the approach of man or dog, their white scuds betraying them. Quite often they venture on to the road and can leap across the bonnet of a car, or crash into it, causing a hazard to themselves and to drivers. They can equally easily leap over the fence of field or garden and cause considerable damage. I have seen a small herd in a field on an autumn evening of early cold, devouring the turnips left there for the sheep. But it's good to hear their ecstatic barking from their hideaways in the plantations up the hill, to know that they're still here, give or take a turnip or two.

The fox is with us too, his depredations occurring mostly among the poultry. In late spring and early summer, often a time of chill east wind and rain, he has young to feed and he and his vixen will make daring raids on chicken runs or on eggs laid carelessly in bush or moss. He'll be at the lambs, too, later on, watching for the weaklings that are easily snatched. But the sight of him standing bright-eyed and alert at the roadside on an early April morning, makes anger hesitate. He has to live, too, and obey the instincts for survival.

Another very attractive, fearless and dangerous predator is the pine marten. He is no longer the shy, elusive, rarely glimpsed animal of legend. His numbers have increased greatly since he became protected and he has adapted to new ways of living, emerging from his den among the rocks or trees to engage, like the fox, in raids on poultry. He can climb, too. High fences cannot keep him out. And he is very determined., even attacking anyone who tries to protect his prey. He has taken, lately, to exploring the contents of roadside litter bins and can be almost tamed, I'm told, by offerings of bread and jam. My nearest encounter was with a family of four, which had taken up residence in an empty croft house, gaining entrance by gnawing a loose plank at the foot of the door and nesting in a torn cushion. Again, anger melts. But, clearly, eviction had to take place.

The badger still prefers an elusive life. He is there in hidden places, almost impossible of access, in the ravine by the big burn. Occasionally he wanders to the roadside, in the evening, and can be picked out as he's dazzled, momentarily, by the headlights of a car. He's a quiet and tidy animal, inoffensive in his ways. He does have a liking for eggs and will help himself, by night, to any laid carelessly by hen, duck or goose. Who can blame him?

It is said that, within living memory, the wildcat was hunting in the upper reaches of the hill ground. My nearest encounter with a creature of any similarity was when I saw something leap and scramble the height of a six-foot fence round a hen-run and disappear across the heather. It could have been a domestic cat with a dash of the wild in his make-up. These crosses did often occur and led to a species of cat which would haunt a doorstep for a drop of milk or a scrap of meat left out, but which depended largely on his hunting skills and would scorn the notion of a summons or a stroke!

A close encounter of a memorable and surprising kind occurred for me one still, frosty morning in November, at Loch Laide. The water was calm, yet there was the sound of splashing. I looked along the bank, from the shelter of the trees and was able to watch, for fully twenty minutes, a family of four otters, disporting themselves in a game of diving, surfacing, chasing, till eventually they swam away to their haunt on the far side, among the reedbeds. For the many times I had seen their tracks, in the mud, sand or snow and come on their droppings, with never a sight of themselves, even at dawn or dusk, this was reward indeed. Keen fishermen, of course, look differently on these creatures, but there are enough trout, and to spare, to provide sport.

The mountain hare keeps to the high tops and the corries where the snow lies long, as he makes his fearless dashes, safe in his winter camouflage of spotless white. He's hunted sometimes, when winter hunger is acute, but not on the scale that was indulged in, in some parts, when beaters would drive scores of hares towards a row of waiting guns.

His counterpart, the brown hare, is a gregarious creature, and loves to take part in mad frolics and mock fights in spring time, in the fields below Tyeantore. He's a master in the art of 'freezing' to deter attack. Sometimes, his young, who seem a little slow-witted, stay too long in the frozen pose and end up between enemy teeth, even those of a domestic cat no bigger than themselves.

Rabbits are back. After years of absence owing to the decimation caused by myxomatosis, they are not unwelcome, as their numbers, so far, are smaller than before and they can take their proportionate place in the scheme of things. To see them suffering from that most unpleasant disease which nearly wiped them out is not, I hope, an experience to be repeated. Now that we are no longer so closely dependent on roe, hare, rabbit or trout to ward off hunger, when rod, gun and trap were the necessary weapons in a war for survival, we can live on good terms with all the wild creatures hereabouts. Some fifty years ago there were many feral goats eking out a living in the wilder places. They were descendants

*of the many goats which crofters kept, along with a few sheep, to provide a sup-
ply of milk, even meat. When the 'improving' lairds began to plant trees for the
embellishment of their estates, goats had to go. Their destructive habits included
the eating of bark, which led to the death of trees. Bigger farmers favoured the
existence of some goats, as they grazed ledges on the hillsides which were dangerous to sheep. The Abriachan goats were well-known as they would wander
the road as far as Inverness for a feast in wayside gardens.*

*In the wild woodland down towards Loch Ness red squirrels live without their
grey cousins. Some come to share an easy meal at a bird-table, most find plenty
of natural food.*

*Down in that milder climate adders are often seen taking a sun-bath on the
road. Everywhere there are slow-worms, snails, grasshoppers, weasels, stoats,
all the small, mostly invisible creatures that make up the population. Bats, like
winged mice, flit about the eaves, field-mice, hedgehogs and moles have gardens
to enjoy. Only rats, which appear some winters in numbers, are not welcome.
They are destructive, even of plastic pipes, and electric cables and can pose a
danger.*

*Up at Loch Laide in the shallow places round the shore, the tadpoles appear,
in early spring, leading, later on, to a profusion of tiny frogs. There are leeches
in the shallows, too. Paddlers are wary of them, but they are being used again, I
believe, in the curing of certain human afflictions.*

*There are still trout enough to keep some anglers happy and, more impor-
tantly, to keep the population of water-birds alive. Sticklebacks help, too. Mal-
lard and tufted duck are the most numerous, managing to rear families each
year. In winter golden-eye and pochard appear and often a party of wild whooper
swans fly in, seeking shelter and respite on their long journey south.*

*In spring the blackheaded gulls return to their nesting-site on the island. Their
joyful clamour is a welcome sound and they do provide a protective element for
our most treasured summerer - the Slavonian grebe. At one time eight pairs of
these lovely birds nested here. Now they are fewer, but even more welcome.*

*The heron, that bird of ill-omen flaps disconsolately up the burn and stands, a
solitary sentinel, in the shallows. The dipper, supremely alert and agile, dives in
after his prey, staying an astonishingly long time submerged, then reappears to
dry off and sing a few lovely staves.*

*Birds make the landscape live - their flight, their song, their colouring, their
transcendental quality as they soar or caper into space. The thrill of spring is in
the sight and sound of returning curlew, peewit standing heads to the wind, and
the sudden ceaseless singing of the larks. These signals are treasured today, as
the numbers of curlew, peewit and lark diminish. The oyster-catcher, the redshank
and the sand-piper which used to haunt the vicinity of the loch, are also seldom*

seen today. Changes in agricultural practice, less cultivation, the use of certain noxious substances are probably to blame. But the hill birds are here, though in reduced numbers - the grouse, the buzzard, the sparrowhawk, kestrel, hen-harrier, raven, owl. Snow bunting have been seen and goldcrests enjoy the thistles. Occasionally an osprey will fly over on his way to Loch Ness and on one memorable occasion a red kite attacked a bag of nuts hung out for the garden birds. It's thought that the red colour of the bag may have been the attraction and, of course, red kite were always known as scavengers.

Blackcock may still be heard 'on the lek' at mating time. Hoodie crows are plentiful. There is the usual garden population of blackbird, robin, wren, the tit family, chaffinch, greenfinch, tree-creeper, starling, wagtail, sparrow. Yellowhammer and siskin are not far away. Crossbill sometimes crack the pine cones at the top of the garden.

Summer comes in from Africa on the dusky backs of swallows and house martins, which we welcome to our eaves. And then the cuckoo calls...

At flocking-times the long-tailed tits and bright bullfinches go roving through the pines. After the quiet of September, when the summer birds have gone, October brings the arrival of the fieldfares and redwing. They strip the rowans in a couple of days, sometimes waxwings assisting at the feast. Then, when the wild geese come in formed battalions out of the north sky, we know winter has signalled its arrival once again.

Spring comes late in the heights of Abriachan, but a keen lookout in the first mild spell will reveal the tiny ardent suns of coltsfoot, then, in sheltered spots, wood sorrel, violets, and half hidden in the moss, among the birch and hazel, banks of primroses. Celandine, wood anemone, wild hyacinths all flourish in the natural woodland on the lower ground. In May there is blossom everywhere - gean, bird cherry, blackthorn, rowan, are all bedecked in delicate bloom. In June and July there is a sudden burst of flowering - red and yellow mimulus by the burn, marigold and ox-eye daisy on the field edge, along the roadside lady's smock to welcome the orange-tip butterflies, columbine, milkwort, vetch, stitchwort, tormentil, stonecrop, speedwell, foxglove, mountain saxifrage, St John's Wort and others too numerous to list.

In later summer bedstraw, scabious and golden rod come into flower and, in the wet patches, ragged robin and meadowsweet. A special delight is the variety of orchids in the marshy ground and the few patches of globe flowers in damp hollows. The two insectivorous plants - sundew and butterwort - are found in various places, and on the moor-ground, among the scattered birches, there is a profusion of mosses and lichens. Moss was used as a dressing for wounds and lichens provided those beautiful soft colours in the dyed wool. Edible fungi of many kinds are found.

Summer brings great splashes of yellow to the landscape when the broom flowers. Whin blooms almost all the year round and was bruised in 'whin-mills' and used as fodder for horses in times of scarcity. Bog-cotton brightens the loch shore in summer time. The silky heads would be gathered to stuff pillows. Myrtle scents the air about the bog cotton. It has always been considered a deterrent to noxious insects. Today, the oil is being used experimentally in an effort to deter that particularly noxious insect - the midge.

The little white Jacobite rose flourishes in the protection of dwarf willow and alder along the roadside. Luckily the roadsides are uneven, boulders protruding, tree-stumps and bushes too - so that the council strimming machines can scarcely operate and plants of all kinds are allowed to flower and seed as they will. Rushes, nettles, thistles are all part of the scheme of things. And the herbs - mint, thyme, garlic, many more are highly valued. Wild raspberries are plentiful, with tiny strawberries in the woodland, while autumn brings a profusion of berried fruit - blaeberry, cranberry, sloe, rose hips.

Late August is the most dramatic flowering time of all when the hills are covered in heather-bloom, and October brings the dazzle of rowan berries among the gold of birch leaves and bracken. Even in the dark of winter these birches provide colour, their skeletal outlines tinged a delicate shade of mauve.

It's good that at the present time efforts are being made in many places and by many agencies, particularly in Abriachan, by the Woodland Trust and the locally run Abriachan Forest Trust, to bring back the native trees. Birch, willow, alder, hazel, rowan, ash, holly, oak, hawthorn, elder were all familiar to the people of the uplands, their unique properties understood.

People living sparse lives, close to all other natural forms of life depended largely on what these other forms could provide. Among the trees they found willow and hazel shoots made linings for their houses and even furnishings in the form of wickerwork, as well as creels and baskets. Birch wood made cradles, roofs and boats. From the alder whistles and pipes were made. The holly, along with the blackthorn, could be used as an impenetrable defence against marauders and was often used as hedging. The elder, like the rowan, was always planted near the house as protection against evil spirits. All these trees, and many plants, were found to have healing qualities, some of which are being resorted to today. Thus, the bark and leaves of the ash make a laxative, the hawthorn is used to treat heart conditions, the alder calms fever. Many plants also promoted positive health by providing natural nutrition. The pine, too, was part of the tree population, the Caledonian forest covering large areas of the country. But these naturally regenerated magnificent trees grew sparsely, allowing for other growth, not in the serried ranks and gloom of the commercial plantings. They provided habitat for many kinds of wildlife, as will the new natural woodlands as they mature.

In Abriachan, even today, we are fortunate in having some stands of all the native trees. With these and the native plants of many kinds that still flourish, it is still a habitat for most forms of life, including insects. Many butterflies, among them the orange-tip, appear in summer, also the painted lady, which thrives on thistles and nettles, the small blue, the Scotch argus, the white cabbage, fritillaries, sometimes a Red Admiral and, of course, the tortoiseshell, which often over-winter in the house. Moths of many kinds are everywhere and up at the loch, dragonflies skim the water on calm days. Wasps make their masterpieces of nests in the garden ivy. Escapee bees live on in hollow tree-trunks.

Changes in farming practice, the lack of cultivation, though it may account for the disappearance of some species of wildlife, is yet helpful to the well-being of others in that fewer chemical substances in the form of pesticides, weed-killers and so on are dispersed. Gardens are worked organically, with provision made for many kinds of creatures, stands of nettles left for butterflies (and to make soup) willow-herb for the bees, rotted logs for the toads, piles of leaves for the hedgehog. A small patch of permaculture, or 'God's acre' can be left to look after itself and to provide a place for essential human relaxation.

It may be that, by looking back to the best practices of the past, with the benefits they provided and adapting them to the present, we may move into a future of great promise.

33

MODERN TIMES

A briachan, like so many small places in the Highlands, has had to move, inexorably, into the modern era. The movement was, of course, expedited by the prevalence of the motor car. For a vehicle with four-wheel drive, not even a steep hill road, often snow-bound in winter, would prove an obstacle. The town, with its promising job opportunities, was only ten miles distant, so, to commuters, the place offered many attractions, a healthy environment, quiet, space. One commuter travelled, for a time, to London for work, coming home every other weekend, the airport being only twenty miles distant.

By the early 1980s the last of those trying to make a living in the traditional way had passed into legend. At the former gamekeeper's place a young woman had worked to establish a pony-trekking and pony-breeding centre. She showed much skill and courage in handling a Connemara stallion and mares. After marrying, she moved away. Several families with long connections with the area do manage to combine work in construction yards and other places with keeping their land in good heart, running sheep and so on. One family still works a croft full-time, finding seasonal work in forestry to provide some extra income.

As the demand for country living grew, the selling of sites and the building of houses began. Efforts to have the area brought under the protection of a conservation order had failed, some years previously, the places of interest being scattered. The mill, however, is protected by Historic Scotland. The tradition of building in stone, well-seasoned timber and slate by local skilled masons, joiners, slaters and other craftsmen had been a long one, but clearly today the cost of such building would be prohibitive. Houses of different styles and built of different materials began to appear. Soon, as private water sources were inadequate for further development, a mains supply was installed. Those with sufficient water for their own use kept to the natural source which they preferred. By this time the hill road had been improved, more passing places and even crash-barriers on some of the more dangerous corners had been provided. As most commuting families had two cars there was a fairly steady flow of traffic.

ABRIACHAN NURSERIES

When I went to the Falkland Islands first in 1962 nobody knew where they were and most of my friends thought that I was somewhere off the West coast and wondered why I only came back every three years. By 1982 it was a different matter, everyone knew where the islands were but they were still a long, long, way away.

In 1983 we decided to return to the U.K. and not wanting to spend months wandering around the country looking for somewhere to live, we advertised for property with land and were offered places from Shetland to Spain and to cut a long story short we ended up at the bottom of the hill at Abriachan in the area known as Kilianan which was then known as Loch Ness Nurseries.

The house was built and the nursery started in the early 1950s by the Woodward family. They established a thriving business growing tomatoes and bedding plants in Dutch light greenhouses. These were heated by electricity provided from a turbine run from water taken from the large stream on our western boundary. Until recently we still used the same turbine to provide power for the house. The 6-inch piping, which brings the water from 300 feet up the hill, was used in Inverness during the last war to provide an emergency water supply.

Abriachan Garden Nursery

When Margaret and I and our three children, Elizabeth, Hamish and Catherine, arrived in September 1983 all that was left of the old nursery were piles of glass from the old greenhouses. We set to and by spring had got plants ready for sale and opened as Abriachan Nurseries which has grown steadily over the years along with the woodland garden which we have built at the same time.

The nursery and garden lie in a sheltered valley just above Loch Ness and the small very old cemetery of Kilianan. The gardens wander among the native trees by a network of paths following the natural contours of the land. At the centre of the garden is the large historic holed stone known as Saint Columba's font stone.

The soil is shallow, sandy and acid but well drained. When the large rocks and stones have been removed from an area and used to make a retaining wall on the slope, the soil is mixed with our own compost and well rotted animal manure to make an excellent growing medium for the large variety of plants that we grow. Some plants, which are considered less hardy, thrive in the conditions that we have created for them.

We grow about 80% of the plants sold in the nursery ourselves, using five small greenhouses, four polytunnels and a large outside standing area. We started with a strong emphasis on alpines, but as fashions in gardening have moved, we have changed our growing patterns to accommodate, or in some cases to antici-pate them, so that most of the time we are growing what the customer wants to buy.

It is a privilege to live and work on the land and be part of the thriving commu-nity that is Abriachan.

Don Davidson,
Abriachan Nurseries.

As the result of an extension over the whole Highland area of improved tel-ecommunication facilities, one house in the uplands has been transformed into what has become known as a 'tele-cottage' equipped with every technological device, where a successful business can be, and is, conducted through the airwaves. The people involved also have the opportunity, and the time, to keep some live-stock and to benefit from life in an ideal environment.

During the years since the completion of the 'Highland Village' project, the school premises had been disused. Having only cold running water, an open fire for heating and outside toilets, they were considered inadequate, by modern stand-ards, for use as a Field Centre on a permanent basis. The big schoolroom was, however, quite suitable for the occasional social gathering, for the Hallowe'en ceilidh, the Christmas party, the Burns supper and, of course, for the monthly prayer meeting, when a minister, or an elder, would come out from Inverness to conduct a service.

Soon, nevertheless, with the arrival of more families in the area, demand grew for the provision of more adequate premises for indoor activities of all kinds - badminton, country dancing and so on. Mains water was just over the road, electric cables were nearby, there were people willing and able to use their skills in renovating property and most importantly, grants were being made available for the provision of village halls. It had always been understood that the museum collection would be removed should it be wished by the community that the hall revert to its original use. The artefacts therefore were put into storage, those formerly in the croft house at Druim had already been removed when the place was sold. Much hard work was put in over the next few years in bringing the hall up to standard, with regular inspections by the authorities. New toilet facilities were installed, kitchen premises evolved out of the anteroom, with hot water on tap and a modern cooking stove. The old oil lamps were furnished with electric bulbs. Wall heaters kept the temperature well above freezing. As time went by various extras were added, and donations made, in cash or kind. Fittingly, in the year 2000, the hall has been extended, and a much needed car park provided.

Meantime, the members of the expanding community had been busily involved in settling into life in the area. Some were of Highland origin, some came from various parts of the world. A few years previously we could have included people from New Zealand, Sweden and Germany as well as those who are still here from Australia and the Czech Republic. All were equally interested in keeping Highland cultural activities going. There had always been music in the place. The Gaelic choir in the school had won fame all over the area. Donald Riddell the piper and fiddler lived close by. Local fiddlers had always played at ceilidhs in Abriachan: Johnnie Findlay, Leault and Willie Grant, Balchraggan, the son of Alexander Grant - 'Sandy Battan,' friend of Scott Skinner, a great fiddle-maker and leader of the Inverness Strathspey and Reel Society. Three brothers - Hugh, Neil and Gregor Borland, pupils of Donnie Riddell - had taken fiddle prizes in Inverness, Aberdeen and elsewhere; their parents, Alistair and Isa Borland, were both very prominent in fiddling circles. Now a new generation of fiddlers had grown, along with two pipers, a brother and sister, accordionists and a clarsach player. Young talented musicians reinterpret traditional music in a modern idiom. There are fiddlers, an accordionist, singers and composers, too, among the older generation.

A country dancing class meets regularly in the hall. Some of the girls are learning step dancing, the original form of Highland dancing now being revived. Several boys, and girls, play shinty. Highland games with a shinty match and a hill race up the Leitir, are held in June. Gaelic, though an acquired language by a few members of the community today, has been studied by several pupils. Gaelic songs are sung on festive occasions, led by the only remaining native speaker,

now in his nineties. Culture, of course embodies so much more, even, than the use of the Gaelic language, marvellously expressive and valued as it is. It is more than the traditions of song, poetry, music, dance. It is in the whole attitude of a community to life itself - to birth, death and all the intervening contingencies - in care for the young, in respect for the old and for the dead, all based on a close association with the earth itself and on the concept and practice of human interdependence. Though the backgrounds of today's members of the community are diverse, yet the feeling of solidarity can still be real, with help offered in adversity and happiness shared in times of celebration. As other developments involving natural heritage are now to the fore, the old sense of community expressed in shared effort is growing steadily and leading to a renewed appreciation of all that working in close partnership with the environment really means.

Katharine Stewart,
Abriachan

above: Abriachan today: gathering sheep

The author of this history, Katharine Stewart, has lived in Abriachan for half a century. For the first years she and her husband Sam worked a croft in Caiplich, and then moved to the old Schoolhouse, where first Sam and then Katharine ran the post office. Together they gathered a collection of crofting artefacts. She has written a number of books relating to the area, published by Mercat Press, and has also published many articles on other aspects of Highland history. She is patron of the Abriachan Forest Trust.

This story of Abriachan has been brought up to date by the following:

Margaret Davidson arrived in Abriachan with her husband Donald and family in 1983. They revived the nursery and have created an extensive woodland garden at Kilianan, the Abriachan Garden Nursery, which has gained a considerable reputation, and been featured on television several times. Margaret joined the local Community Council in 1988, and stood successfully for election to Highland Council in 1995.

Jim Barr and his family live at Tyeantore in Abriachan. He is the chairman of the Abriachan Forest Trust, which he runs with fellow directors, George Hawco, Margaret Davidson, Andrew McMillan, Charlie Webster, Mary Hesling, David Somerville, Helen Wood, Christine Matheson, Hamish Davidson.

Suzann Barr, Tyeantore, runs the local youth group, Active Abriachan.

above: hay-making at Loch Laide - Carn na Leitir in background

ABRIACHAN TODAY

34

CHANGING LAND USE IN ABRIACHAN

There is a sense of satisfaction in seeing the turn of a great circle. It is still hard to see when you look at the hills around Abriachan, but change has begun and though I will not live to see the land look as it did a millennium ago, my grandchildren will.

What did Abriachan look like a millennium ago? Some areas were much as they are now. On the slopes above Loch Ness the native woodlands would have been very similar to what we have now, hazel, alder, rowan and ash with a rich and varied undergrowth of fern, woodland grasses and beautiful herbaceous plants.

As you climbed the hill the woodlands continued, but the species change; first oak, the occasional gean and aspen and then downy birch began to dominate. Further up the fertile loam soils of Balchraggan run out and the soils were then, as now, acid and peaty with patches of poor drainage. Looking across the sweep of the hills a millennium ago you would have seen a patchwork of heather clearings, birch clad slopes, juniper valleys and sphagnum rich bogs with the climax of the vegetation: fine specimens of Scots Pine. This is all very well, but can you make a living out of it? Well, ever since he arrived, man has found it necessary to modify the landscape and attempt to make it more productive. Here we have the harsh realities of 5-6 month growing seasons and long, cold winters. It is no wonder men began to clear fields and keep grazing animals.

At first the settlements seem to have been around the Loch Laide area, and the other watercourses of Allt Loch Laide, Balmore Burn and near the shores of Loch Ness at Kilianan. 1 suspect the appearance of the land did not alter much until the 18th and early 19th centuries, when the population seems to have increased with a consequent rise in grazing animals, cattle and the arrival of sheep. More fields were cleared and the field system we see now probably emerged from the woodland cover at that time. The fertile areas of the slopes at Balchraggan and the flatter areas of Balmore, Caiplich and Loch Laide must have been used for crops and at one stage the grain crops kept the mill operating at Balbeg. Potatoes grow well in Abriachan, the open aspect keeping aphids and potato blight to a minimum, and they must have formed a staple in the lives of most families after their introduction.

Fuel for many years must have been a mixture of wood and peat. The flat tops of Carn na Leitir are criss-crossed with old peat tracks and the signs of old peat workings.

As the population increased, the school was built and filled up and farming became more intense and probably hit a peak around the time of the Second World War when the whole country was being exhorted to produce food. Abriachan appeared on the maps then all right for another crop, timber. The Canadian loggers arrived with clear instructions to harvest timber. Along these north shores of Loch Ness, they took out oak and the Caledonian pine, as it had never been harvested before. Local sawmills operated steadily and efficiently.

After the war mobility increased and families moved out for work, the number of boarded-out children dropped and the labour to crop the land intensively fell away. The sheep began to have its day. Grazing became more extensive and the fertility of the ground and productivity lessened. It was a hard time to make a living off the land and it is no wonder that when the Forestry Commission with its cheque book came along and asked to buy the ground it must have seemed the only thing to do.

This post-war period was also a time of some novelty. Men came back from overseas and they had energy, sometimes a little cash in their pockets and always plenty of dreams. This was the time of the strawberry farm, the daffodil enterprise and the beginning of the garden at Kilianan. The ground of Abriachan cannot compete with the fine soils of vegetable and fruit growing areas and the season is short. What it can do is produce early crops for the local market on the sunny, south-facing slopes of the lochside hills. This made a living for the Woodwards at the nurseries with their early strawberries and tomatoes for some years, but as distribution of goods throughout the country changed and the profit dropped they too had to change. Since then the nursery has survived as a producer of bedding and ornamental plants and the strawberry farm up the hill slowly reverted to grazing and woodland.

from the Leitir: a 1960s view: the green fields of the former croft lots of Lochlait

above: from left - former croftlands, now afforested, a working farm, felled woodland

1960s - Forestry Commission machinery moves in to plant the moor above the postie's croft

continuing: the dark mass of the Leitir, conifer plantations and the hill farm of Achpopuli   201

The Forestry Commission left a bigger mark on the landscape and one we still live with. They planted many acres of lodgepole pine, sitka spruce and a scattering of other species throughout the 1960s and 70s. As they matured they have come to dominate the landscape with their dark presence, especially around Achpopuli and Loch Laide and behind the back of Carn na Leitir. Alongside a dramatic change in the appearance of the hills came disruption to watercourses as had never happened before. Their deep ploughing altered the direction of run-off from the hills and greatly increased the volume of peat particles running into Loch Laide and the feeder streams. It has taken 25 years for that Loch to recover some of its rich wildlife.

On the heels of the Forestry Commission came private forestry. Various governments made it fiscally attractive for the rich to plant forestry by providing a variety of tax incentives. Hundreds more acres of land disappeared under conifers, particularly the areas of Blackfold and Craggan Valley.

Living with these dark forests has a strange effect. They estrange you from the land, climbing over the deer fencing and trying to walk over the deep ploughing and find your way out of the dense plantings does not give me a feeling of intimacy with the land. You begin to feel that they have always been there and that you are the intruder. But they are not all bad. Sitka spruce grows well and can provide a "fast" crop of timber. If the timber price is right that means jobs and the sustaining of families. Open, overgrazed moorland has little more to offer the eye.

If you walk up through Abriachan on a clear winter day, now, at the turn of the millennium, that is the land pattern you will see: deciduous woodland moving up onto poor open pastureland and substantial areas of conifers.

So what is turning the wheel and closing the circle is a dramatic change in ownership and government subsidies.

Two years ago the community purchased over one thousand acres of forest from the Forestry Commission. With the availability of Woodland Grant Schemes we are now able to harvest some of the poorer areas of conifers and either replant or allow natural regeneration of native species. At the same time we will gradually thin the better plantings of sitka spruce and hence providing some continuous cover and work availability over a longer timescale. We even intend to re-plant some of the sitka with another crop of conifers in due course, to see if we can keep a steady supply of timber for local use and harvest.

Simultaneously some of the private woodlands have been harvested and have been grant-aided to allow for natural regeneration. That began only two years ago and we will watch the results with interest. All of this planting and regeneration has been accompanied by increased culling of deer and hence an increased ability for native plants to regenerate.

Put alongside that there is a disastrous fall in the price of sheep and cattle and a change in emphasis of subsidies and the result is that dramatic changes will occur in the landscape over the next 10-20 years. The landscape will begin to look much closer to what it was a thousand years ago. The conifer crops may be an incident in the course of events.

It won't be the same. There are more and larger houses and many more wide tracks and roads across the landscape. Modern life demands mobility.

Maybe this change in landscape will sit comfortably with an increased awareness of our environment and will fit well with the growth in outdoor recreation. If it does then it will be sustained. If it doesn't and again people have trouble making a living, then it may change again.

Ask my grandchildren.....

> Margaret Davidson
> Kilianan
> Abriachan
> November, 1999.

overleaf: map of the Abriachan Forest, and the Abriachan Woodlands. These areas, formerly belonging to Forest Enterprise - the old Forestry Commission - are now in the care of the Woodland Trust (Abriachan Woodlands) and the community-led Abriachan Forest Trust (Abriachan Forest). The history of these developments is outlined in the following pages.

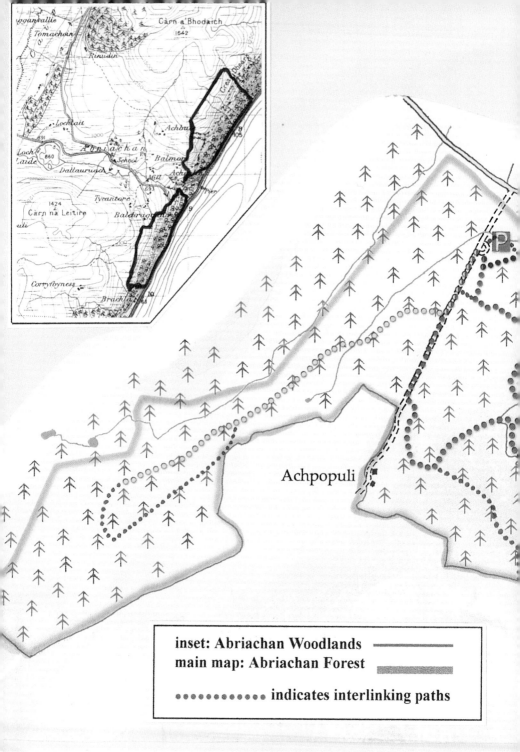

Achpopuli

inset: Abriachan Woodlands ───

main map: Abriachan Forest ▬▬▬

••••••••••• indicates interlinking paths

204

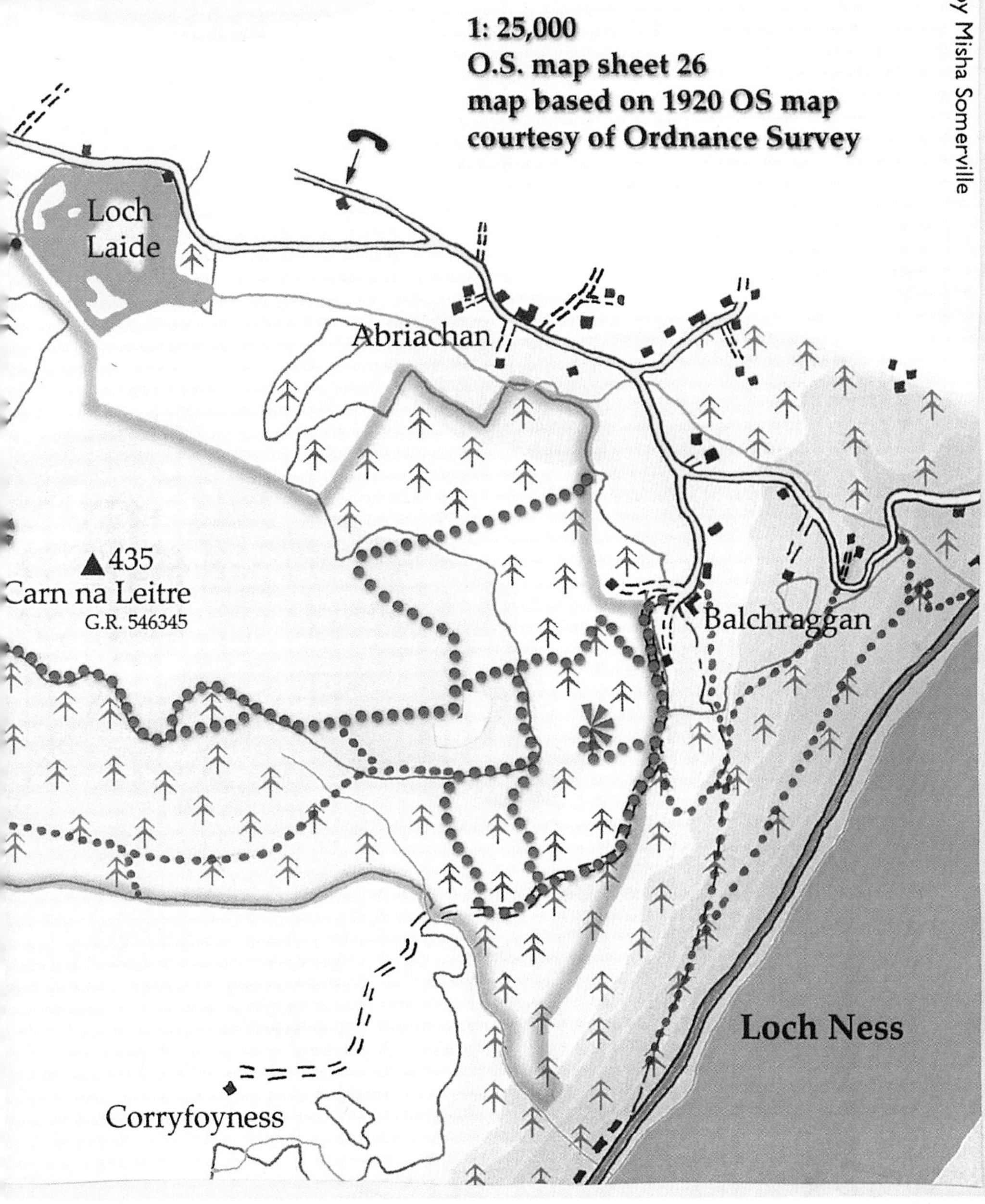
1: 25,000
O.S. map sheet 26
map based on 1920 OS map
courtesy of Ordnance Survey
Loch Laide
Abriachan
▲435
Carn na Leitre
G.R. 546345
Balchraggan
Loch Ness
Corryfoyness

Design and Production by Misha Somerville

35

ABRIACHAN WOODLANDS AND THE WOODLAND TRUST

We all take things for granted and in Abriachan it was our woodlands and forests. For over 40 years large tracts of woodland and open ground had been in the ownership of the Forestry Commission. Much of the area had been densely planted with non-native conifers. As neighbours, the Forestry Commission had their faults, but they also had their virtues, not least of which was their relaxed attitude to access. We could walk through their ground whenever we wanted.

Abriachan Woodlands are 163 hectares (403 acres) of predominantly native woodland in 2 separate blocks. About half of the acreage is on the shoulders of the south-west corner of Carn a' Bhodaich. The area is very steep, predominantly birch woodland and open moorland that has a high landscape value. The second area is on the loch side between the Nursery Gardens and the Clansman Hotel. This is a very special area, a rich mixture of species and old hazel and alder coppices. The woodland is renowned for the spring display of primroses, violets and wood anemones. Diagonally through the woodland is a proven and registered Right of Way, the "Funeral Road". This steep, old path on which the coffins were carried to the road for conveyance to the burial ground at Kilmore, links Balchraggan, Abriachan with the old croft at Brackla on the lochside road.

Abriachan has long had a finger or two or three in the political pie. 1990 was the time of Forestry Commission "disposals." There were two of us on Inverness West Community Council and it was there that we learnt that the whispers we were hearing, about Forest Enterprise's intending to sell large areas of the land around the village, were true. It was also there that we first learnt of the idea of a sponsored sale. In those days a sponsored sale meant that Scottish Natural Heritage would assess the natural history and/or landscape significance of a proposed sale area and if it was of sufficient stature they would give the green light for a closed or sponsored sale to an approved conservation body.

Here the Woodland Trust came in. They were alerted to the potential sale and began approaching the Forestry Commission and Scottish Natural Heritage. The Woodland Trust already had a presence in the area, having purchased the Balmacaan Woods and the Site of Special Scientific Interest, the Cover, at Drumnadrochit, two years previously.

As a community we were concerned on three counts. Firstly, we were used to full and free access and if a private buyer took control we had an uncertain future. We had local examples of restricted access when sporting interests had control. Next, we were concerned that some of the woodlands would come under pressure from developers for housing. Finally, the area proposed for sale had no conservation status. We were not confident that woodlands would remain essentially as they were.

So the Woodland Trust with its policies of public access, conservation and track record of non-sale to developers looked a good option. However, we needed help raising the money. The purchase price was £20,000. Scottish Natural Heritage grant aided £7,500. We were lucky; this was the last land purchase to which SNH were able to contribute until the change of government in 1997.

The community was set the target of raising £7,500. To remind you, Abriachan is a community of around 130 souls and just the previous year we had put our hands deep into our pockets to reclaim and refurbish the old village hall. So, we had a fund-raising launch at the hall and cast the funding net on a wider front. I remember Suzanne MacEwan, the young woman who co-ordinated the fund-raising for the Woodland Trust. She was excellent, keeping us informed and maintaining the momentum. Early in 1995, Suzanne found us a benefactress: she was Mrs Howman from Pitlochry in Perthshire and she had connections with Inverness and the Loch Ness area. She kindly agreed to close the gap that was left in the funding and the deal was done, alongside some local negotiations for grazing and boundaries. We celebrated the sale with a walk up and down the funeral road, a barbecue, story-telling and dancing. Charlie Webster, a local crofter, performed a splendid, spirited tune that he had written to acclaim the purchase. It was a great day.

Since that date things have moved forward. A management plan was drawn up and consulted upon. Now, at the turn of the Millennium we are seeing some real progress under the guidance of Paul Young, the officer for the Woodland Trust in the Highlands. We have a network of paths in the lochside woods; the funeral road is clear and wide, the old cart track has been opened after decades of neglect and there are excellent new link tracks. There is also a selective felling of non-natives, which has opened up the views and woodlands very well. Our first walk leaflet is being produced for Abriachan and will include the walks through the large community forest and the network in the Abriachan Woodlands.

Since the purchase of Abriachan the Woodland Trust has grown significantly. There is now a separate Scottish division to reflect large land acquisitions in Scotland. It will be interesting to watch as the organisation develops and I hope to see more Scottish directors on their main board and more regional management within Scotland involving their membership and members of the communities where they have a presence. Since the buying of the woodlands the Abriachan community has moved on, too. We have purchased the much larger area, the Abriachan Forest, the largest community forest in the whole of the United Kingdom, and we are developing and planning the future ourselves. Meanwhile we can all be sure that the Abriachan Woodlands are safe for the next generation and that they, too, can take a hand in their future.

Margaret Davidson.
Kilianan, Abriachan
December 1999

native woodland at Balchraggan, fields and the bare moorland tops

facing page: workdays in the Abriachan Forest

36

ABRIACHAN FOREST

The story of the modern day Abriachan Forest really began in 1942 when the Countess of Seafield was divesting herself of some far-flung parts of her estate in Abriachan and Glen Urquhart, known collectively as the Balmacaan Estate. The tenants at the time were offered first refusal on their houses and cultivated land if they gave up their rights to certain areas of common grazing. This was an attractive offer but only to some, mostly those for whom crofting was truly a part time occupation. Also lost in this transaction were the rights to peat-cutting on the grazings.

Once the tenants had made their decisions, the lion's share of what remained, including many crofts with sitting tenants, was bought by Gillett Stephen and Company, a Surrey-based property company who had thoughts of turning the common grazings into a grouse moor. The grouse moor never became a reality and between 1942 and 1947 Gillett Stephen gradually sold off parcels of land and effectively withdrew from the Abriachan scene with a major transaction to Mr. Ronald Forbes Pearson in July 1947 in which several parcels with sitting tenants were sold. This latter-day laird continued the piecemeal sell-off of Abriachan properties as tenancies became vacant but there was emerging an even bigger player in the land market in the shape of the Secretary of State for Scotland. Complete with his post-war 'Forestry Fund,' the Secretary of State had already acquired some vacant land in Abriachan from Gillett Stephen and the Forestry Commission continued to expand and consolidate.

As the Forestry Commission sought to rationalise its boundaries, a mechanism called 'a contract of excambion' was frequently used to swop parcels and pieces of land and generally confuse long-established boundaries almost to the point of anarchy. While the Forestry Commission successfully delineated its major boundaries with 8 feet high deer-fencing, those outside were left to pick their way through title deeds as long as Jeremiah and as confusing as Job. There is no question that one man's successful excambion was another's source of deep suspicion. In very recent times the Abriachan Village Hall nearly fell victim to a contract of excambion between the Secretary of State and the aforesaid Ronald Forbes Pearson when his descendants attempted to claim its solum for their very own. The Countess of Seafield had granted the land in question on lease in perpetuity to the residents of Abriachan in 1933 and the great post-war land shuffle had seen the feudal rights pass by exchange into private and potentially less benevolent hands. Suffice it to say that the robustness of the Community response to this attempt to resurrect the laird's legacy was sufficient for the realities of the present day to be recognised and for the Village Hall to resurrect itself unburdened from a period of dormancy.

By the middle of the sixties, the Forestry Commission had acquired, by purchase or swop, sufficient land to the south of Abriachan from Ronald Forbes Pearson, Finlay Maclean, William Grant, among others, to fix a boundary and commence cultivation. Together with the plantings between Corriefoyness and Creag Nay this was known as the Abriachan Forest and stretched to approximately 2132 acres. Plantings of the areas adjacent to Abriachan and Achpopuli took place between 1970 and 1980 and consisted predominantly of lodgepole pine and sitka spruce with some Scots pine and larch. Little then happened in the forest for over 10 years except for the occasional visit of a local forester or the keeper.

However in 1992, at the height of Thatcherism, an apparently innocuous circular was received by the Inverness West Community Council advising them that Forest Enterprise was considering the sale of parcels of land which no longer fitted its management portfolio. It was requested that, as a general exercise in conjunction with Highland Regional Council, local communities indicate whether they wished to retain access rights to adjoining land in the event of any disposal. The Community Council canvassed its constituents and requested that any individuals concerned with access also write directly to Highland Regional Council who were charged with co-ordinating the responses. This was done by several local residents who all expressed their support for continued amenity access to the adjacent hill and forest for a variety of hobbies ranging from walking, cross-country skiing to horse riding.

Peace reigned once more in the Forest until October 1995 when adverts appeared in the local press advertising the proposed sale of Abriachan Forest by Forest Enterprise. One or two individuals sent for details to the selling agents, Finlayson and Hughes, expecting to find rights of public access safely enshrined in the terms of the sale. Had this been the case, it is likely that direct action by the Abriachan Community would have been confined to a few expressions of

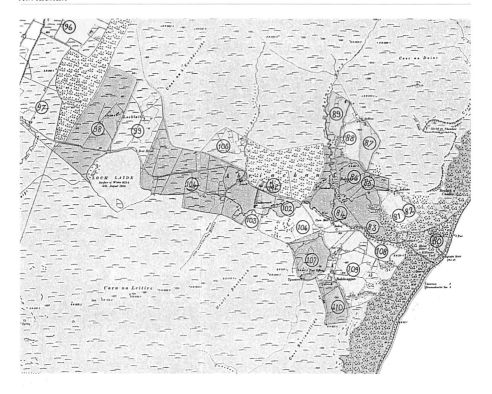

mutual regret at the Christmas Ceilidh later that year at the loss of Forest Enterprise, who were universally recognised as good neighbours. However, given that there was absolutely no mention of any form of access in the sale particulars, there was an immediate sense of outrage. What had the consultation exercise been all about? Why did we bother writing those letters? Had we been deliberately ignored? All these questions and more were echoed throughout the valley, with sufficient heat being generated to animate the conversation. Little was it realised that this signalled the first drips falling slowly from a communal glacier shortly to be on the move.

The first action was to refresh memories and confirm recall of the 1992 consultation exercise. Computers and word processors came into their own as individuals searched back through hard disks and dusty floppies to locate the precious missives to Highland Regional Council (HRC), with some success. Armed with this hard evidence of participation in the consultation process, Forest Enterprise were tackled to find out whether the particulars of sale had been misunderstood. Forest Enterprise (FE) were adamant that they had received no indication of interest regarding access for this land from HRC and hence had no reason to clutter their sales document or devalue their property with such irrelevances.

above: 'the lands of Abriachan' - Balmacaan Estate sale

Eventually HRC admitted that the consultation process had stalled at their door and there had been a breakdown in communication with FE. Everyone involved, with the notable exception of FE, believed that the obvious way forward was to halt the sale, draw up a formal public access agreement and then put the property back on the market with full particulars. However, it was now well into November, expressions of interest for the property had been received, including some from abroad, FE were relying on disposals to balance their budget and were keen to set a closing date. More local outrage followed and the power of the pen and political lobbying went into full swing. Local Councillors, local M.P.s and the Secretary of State for Scotland were all sent details of the sorry tale with requests to intervene. Further meetings with FE were held and they agreed to a brief stay of execution until political soundings had been taken. For the first time the suggestion of community ownership was raised which FE volunteered as an option if Scottish Natural Heritage (SNH) considered the area sufficiently interesting to provide technical sponsorship. At an asking price of over £500,000, this was considered to be an extremely tall order and an unlikely outcome.

Immediately after this, the resistance movement began to organise and the first public meeting on the topic was held in Abriachan on the 10th December 1995

young Abriachan resident Milo Farragher-Hanks and Deputy First Minister Jim Wallace at the launch of the White Paper on Scottish land reform in Abriachan Village Hall, summer 1999

213

which elected a steering committee to explore the feasibility of purchase and other options. A political champion came forward from an unlikely source in the shape of Michael Forsyth, an embattled Tory Secretary of State in a hostile Scotland, facing an inevitable and unenviable election. As a consequence, the property was temporarily taken off the market until the Community had the opportunity to complete a feasibility study. FE still harboured the hope of a sale within that financial year but, with an election looming sooner rather than later in 1996, time was definitely on the side of the Community. A survey of the site from SNH confirmed what the Community had long believed, that there were some special features on the hill and in the forest worth protecting and nurturing. Consequently technical sponsorship and support was forthcoming at an early stage and the personal enthusiasm of Iain Findlay, the SNH officer who conducted the initial survey, was a source of great encouragement. Funding was found from a variety of sources to enable a feasibility study to be carried out and bring in a local forest consultant to put some facts and figures alongside the environmental gems.

So began a long haul of meetings, funding requests and more meetings, all chasing the elusive prospect of raising half a million pounds. The hopes of a lower asking price being set by the District Valuer, as opposed to the market, proved to be only partially fulfilled with £425,000 + costs becoming the actual target. The funding roller coaster began for real towards the end of 1996. Just as it looked as though a way forward had been found, a door would close and it would be back to square one. However, the steering group was sufficiently encouraged to recommend formation of a fully constituted body and thus the Abriachan Forest Trust (AFT) was brought into being as a registered company in January 1997. Towards the middle of 1997, funding pledges had been received from the Scottish Office and SNH, together with high hopes of major financial support from the Heritage Lottery Fund (HLF), with whom work and correspondence had been ongoing for several months. However, one of the darkest hours for AFT was around the corner when the HLF suddenly changed their tone one week before the application was due to be considered in November 1997. The inevitable happened and the application for £320,000 went down on the day with all hands for reasons as yet to be fully explained.

However, after a brief period of despair and with the clock ticking on existing funding pledges which expired at the end of that financial year, an option for part purchase of the forest was then pursued. The General Election in May 1997 had brought a new government, new policies and consequently less pressure on the timetable. Indeed, with disposals to private individuals completely frozen, a sale to a Community group was suddenly very attractive to FE whose budget strategies were obviously impacted by the new policies. The pace picked up significantly and funding rolled in from Highland Council (Land Fill Tax), Highlands and Islands Enterprise (Land Unit), BP Exploration and a final top up from SNH. This culminated in the formal hand-over of 1336 acres of forest and open hill from Forest Enterprise to the Abriachan Community on March 24th 1998 for the sum of £152,000, to create the largest community owned forest in the UK.

After a brief pause to regroup, a development project valued at nearly £450,000 was commenced with assistance from SNH, Millennium Forest for Scotland, Highland Partnership (Objective 1), Leader 2, Crofter's Commission, HIE Land Unit, Rural Challenge, Landfill Tax and the Forest Authority. The project is aimed at naturalising the Forest with native species and improving amenity access for all. The bulk of the works will be completed in the year 2000 in fitting celebration of the Millennium.

A highlight for the Abriachan Forest Trust was being chosen in July 1999 as the site for launching the Land Reform Bill for Scotland by Deputy First Minister, Jim Wallace. It proved to be a proud and inspiring event well attended by young and old.

The remaining piece of Abriachan Forest remains under the stewardship of Forest Enterprise but a management agreement has been prepared with AFT to ensure that the properties are developed in harmony and with similar principles of management.

Abriachan Forest Trust remains a fledgling organisation despite its robust and very energetic beginnings. It remains to be seen if AFT will fulfil in the long term its stated objectives relating to care of the environment, amenity access for all, local job creation, education and encouragement of a wide variety of Community activities.

The initiative was born out of outrage and is sustained by a vision of opportunity but will be judged by the dispassionate and critical eye of history.

Jim Barr
26 November
1999

37

ACTIVE ABRIACHAN - THE YOUTH OF TODAY

By the early nineties the number of children in Abriachan had risen very quickly. From there being only one child in the early seventies there were, by 1991, enough potential clients for a youth group. An inaugural meeting was held in the barn of Tyeantore on a cold January day in 1991 and a constitution was drawn up. Children who were pupils and ex-pupils of Dochgarroch primary school were welcome to join and a committee of parents was elected. Active Abriachan was chosen as the best name for the group and suggestions for activities which all ages could participate in were asked for. It was felt to be important that there was an opportunity for the young people of the community to meet *within* the community - otherwise they would find all their entertainment in the big city of Inverness. Starting a youth group helped to reduce the risk of our village becoming a dormitory to Inverness.

For the first two years the club met at Tyeantore. A lot of the early activities were held outdoors on a Saturday morning, this avoided the hiring of a hall and extra expenses. The names on the register were marked off, two leaders were present but the word 'policy' was never heard of. Unfortunately nine years later,

above: members of Active Abriachan: Andrew Hawco, John Barr, Jack Coe, Michael Hawco, Hayley Coe, Mary Somerville, Louise Coe and Eilidh Barr

facing page: Active Abriachan

there are many more policies and procedures to be carried out in a politically correct manner, than we ever dreamed were possible. We meet regularly on a Friday night or Saturday morning in the village hall and comply with all the required legislation pertaining to running a club for children over eight years old. The ethos of the group remains the same, the activities are often suggested by the members and regularly run by some of the older children.

One of the aims of the group is to enable the young people to enjoy activities in the environment immediately outside their own homes. To this end there are regular orienteering, treasure hunts, map work and wide (chasing) games which entail hordes of shouting children running about over the hills and fields frightening all the wildlife for miles. In contrast to this, a group of the junior members have been leading "Ranger Tours" of friends, family and visitors on quieter walks around the woods and up on the hills. This has been very rewarding and the young experts now point out features which they had previously walked past. They have taken on the role of interpreters of the environment.

As part of the necessary policies, the club members must show consideration for their fellow humans as well as for their environment. This is highlighted during the year by various 'good works' ranging from doing Christmas baking, litter picking, wood chopping and some sponsored activities for different charities. The children are always quite amenable to getting involved and are willing to help others. The fact that they all go to school together and have been in composite classes, with the older pupils being there to help the younger ones, plays an important part in their attitude to others. Even when they go from primary school to secondary and are waiting for the school bus with the older teenagers they still talk 'across the age divide' - not too common in young people of a certain age!

Of necessity, the activities must sometimes be split according to age. Over the years there have been winter skiing weekends and summer adventure weeks for the over twelves. These were run with the help of Outdoor Education instructors and provided some big challenges for leaders and young people alike. Summer trips have included camping at Corriefoyness, camping/canoeing at Findhorn, camping/cycling at Rumster and Loch Insh and, most memorably, weeks at Gairloch where we catered for thirty nine appetites! During the winter months there are a variety of craft activities on offer and these are usually tailored to the different abilities and ages coming to the hall. They are often adapted to use recycled materials thus fulfilling the 'is your group running along sustainable lines..?' question when it is asked. The day to day running is funded by annual subscription(£1.50) and a nightly 50p. The hire of the village hall is recoverable from Highland Council and thus makes the low fees viable.

One disadvantage of the small village hall is that the craft activities preclude the development of sporting prowess so compromise must be made..... basketball, unihoc, badminton or skipping first, then, after the aerobic exercise, the art and craft. In the summer the bottom Tyeantore field is mown to provide a multi-sport pitch - some weeks shinty, others rugby and occasionally a community rounders play-off. Recently it hosted a group of Swedish teenagers and a team of children from Chernobyl - both nationalities choosing to play football. The disadvantages of playing ground-contact sports where sheep have just been grazing are obvious! The top field, when properly groomed, has been the venue for days and flood-lit nights of snow sports - après-ski barbecues and bath tub Cresta runs were recent successes.

Sometimes the whole group uproots and goes urban with a visit to the town and its swimming pool or to the Charleston Community Complex for use of its huge gym hall or even to the pictures or theatre for a spot of culture. The musical and thespian talents of some of the children have provided the community with the basis of some first class concerts and dances - unfortunately the maturing of the maestros has meant that we do not hear them as often as we would like because they are moving away to further education and employment at an alarming rate. There are still enough singers and musicians to go round guising at Hallowe'en but there is a higher proportion of joke tellers which is disappointing for some of the houses visited. Do the television and computer take the blame for this?

The community purchase of the surrounding forest has led to more youth activity within it. Some of the ex-members are actually employed either during their holidays from university or are working full-time on paths construction. The Abriachan Forest Trust monthly work days are attended by regular junior workers helping to clear paths or bag firewood. Over a period of nine weeks in August and September 1999, a group of the senior members constructed a replica Bronze Age dwelling. This entailed research, help from within and without the community and a lot of hard work but the end result has been a rain shelter for the use of visitors to the forest. This project won first prize in the Youth Clubs Scotland / BP Amoco Grizzly Challenge competition and the group members have won a trip abroad. The younger team also won through to the final four with their junior rangers' project so the sense of achievement at having two teams from over eighty selected as finalists has been gratifying for all concerned.

It is always a pleasure to observe the youth group in action on a good night to see the activities flow, being youth led with the adult leaders only there in an emergency capacity. The fact that sometimes these leaders are actually former members and are willing to come in and help out is even more satisfying and hopefully they will be there to carry on the running of Active Abriachan in the future. We try not to pass critical comments about "the youth of today".…. in Abriachan, and rural deprivation is only mentioned in funding applications.

Suzann Barr, Tyeantore

38

BRONZE AGE SUMMER

In April 1999, we arranged at the youth club to enter the BP/Youth Clubs Scotland Grizzly challenge with a team of four constructing a Bronze Age dwelling. During the summer of 1998 youth club members had helped the Corbett Centre clear heather from the original hut circles at Caiplich and although this would have been a very appropriate place for our hut it was a protected historical site. The Abriachan Forest Trust offered us a clearing, with a very boggy access, near the new car park on the Achpopuli road. After much research and a site visit to Archaeolink, near Huntly, we decided our hut was definitely going to be one of the smaller authentic Bronze Age reconstructions!

Over the first few weeks our elaborate plans were drawn up, with architectural assistance and advice from helpful people contacted at the library, museum and every other historical organisation in the Highlands. We started by erecting the structure, digging turfs and weaving wattle with parents and Liam (our support worker) looking on. The roof timbers needed slightly more assistance and by week three we were flying and adding extra items to our summer plans by the minute. Instead of conventional notice boards we opted for less usual 'sack signs' on which we printed information we had gathered from site visits, archaeologists, books and pictures. We made these and our drama costumes very simply in a couple of days. Jenny Hardy, a local dramatist, gave us advice on the performance. With a much praised frame work standing proud in the middle of our clearing all that was needed was thatch, stone work and an entrance path.

We began pulling heather three weeks before Brian (our thatcher) arrived, thinking that once we had finished we would simply lend a hand thatching the hut and admire the finished result. Little did we know that we would be pulling heather for so hard, for so long. After arranging to stay for only two days our two hard working thatchers ended up staying for six. With a perfect thatch and quickly built dry stone wall, all that was needed was the path to be surfaced and a Bronze Age drama and ceilidh to end the project. This resulted in the car park being filled to overflowing on the opening night.

We were thrilled to be chosen to attend the final in Dynamic Earth, Edinburgh and set off complete with our hut's doors and a Bronze Age chant to drums to perform in front of VIPs. We all enjoyed the project even after the hard work over the summer but there is one thing we will make sure of - we will not be in Abriachan in ten years time when the renewal of the heather thatching of our hut is due! The hut is now the first in a series of rain shelters which the Forest Trust will use for interpretation. Our plans for next summer will be to travel the world to research some other thatching techniques as our first prize.

Eilidh Barr
Tyeantore

Bronze Age Builders: from left - Jack Coe, Mary Somerville, Eilidh Barr, John Barr

39

POSTSCRIPT

I came to Abriachan almost exactly fifty years ago, in the summer of 1950. I was a small child with my mother and father - this was unusual in a community where the only other children were from the Central Belt, boarded out in the country. Our playground games owed more to traditional Glasgow street songs than to Highland folklore.

I walked to school every day on the high road past the postie's croft, with its grey Ferguson tractor, and tiny, neat fields, rows of cornstooks so precise and black cattle so diminutive that they seemed to belong to a giant model farm set. As a child you cannot know that the elderly people whose houses we visited were a last generation of crofting people. I remember them as small and stooped, nearly always dressed in black. Unfailingly kindly, they pressed towering piles of home-made pancakes and van-bought fruit cake on a small child, but I would fidget increasingly as the grown-ups' conversation swirled over my head and I would nod in time to the wag-at-the-wa' whose hands dragged ever more slowly towards the promised time of departure. At New Year they dispensed a thick sweet fruit cordial to the children and I remember the illicit thrill of the time when an unsteady hand mistook this for the glass of port intended for my mother. They spoke with all the cadences of their native Gaelic, and referred to their neighbours by bye-name, occupation or locality. Thus it was that my school-teacher, Miss Fraser, was always referred to as Lizzie Taylor after her grandfather's trade. This could, and indeed did, cause confusion to incoming parents. This small, upright and sprightly lady, a former member of the legendary Abriachan School Gaelic choir, taught us wonderful songs with the aid only of a tuning fork, struck forcibly on the edge of the tall dominie's desk.

Meantime, back on the farm, my parents worked hard at a time of post-war austerity to make a living from the land. My mother had started the writing career that would bring her accounts of crofting life to people all over the country and later my father would dispense wisdom, humour and hospitality to visitors to their small collection of country artefacts.

Now reaching an age when the past has fascination, I would give a great deal to be able to return to those remembered firesides and ask the questions which would enable me to unravel the fabric of the complex relationships engendered by this small place, and to hear at first hand the rich store of tales and legends, to flesh out the bare bones of statistics and archival evidence.

When I left Abriachan in 1970, the school had closed, and the place seemed set to become merely a location for second, holiday homes for the affluent. Our postman would gleefully recount that one family would send postcards 'from our Highland estate' - in fact a few acres of rushes and bog! But nothing is ever static, and the loops and spirals of history mean that the 1980s have brought in new families, with a dedicated commitment to making a living in the area, and keen to raise their children with all the opportunities of today combined with a sense of respect for the traditions and values of the past. It is still a source of enormous pleasure for me to hear the shouts and laughter of children at play in Abriachan, and to realise these are not holidaymakers or visitors, but the young-sters who have grown here. Not everything is perfect. It is concerning that those of the young people who choose to stay will find that houses in this now popular commuting area are at the very expensive end of the market.

It has been a great privilege to put together my mother's account of the history of Abriachan. For half a century she has lovingly accumulated a treasure-house of information and lore and we are indebted to the Abriachan Forest Trust for sponsoring this book. Many things stand out: the strength and resilience of past generations, the courage of those who bore losses with fortitude and endured a hard life with few grumbles; then the value of story and song, music and dance, homespun entertainment which lightened their lives; and also the importance of a sense of community, whether in petitioning for a new school in 1825, the establishment of a post office in the 1880s, the building of a village hall in the 1930s; people finding confidence when they can rely on the steadfast support of neighbours. The Abriachan Forest Trust of today has been built on such interde-pendence; I am sure those involved would not claim to be heroes, but they are certainly trailblazers. They are writing a new chapter in the history of land-holding in the Highlands and bring a refreshing optimism as they work hard to realise their vision. To them, and to all the youngsters of Abriachan, we dedicate this book.

Hilda Hesling
Abriachan 2000

40

Dear Mrs Stewart...

'I spend my time playing with my toys and going on my pony and playing with my sister and helping Dad with the crofts.....' - Katy

'I like living in Abriachan because there is loads to do. There is youth club every week and I am a Junior Ranger. We take people on walks and share our knowledge with other people......' - Hayley

'In the winter I go sledging because in Abriachan there are lots of hills. In the spring I have to help with the lambs, sometimes we get a pet lamb, the worst one is Mary Rose, a bad gimmer breaking into my Mum's garden......' - Katie

'In the summer I have lots of fun playing in the loch by swimming, fishing and canoeing etc. On the farm I help take in the bales to the barn. I like to watch and take photos of the wildlife on the loch, the birds and in the winter the otter (sometimes).....' - Mark

'I really like living in Abriachan because it is great for wildlife watching and bike riding. It is very quiet and peaceful most of the time, but sometimes we have great big fun events like ceilidhs. All in all I would say that Abriachan is a really good place to live.' - Michael

above: from back row, left - Duncan Wood, Kayleigh McCrory, Mark Foster, Eleanor Robertson, Katie Barr, Euan Coe, Ishbel Barr, Katy Hardiment, Jonathon Milton, Harry Milton, Jill Hardiment, Keana Mackenzie wait at Dochgarroch Primary School for the Abriachan bus home.